A JavaScript beginner learns React.js ecosystem

React Hooks Redux

in 48 hours

Copyright © 2021 by Satoshi Yoshida

All rights reserved. No part of this book may be reproduced or used in any manner without the written permission of the copyright owner except for the use of quotations in a book review. However, all code examples in the CodeSandbox created for this book are free to fork. For more information, email address: react3001@gmail.com

Release History:
                FIRST EDITION June 2021

Cover design: Inspired by Piet Mondrian (1872-1944) Composition No. III, with Red, Blue, Yellow, and Black, and modified design by Vanessa Celik.

All men by nature desire to know.

(Aristotle 384-322BC)

About this book

React (also known as React.js or ReactJS) is a JavaScript library for building UIs. React was created and is maintained by Facebook, a community of individual developers and companies. Facebook, Instagram, Netflix, WhatsApp, Airbnb, and many startup companies are using React.

One of the advantages of React is its flexibility. React could be used for client-side rendering or server-side rendering. Although React is a UI library, many developers consider it a framework because React imposes the component-based architecture that developers must adopt. React has a considerable architectural impact on every aspect of an app that would use them.

Unlike Angular, React is not a complete framework, and advanced features require additional libraries for state management, routing, and interaction with an API. This makes the basic core React simple and the learning curve not so steep. However, depending on the path you take with additional libraries, the learning curve can be very steep.

This book helps you understand React, React Hooks, Redux, Redux Middleware, Redux-Thunk, Redux-Saga, RTK, Recoil, XState, SWR, and various React related technology.

With CodeSandbox examples, you can run sample programs in your browser, no need to waste your time by setting up the environment. The example codes used in this book are not for production projects but only for learning the concept. Many diagrams also help you understand visually. The goal is to help you learn the React ecosystem quickly and guide you in the right direction.

This book is for:

- JavaScript beginners: some experience in Web design using HTML, CSS, and JavaScript.

- JavaScript programmers who do not know closure, functional programming, and ES6.

- Busy developers who do not have time to go through React/Redux official documentations.

- Non-Web software engineers or system architects know at least one of the high-level languages.

This book is not recommended for:

- No experience in any programming: JavaScript is a confusing language for beginners, and most of the free online courses do not explain essential concepts required for React.

    For programming beginners, we recommend
    "Head First JavaScript Programming".
    O'Reilly (Eric T. Freeman, Elisabeth Robson)

- React experts: Please refer to the React and Redux official docs.

Learning programming with CodeSandbox:

We have created 99 code examples in the CodeSandbox for this book. You will need Windows PC, Mac, Chromebook, or Linux-based computers to run the code. We have tested all code on Chrome, Firefox, and Edge browser.

TABLE OF CONTENTS

1. OVERVIEW 19
    1.1 JavaScript 20
        JavaScript Environment in Web 23
        ECMAScript 2015 (or ES6) and TypeScript 25
    1.2 React Overview 26
        Why using React? 26
        React Elements 27
        React Components 28
        Virtual DOM 29
        How can data be exchanged among components? 30
        Props and State 31
        Local State and Global State 32
        Functional Components 33
        ES6 Class-based Components 33
        Functional Components with Hooks 34
        Flux 35
        Redux 36
        Redux-Thunk 38
        Redux-Saga 39
        Recoil 40
        Concurrency in rendering 41
    1.3 Server-Client Architecture 42

    Legacy Server Side Rendering (Multiple-Page Application) 42

    Single-Page Application (SPA) 44

    Universal Server-Side Rendering (or simply referred to as SSR) 46

    JAMstack and Static Rendering 47

  1.4 Mobile Apps 48

    React Native 48

    PWA (Progressive Mobile Application) 49

  1.5 Tools used in this book 50

    CodeSandbox 50

    Babel 52

    Webpack 53

2. INTERMEDIATE JAVASCRIPT 54

  2.1 Data Types 55

    Primitive data type 55

    Reference data type (Complex data type or simply called Object) 56

    Strings & Literals 58

    Template Literal (ES6) 58

    Variables and constant 59

    Block scope of var, let, and const 61

  2.2 Expressions and Statements 62

  2.3 Shorthand expression 62

  2.4 Iterators 63

    for...of iterator (ES6) 63

Symbol.iterator (ES6) 64

2.5 Functions 66

Function Declaration (Function Statement) 67

Function declaration 67

Function Expression 68

IIFE (Immediately Invoked Function Expression) 69

Arrow function (ES6) 70

Arrow Function Return 71

Methods 72

Arguments 73

Arguments Object 73

Function Rest parameter (ES6) 74

Default parameter values and optional parameters (ES6) 74

Functions as Values 75

Passing Anonymous functions as values (callback) 76

Use cases of callbacks 77

Higher-Order Functions 78

Function declaration hoisting 78

Constructors 79

'this' keyword in function 80

'this' behavior in ES6 Arrow function 81

call & apply 82

Bind 83

Recursive function 85

Memoization 85

Enhanced Object Properties 87

Property shorthand 87

ES6 Shorthand for Function Declarations 88

Object.assign (ES6) 89

Destructuring Assignment (ES6) 90

Spread Operator (ES6) 92

2.6 Arrays Methods 93

Includes( ) method 93

Some( ) method 93

every( ) method 94

forEach( ) method 94

map( ) method 95

Filter( ) method 96

reduce( ) method 97

map.filter.reduce chaining example 98

2.7 Function Scope & Closure 100

Execution Context 101

Lexical Environment 101

Closure 102

Curry 109

Partial Application 110

- Prototypes and ES6 Classes 111
- ES6 Classes 112
- Subclassing 113
- 2.8 Asynchronous systems 114
  - Nested callbacks - Callback hell 116
  - Promise 117
  - Creating Promise 118
  - Promise Consumer - Promise.then 118
  - Promise consumer - Promise.catch 120
  - Promise consumer - Promise.all 120
  - Promise consumer - Promise.race 121
  - Generators (ES6) 123
  - async/await (ES8) 125
  - async 126
  - await 127
- 2.9 Making HTTP requests 129
  - Fetch API 129
  - Axios library 130
- 2.10 Modules 131
  - Named exports 131
  - Default export 132
3. REACT FUNDAMENTALS 134
  - 3.1 JSX 135

    Naming Convention 136

    Multiple Elements 137

    Attributes 137

    JavaScript Expressions 138

    Styling 140

    Comments 141

3.2 Props and State 142

3.3 Components 144

    Functional Components and Class Components 144

    Rendering a component 145

    Component reuse 146

    React Element 147

    Fragment Component 148

    Passing data using props 149

    Values that can be passed as props 150

    String 150

    Numeric value, Boolean value 150

    Object, Array, Function 151

    Variable 151

    Children 151

    Nested example 152

    Passing multiple values 153

    Default Props 155

Conditional Rendering 156

Stateless Component 158

Stateful Component 158

Inter Components Communication 161

Unidirectional Data Flow in components tree 162

Passing props down components tree 163

Talking to siblings - lifting state in components tree 164

Combining state and props examples 164

Events - Working with DOM events in React 167

onClick event example 170

initializing state 171

updating state 171

Component initialization/updating example 173

setState() confusing part 175

Stateful Class Component Design Patterns 177

Child Events update the states of the parent component 182

3.4 Component Life Cycle 183

Lifecycle Methods 183

3.5 Form 188

HTML Form and React Form example 190

React Controlled component example without <form> element 191

React Controlled component example with <form> element 192

3.6 Refs Attribute 193

3.7 Keys 195

3.8 Higher-Order Components (HOC) 199

3.9 Context API 201

3.10 Props Validation 204

3.11 Server-Side Rendering 207

    ReactDOMServer API 207

    ReactDOM.hydrate( ) 207

4. REACT HOOKS 209

4.1 useState 212

    useState() confusing part 216

4.2 useEffect 218

    Cleanup after the effect execution 219

    Run the effect on every render 220

    Run the effect only once 221

    Run the effect when data changes 222

    Using setInterval( ) in useEffect. (a bit tricky) 223

4.3 useContext 226

4.4 useRef 228

4.5 useReducer 230

    Counter example 1 231

    Counter example 2 232

    Todo list example 233

4.6 useMemo 235

4.7 useCallback 237

4.8 Custom Hooks 239

4.9 React Hook Form library 242

4.10 SWR 243

5. REACT ROUTER..244

    React Router Example 247

6. TEST DRIVEN DEVELOPMENT 250

    Jest..251

    React Testing library 252

7. REDUX...257

    7.1 Redux Concept..258

        Rule 1 — Single source of truth (single Store)..259

        Rule 2 — State is read-only (Actions) 260

        Rule 3 — Changes are made with pure functions (Reducers) 261

        Redux data flow 262

        View/UI Layer - Presentational and Container Components..................................263

    7.2 Learn Redux implementation..264

        Store 264

        Actions 265

        Action creators 265

        Reducers..266

        Connecting React with Redux...268

    7.3 Learn Redux with ToDoList 275

User interface and usages example 275

Data and Control Flow 276

Entry point and Store Creation 278

Action Creators 279

Reducers 280

Container Components 283

Presentation Components 285

Other Components (mixture of Presentation and Container) 289

7.4 Middleware 290

Creating a custom Redux middleware   (store => next => action) 292

createStore API 294

Middleware example 295

7.5 Redux-Thunk 296

Redux-Thunk example 297

Entry point, Store creation and UI 298

Container Component 299

Action Creators 301

Reducer 302

Redux-Thunk library 303

7.6 Redux with Hooks 304

useSelector 304

useDispatch 305

Data flow 306

Redux-Thunk Hooks example 307

Entry Point 307

Store 308

Presentation and Container 309

Actions 310

Reducers 310

Redux-Thunk Hooks Asynchronous example 311

Pros and Cons of using useSelector and useDispatch 313

7.7 Redux-Saga 314

Saga architecture 316

Effects Library 316

7.8 React Saga counters example 318

Entry point and create store 318

Presentation and container 320

Reducers 321

Sagas watcher and worker 322

7.9 React Saga external resources access example 323

Entry point and creating store 323

Reducers 325

Saga watcher and worker 326

7.10 Reselect library 327

Reselect library example 329

7.11 Immer 330

  Immer library example 331

 7.12 Redux Toolkit (RTK) 333

 7.13 Connected-React-Router 337

8. Recoil 338

 8.1 RecoilRoot 340

 8.2 Atoms 341

  Declaring Atoms 341

  Using Atoms 341

  Atoms example 343

 8.3 Selectors 346

  Defining selectors 347

  Using selector value 348

  Selectors example 348

  Writable Selector 350

  Asynchronous Selector 350

9. Various State Management Libraries 351

 9.1 MobX 352

 9.2 React Query 353

 9.3 GraphQL 354

 9.4 XState 355

 9.5 Summary 359

  State Management Solutions 359

  Data Query/Fetching Libraries 359

APPENDIX 360

Installation 360

Node.js and npm 361

Yarn 362

Create React App 363

Developer tools 367

React Developer Tools (React DevTools Extension) 367

Redux Developer Tools (Redux DevTools Extension) 368

React UI Component Libraries/Frameworks 369

Material UI 369

React Bootstrap 369

Ant Design 369

Grommet 370

Fluent UI 370

Shards React 370

Tailwind CSS 371

react-admin 371

SSG/SSR Frameworks 372

Gatsby.js 372

Next.js 373

1. OVERVIEW

(one hour reading)

Divide each difficulty into as many parts as is feasible and necessary to resolve it.

(René Descartes 1596-1650)

1.1 JavaScript

As React is not a full-fledged framework, it is relatively easy to learn. Instead of working in a preset pattern, a developer can add any library according to their preferences. For example, Redux is widely used by developers as state management.

JavaScript ecosystems come and go. But learning React also means you will have to learn JavaScript. Being a react developer will make you a good JavaScript developer automatically. Even if React became obsolete in the future, your JavaScript skills are still relevant and re-usable.

JavaScript is a dynamically typed programming language, meaning that the variables can be reassigned with a value of a different data type after initialization. JavaScript runs natively in the browser and is quite a strange language compared to current mainstream languages.

JavaScript is a broad language that continually evolves, and it is challenging to keep up with the changes. It is a multi-paradigm language whose syntax is based on the C language family. It supports the following programming paradigms:

- **Functional programming (FP)** –The most common pattern used in recently released React. Functions are objects, giving functions the capacity to hold executable code and be passed around like any other object. React's primary flavor is functional programming, which means that components are built through composition, not inheritance. By default, records (state) are immutable. FP consumes extra memory space. However, as memory costs have dropped drastically recently, it is not a problem any longer.

- **Prototype-based object-oriented programming** –You can use objects without defining a static class. JavaScript is the only mainstream language to support the Prototype-based OOP. As ES6 introduced Classical OOP, you can avoid it. One of the advantages of Prototype-based object-oriented programming is to save memory usage. However, considering memory costs these days, this advantage may not be relevant.

- **Classical object-oriented programming (OOP)** - ES6 introduced Class syntax, which is more understandable to many programmers. However, after Hooks released in 2019, React is shifting towards Functional programming.

- **Procedural programming** - It is still a commonly used technique for low-level, timing-critical embedded firmware. But not recommended to use this pattern in the JavaScript environment.

- **Metaprogramming** - ES6 supports the Proxy and Reflect objects, which allow you to intercept and define custom behavior for fundamental language operations. Metaprogramming is useful when developing a new language based on JavaScript.

Recently there has been a growing trend toward Functional Programming. With libraries like React/Redux, you will achieve clean software by using immutable data structures. Immutability is a core concept of Functional Programming. Overall, there are many advantages to Functional Programming in JavaScript. Douglas Crockford says that JavaScript is "Lisp in C's Clothing." In fact, JavaScript may be a bit cheaply looking Functional Programming language. React Hooks and Redux are influenced by Functional Programming. The problem is that many programmers who come from an object-oriented background seem to have difficulties in adopting Functional Programming principles in the first place.

React relies heavily on JavaScript. It takes a component's state, JavaScript objects, and using JavaScript functions to manipulate the state. The page is then rendered to reflect those changes. The fact that React relies heavily on plain JavaScript can be good and bad, depending on how strong your JavaScript skills are. The closure, classes, event handling, importing, exporting, callback functions, higher-order functions, curry, etc., are used in React. If you don't know JavaScript, you will get stuck and return to JavaScript tutorials many times. In the end, you might end up wasting your time.

JavaScript Environment in Web

When you are developing web apps, you don't write isolated JavaScript code that runs on its own. JavaScript is for interacting with the user environment, so understanding this environment will allow you to build better apps and be well-prepared for potential issues that might arise once your apps are released commercially.

The following diagram shows the client-side architecture. For the browser, JavaScript is like a machine code that runs under the CPU.

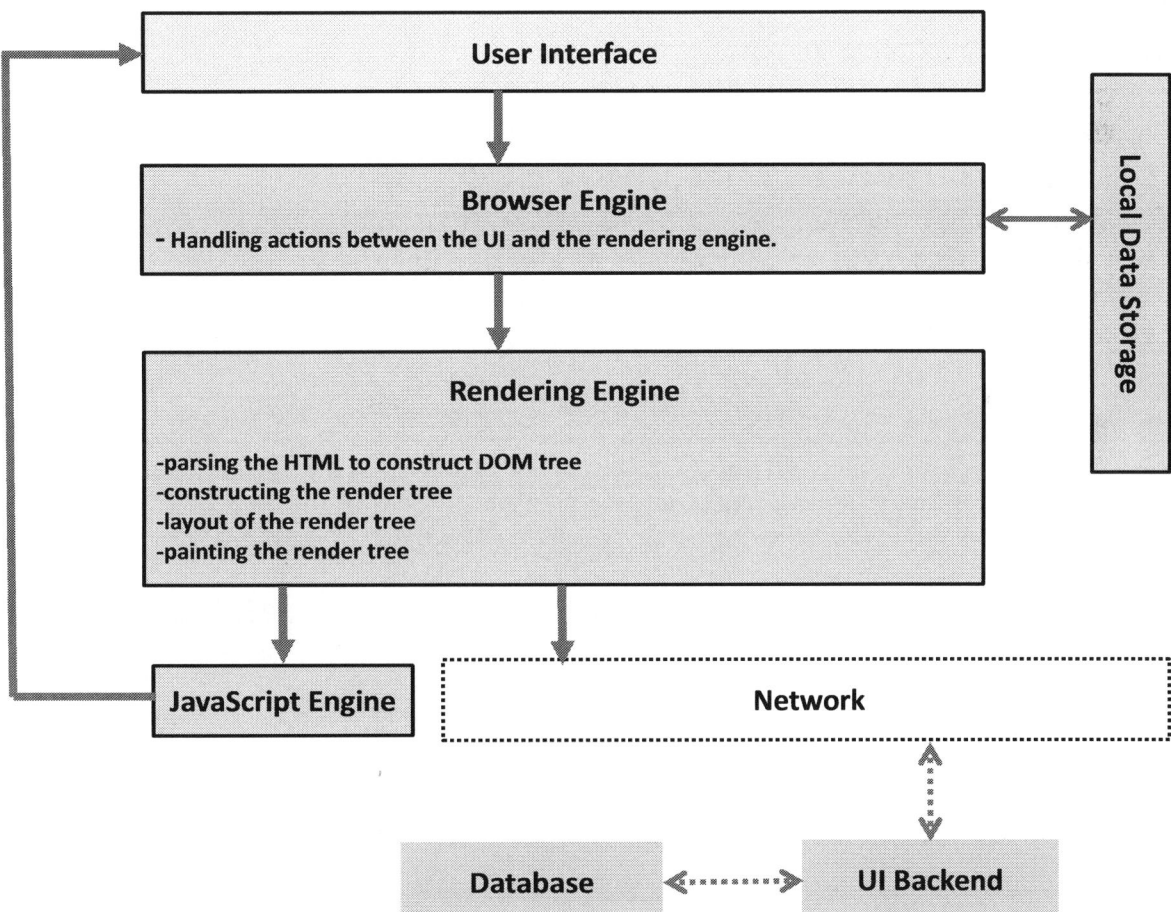

The browser's main components are:

- **User interface (UI)**: It includes the address bar, the back, forward buttons, text input, radio button, submit button, etc. It is every part of the browser display except for the window where you see the web page itself.

- **Browser engine**: The interactions between the user interface and the rendering engine.

- **Rendering engine**: It is for displaying the web page. The rendering engine parses the HTML and the CSS and displays the parsed content on the screen. The rendering engine receives the contents of the requested document from the networking layer.

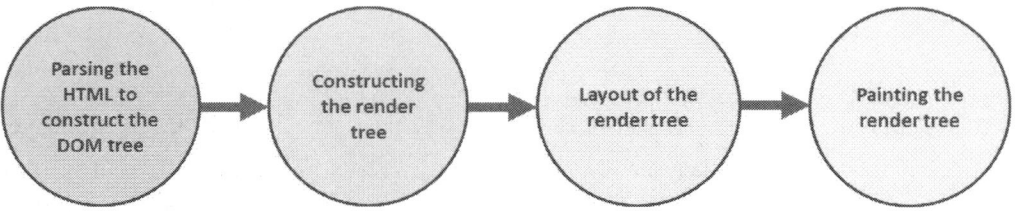

- **JavaScript engine**: This is where the JavaScript gets executed. Modern browsers don't use a conventional interpreter. For example, Google Chrome's V8 compiles JavaScript directly to CPU machine code using just-in-time (JIT) compilation before executing it. The compiled code is additionally optimized dynamically at runtime.

- **Networking**: These are network protocols such as XHR requests, which are a platform-independent interface.

- **UI backend**: The backend exposes a generic interface that is not platform-specific. It uses operating system UI methods underneath.

- **Local Data storage**: The apps may need to store all data locally. The supported types of storage mechanisms include localStorage, indexDB, WebSQL, and FileSystem.

ECMAScript 2015 (or ES6) and TypeScript

ECMAScript is a standard that extracted only pure language specification from JavaScript and removed extras features such as DOM. ECMA-262 5th Edition (commonly known as ES5), released in 2009, had been used for a long time. ECMAScript up to ES5 had features that are not often found in other languages. Many developers had been suffering from these features, which were significant barriers for JavaScript novices. However, since the ECMAScript 2015 (ES6) was approved in 2015, it became a modern and practical language. Countless improvements have been made.

ECMAScript (ES2016, ES2017, ES2018, ES2019, and ES2020) has been updated every year. The good news is that no large-scale additions have been made at present because the change from ES5 to ES6 was too drastic. It has been released every year to improve it gradually. This makes it very easy for users to follow the new specifications.

ECMAScript does not have a static type, but the type checking is feasible using a superset of ECMAScript called TypeScript that adds a type definition to ECMAScript. The main benefit of TypeScript is that a compiler detects descriptive errors in case of type violations. However, if you are new to JavaScript, we recommend learning the native JavaScript first to understand JavaScript's runtime behaviors. Since TypeScript is compiled to JavaScript, you still have to learn how JavaScript works anyway.

Much like Java/C#, TypeScript emphasizes a class-based type system, which promotes creating classes with methods that you need to instantiate.

React also have their own way of enforcing type (prop-types to ensure correct types at component interfaces), unit testing for components and logic, so TypeScript is not mandatory. Typescript comes in handy when you develop large-scale apps.

1.2 React Overview

React, created by Facebook, is an open-source JavaScript library for building fast and interactive user interfaces for web and mobile applications. It is a component-based, front-end library responsible only for the application's view layer.

Why using React?

One-way data binding
React imposes a strict one-way data flow to the developer. React makes it possible to structure a project and defines how the data should flow across the UI by enforcing a clear structure and a strict one-way data flow.

A declarative approach to building UIs
React can build UIs a lot more declaratively than with classic HTML templates. You can build Web-based UIs without even accessing the DOM directly.

Component-Based
Components are the building blocks of any React application, and a single app usually consists of multiple components. React splits the UI into independent, reusable parts that can process separately. You can build encapsulated components that manage their own state, then compose them to make complex UIs.

Virtual DOM
The virtual DOM stores a representation of the UI in memory and is synchronized with the actual DOM. The virtual DOM compares the components' previous states and updates only the Real DOM items that were changed, instead of updating all of the components again, as conventional web applications. It makes web applications faster.

Supports both web and mobile apps
A framework called React Native, derived from React itself, can be used for creating mobile applications.

Supports server-side rendering
Server-side rendering renders the React components on the Node.js server. By combining Client-side rendering and Server-side rendering, you can create a universal application.

React Elements

The browser DOM is made up of DOM elements. Similarly, the React DOM consists of React elements. They may look the same, but they are quite different in concept. **React element is a representation of a DOM element in the virtual DOM and is an instruction for how real DOM should be created.**

Let's say there is a <div> somewhere in your HTML file:
<div id="root"></div>

We call this a "root" DOM node because everything inside will be managed by React DOM. Applications built with React usually have a single root DOM node. If you are integrating React into an existing app, you may have as many isolated root DOM nodes as you like.

To render a React element into a root DOM node, two parameters are required in method **ReactDOM.render([*what*], [*where*]).** A React element using JSX syntax is like below. It looks just like HTML, but there is more than that:

```
const element = <h1>Hello, world</h1>;
ReactDOM.render(element, document.getElementById('root'));
```

<h1>Hello, world</h1> is transpiled to JavaScript code like this:

```
React.createElement("h1", null, "Hello world")
```

React.createElement is a method included in the React library. You can build React apps without using JSX. However, using JSX is strongly recommended for readability and maintenance.

An element is a plain object describing a component instance or DOM node and its desired properties. It contains only information about the component type, its properties, and any child elements inside it. A React element is not an actual instance. It is more like a way to instruct React what you want to see on the screen. You can't call any methods on the element.

React Components

A component is a function or a class that optionally accepts input and returns a React element. A component is an abstraction over an element. They may carry some internal state, and they may behave differently depending on the props they receive. When asked to render, components return elements.

A component is an independent entity that describes a part of your UI. An application's UI can be split into smaller components. Each component has its code, structure, and API. Components encapsulate their state and then compose them to make complex UIs.

Conceptually, components are like JavaScript functions. They accept arbitrary inputs and return React elements describing what should appear on the screen. For example, Facebook has thousands of pieces of components interfaced together when you view their web application. The component-based architecture allows you to think of each block in isolation. Each component can update everything in its scope without being concerned about how it affects other components.

React components are reusable and can be injected into interfaces if necessary. For a better understanding, consider the entire UI as a tree-like structure below. Here the starting component becomes the root, and each of the independent pieces becomes branches, which can be further divided into sub-branches.

React's mechanisms for communicating among components are simple and effective. Props allow data to flow down the component hierarchy from parent to child. When a child wants to talk back up to a parent, a callback function is passed through props.

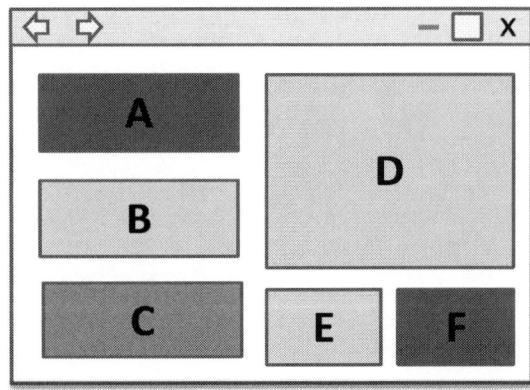
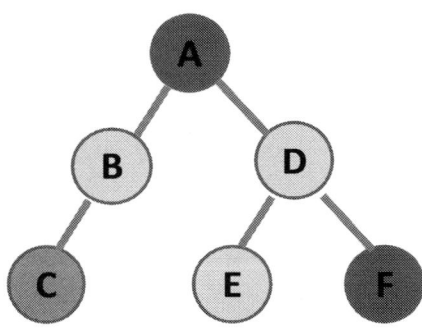

Virtual DOM

In React, instead of directly accessing the real DOM (Document Object Model), it manipulates the virtual DOM. The virtual DOM is a node tree listing of components created in memory. It is a memory area corresponding to the real DOM. The **render( )** method in React creates the Virtual DOM.

Each time the underlying data changes, new Virtual DOM is created, comparing the previous virtual DOM and the current virtual DOM, and only the changes are updated in real DOM. **ReactDOM.render( )** method updates DOM elements that have changed.

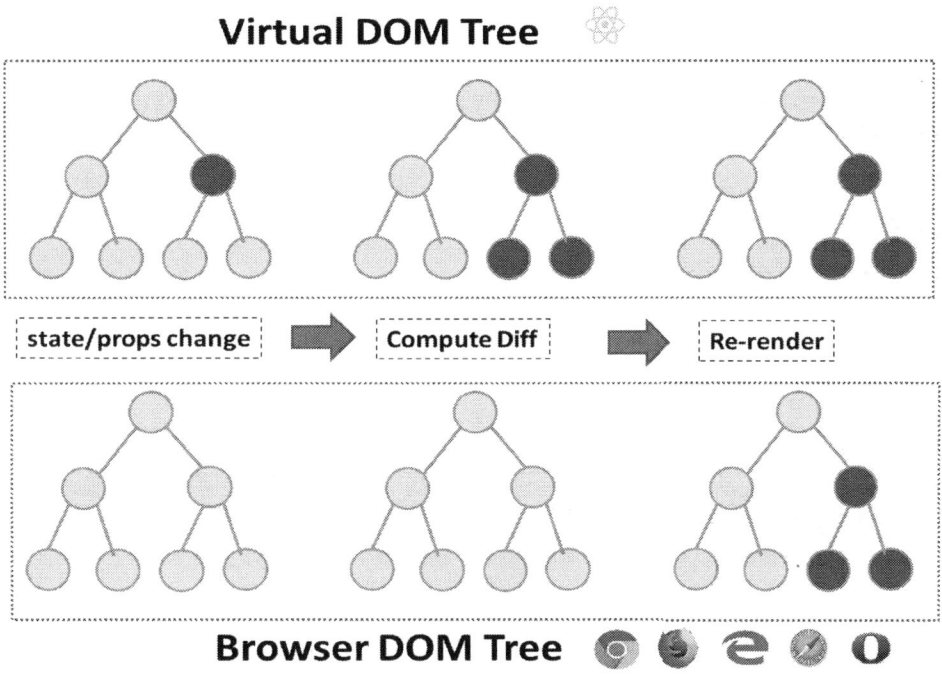

This process that React updates the DOM is referred to as Reconciliation.

How can data be exchanged among components?

In React, there are various ways we can pass data to/from components:
1. Render Props
2. Context API
3. React Hooks (useContext API)
4. React-Redux/Redux
5. Other state management libraries (i.e., XState, MobX)

In the typical React dataflow, props are the only way that parent components interact with their children. To modify a child, you re-render it with new props.

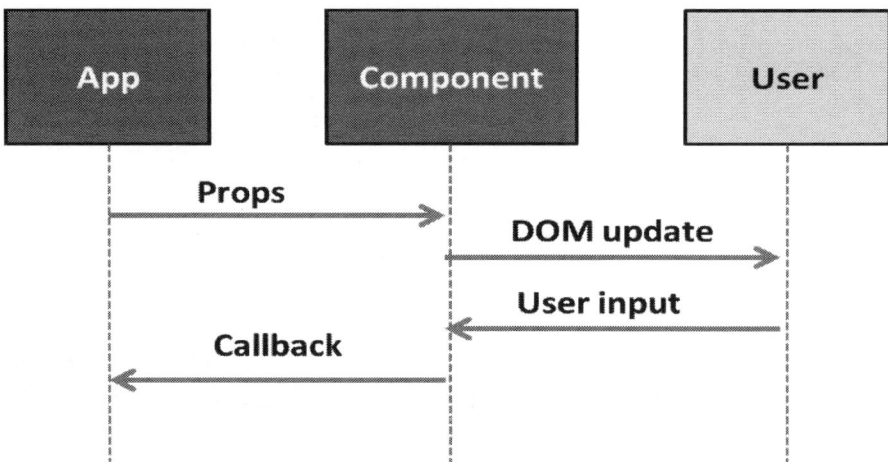

Props and State

In a React component, *state* holds data that can be rendered to the user. *State* is a structure that keeps track of how data changes over time in your application. *Props* stand for properties and are being used for passing data from one component to another.

Data is updated and manipulated by using *props* and *state*. *Props* and *state* determine how a component renders and how it behaves. If components are plain JavaScript functions, then props would be the function input. A component accepts an input (what we call props), processes it, and then renders some JSX code.

props is passed from a parent component and read-only.

In principle, *props* should be immutable data and top-down direction. This means that the parent component can pass on whatever data it needs to its child component as *props*, but the child component cannot modify its *props*.

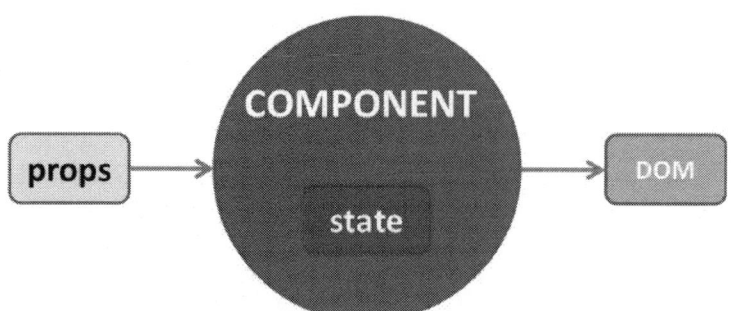

State is used for internal communication inside a component.

On the other hand, *state* is an object owned by the component where it is declared. Unlike props, state is local to the component and can only be initialized and updated within the component. **When the state object changes, the component re-render.** When *state* is passed out of the current scope, it is referred to as *props*. The state of the parent component usually ends up being props of the child component.

Local State and Global State

Local state encapsulates the dataflow within the React component. In other words, the local state in React holds information in a component that might affect its rendering. The local state is much less manageable and testable in a complicated application.

Global state in React means our state is accessible by every element/component of the application. But the important fact is that it could pollute the whole app since every component can access and update it.

Functional Components

A component is a JavaScript ES6 class or function that optionally accepts inputs (*props*) and returns a React element that describes how a section of the UI should appear. Functional components are just JavaScript functions. They take in an optional input (*props*) and return some JSX directly for rendering. **The Functional component does not support** *state*.

ES6 Class-based Components

ES6 class components have more features. The primary reason to choose Class-based components over Functional components is that they can have *state*. Class components can be used without *state* too. Class components implement a render function to return some JSX.

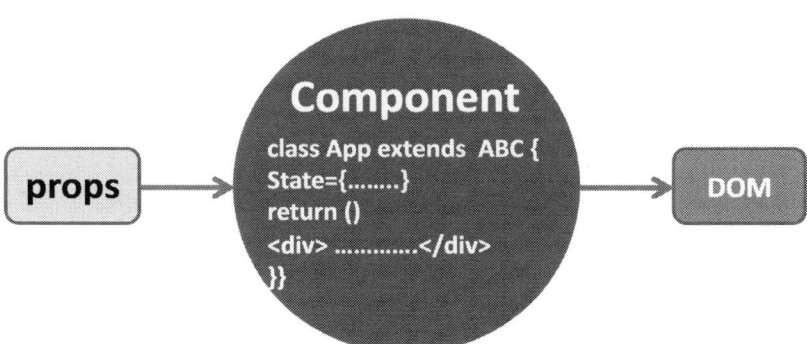

Functional Components with Hooks

Hooks is a new addition in React 16.8 that lets you use *state* and other React features in the functional component without writing a class component. Hooks brings all previously available features in class components into functional components.

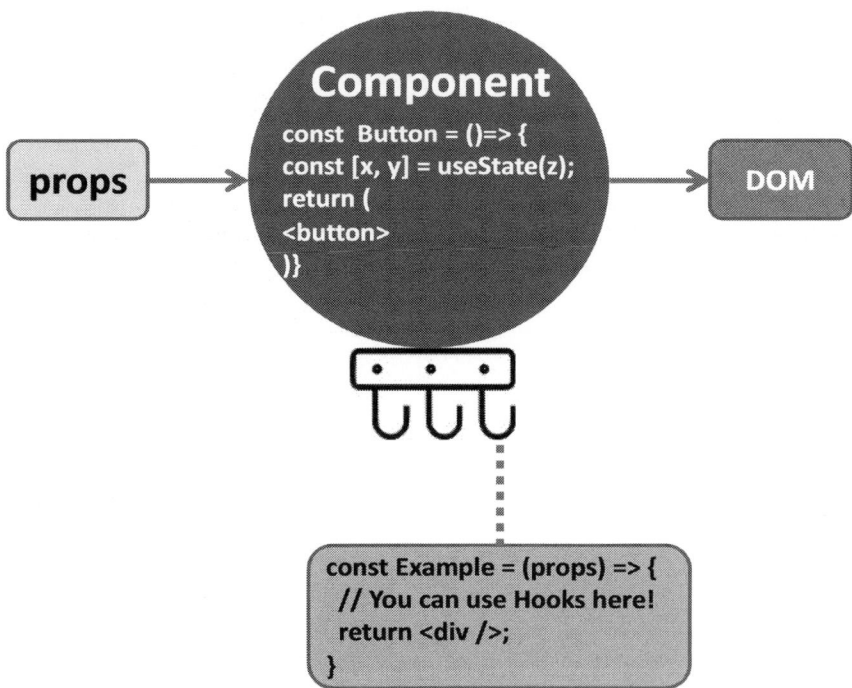

Flux

After having learned the complexity of the MVC (Model View Controller) architecture, the Facebook team developed Flux as an alternative to MVC architecture. Flux follows unidirectional data flow, which supports a composable view of React's components. The Flux architecture is based on the following blocks:

- **Action:** Every change to state starts with an action, which is a JavaScript object describing an event in your application. The actions are typically generated by user interaction or by a server event, such as an HTTP response.
- **Dispatcher:** coordinates actions and updates the store.
- **Store:** manages the application's state and decides how the state will be updated. An application has multiple state portions, and each of them is dependent on the numerous stores of the application.
- **View:** the user interface component, which is responsible for rendering the user interface and handling the user interaction.

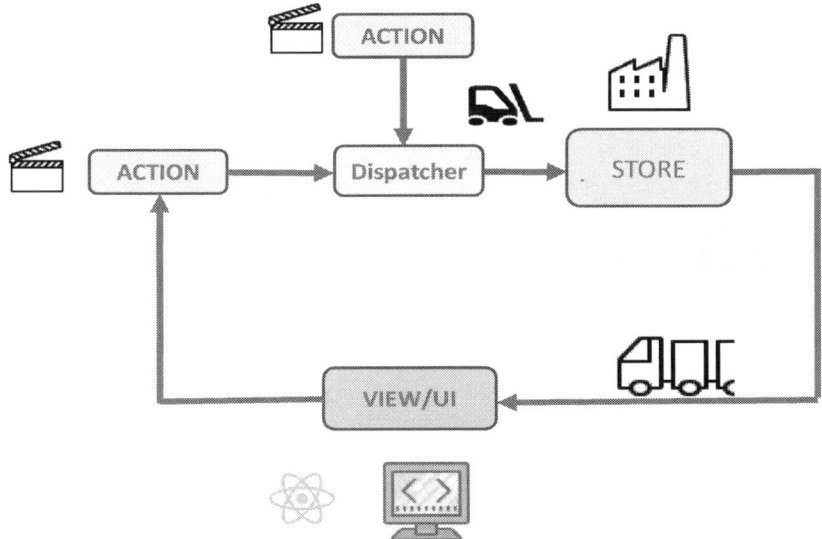

Redux

Redux was created by Dan Abramov and Andrew Clark in 2015. Redux is a library based on Flux architecture. The major difference between Flux and Redux is that Flux can include multiple Stores per app, but Redux includes a single Store per app.

Redux is a predictable state management library to store your app state in one place and manipulate it from anywhere in your app. It helps us write applications that behave consistently, run in different environments (client, server, and native), build more maintainable code, and much easier track down the root cause when something goes wrong. Redux architecture is based on the following components:

- **Action creators:** The actions are typically generated by user interaction or by a server event, such as a server response. The action creators are functions that return actions. Actions are JavaScript objects containing a type and an optional payload. For example, the format of action is like this:
  {**type**: 'ADD_ToDoList', **payload**: 'study Redux'}

- **Reducer**: A reducer is a pure function that determines changes to an application state (based on the new action). It returns a new state object rather than mutating the original state. As our app grows, a single reducer will be split into smaller reducers that manage certain parts of the state tree.

- **Store:** A store is a state container that stores the whole state of the apps in an immutable object tree. Whenever the store is updated, it will update the React components which are subscribed to it. Redux enforces a single global store.

- **View:** The user interface component, which is responsible for rendering the user interface and for handling the user interaction. The views emit actions that describe what happened. Your app reads the state from the store.

ACTION → REDUCER → STORE → VIEW/UI → ACTION

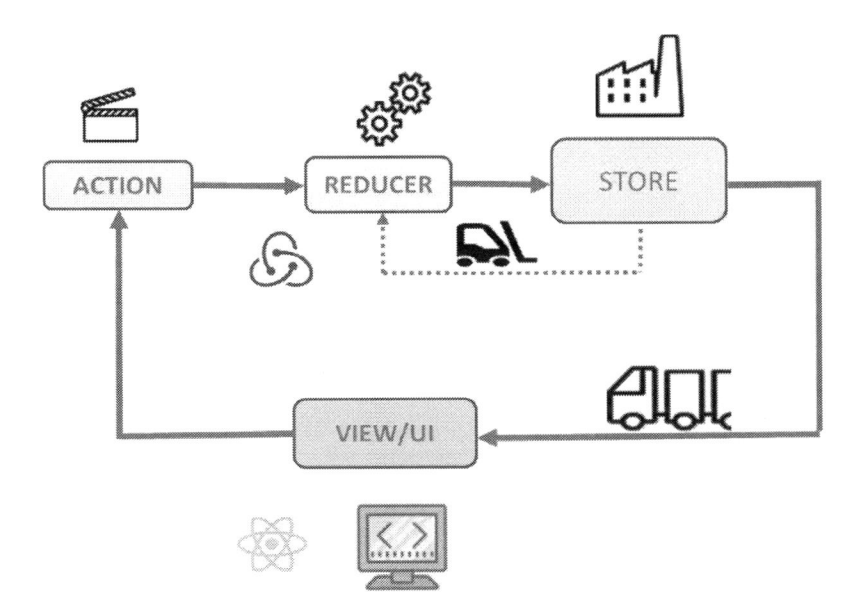

As the data flow in redux is predefined, you have to stick with it. In smaller applications, the amount of boilerplate seems to be excessive. On the other hand, in larger applications, the predefined factory-like data flow helps us. With Redux, you have a centralized location where your application's global state is stored, and the state can only be changed by dispatching actions. When an action is dispatched, the state is updated, and components rerender accordingly. It is easy to reason about and to keep track.

You may not always need Redux for every app. If your app consists of a single view, does not save or load state, and has no complicated asynchronous I/O, you may not find a good reason to add the boilerplate of Redux. Some people think that Hooks (useContext and useReducer) will replace Redux. But Redux is application-level global state management. Hooks are mostly for managing state in components themselves, so usages are completely different. As the complexity of an app increases, more data needs to be managed across the app. In many cases, the state management with one global state container can simplify your application.

According to the "State of Frontend 2020" survey, 48% of React apps use Redux. If you are working on your own project, Redux is not mandatory for simple react applications. However, if you are working with other React developers or preparing for a job interview, you might as well know Redux, even if you decide not to use it.

Redux-Thunk

By default, actions in Redux are dispatched synchronously, which is a problem for any app that needs to communicate with an external API or perform side effects. Redux-Thunk provides a good way of solving the complexity of asynchronous nature in JavaScript via dispatch chaining.

Thunk is a concept in programming where a function is used to delay the evaluation/calculation of an operation. Redux-Thunk acts as a middleware that allows developers to separate any business logic, like Ajax, data manipulation, or any other asynchronous operations, which may not seem to be appropriate in reducers.

In Redux, actions are defined with simple objects or action creator functions that return an object. **Redux-Thunk lets us call action creators that return a callback function instead of an action object.** The Thunk function receives the dispatch method, which is then used to dispatch regular synchronous actions inside the body of the function once the asynchronous operations have been completed.

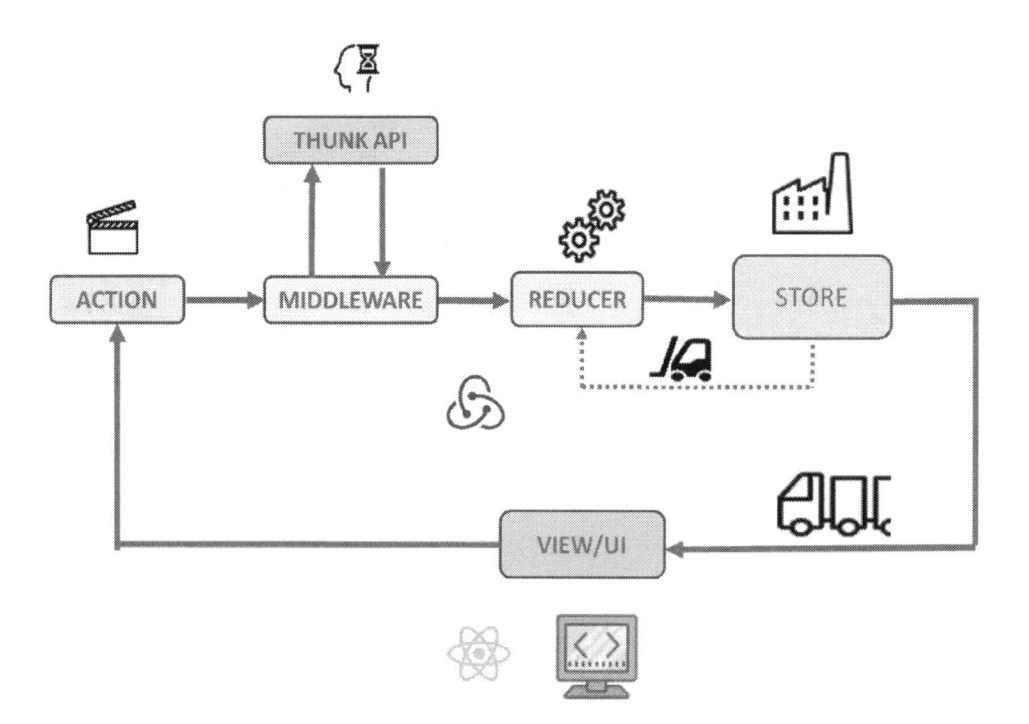

Redux-Saga

Redux-Saga is a library bringing the concept of "task" to Redux. If you have experience in embedded software with an RTOS environment, it is a relatively straightforward concept.

Redux-Saga acts as a middleware that allows developers to separate any business logic, Ajax, data manipulation, or any other asynchronous operations, which may not seem appropriate to processing in reducers directly.

In comparison to Thunk, the benefit of Saga is that we can avoid callback hell. We could avoid passing in functions and calling them inside. Additionally, we can test our asynchronous data flow more easily. Saga can be used to set up complex control flows within our state management system. Saga is suited for complex/large-size applications. The downside is that a bit steep learning curve is expected.

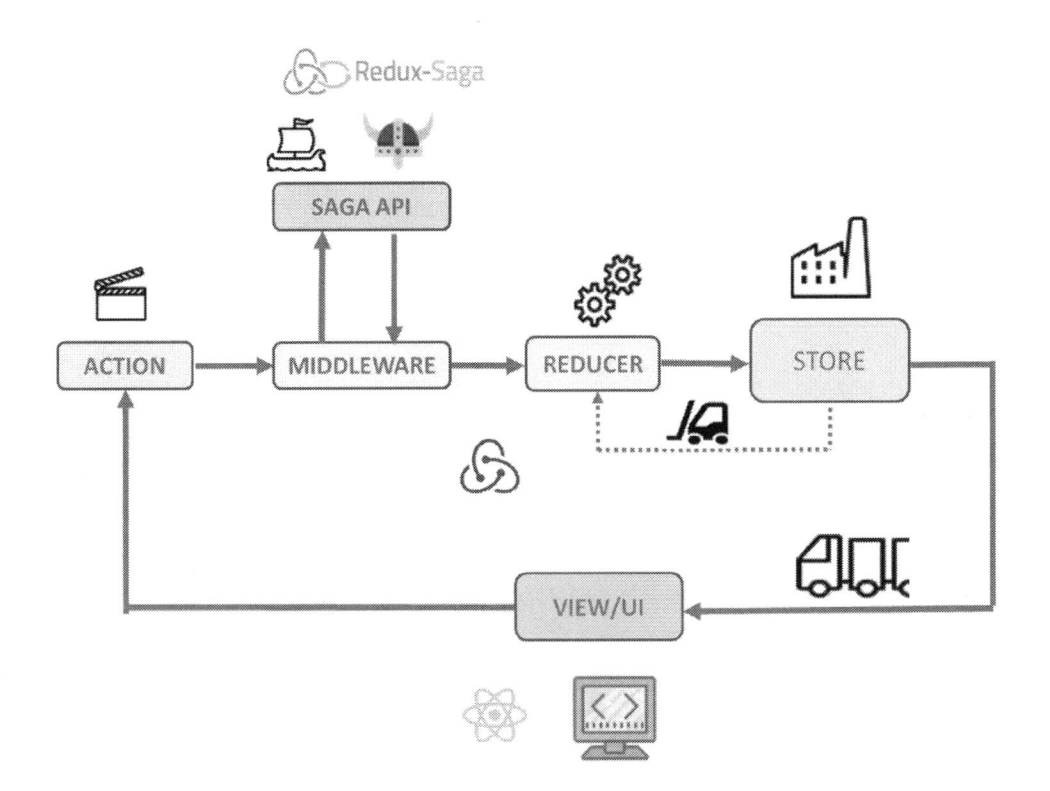

Recoil

Recoil is an experimental state management library introduced by the Facebook team. Just like Redux, Recoil is not an official state management library for React.

Recoil provides several capabilities that are difficult to achieve with React alone. Recoil lets us create a data-flow graph that flows from atoms (shared state) through selectors (pure functions) and down into our React components. Atoms are pieces of React state that can be subscribed to by any component inside the root component. Selectors are pure functions that can receive atoms and selectors and return derived state (computed values or transformation of state). The Recoil hooks are designed to be easily incorporated into custom hooks.

The concept of atoms is to isolate the state in small pieces, making it very flexible. Using selectors, we can easily combine pieces of state and move between being synchronous and asynchronous without modifying the components.

In a nutshell, Recoil is like a global version of React's useState hook. It also supports Concurrent Mode, which is still in the works at the time of writing.

Concurrency in rendering

React, and its libraries are written in JavaScript that runs on the main thread. The main thread also runs DOM updates, browser paints, etc. JavaScript runs on a single main thread, which blocks the react rendering and updating.

In Concurrent Mode, React can work on several state updates concurrently. It means that React can render multiple trees simultaneously, interrupt, delay, or dismiss an ongoing render and defer state updates.

- For CPU-bound updates (such as creating DOM nodes and running component code), concurrency means that a more urgent update can "interrupt" rendering that has already started.
- For IO-bound updates (such as fetching code or data from the network), concurrency means that React can start rendering in memory even before all the data arrives and skip showing empty loading states.

Note: The Concurrent mode is still in the experimental stage at the time of writing in March 2021.

1.3 Server-Client Architecture

Legacy Server Side Rendering (Multiple-Page Application)

Before the time of JavaScript frameworks like Angular, React, Vue…., all the web applications were server-side rendered. When a visitor enters the URL on a browser or visits the website through a link, a request is sent to the Web server. The server gathers the required data through necessary database queries and generates an HTML file for our browser to display. Every page is coming from the Web server, every time we click something, a new request is made to the server, and the browser subsequently loads the new page.

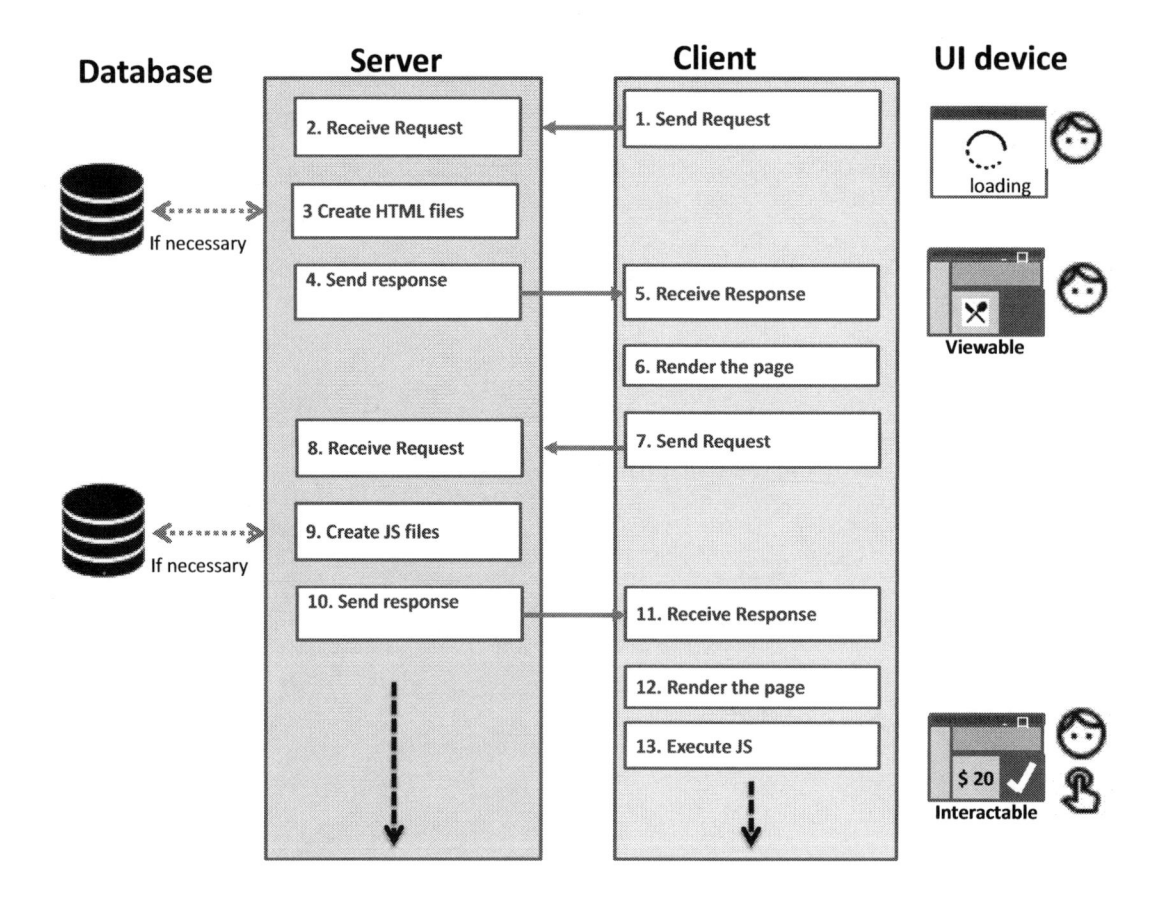

Conventional Server Side Rendering has the following advantages and disadvantages.

PROS
- Advantage in SEO (Search Engine Optimization).
- Initial load duration is shorter.

CONS
- Second and further page load takes time.
- Difficult to handle heavy user interactions.
- Partial real-time updates can be difficult.
- Synchronous rendering, which blocks other processes.
- In the case of a large number of requests, performance will decrease due to the data communication delay and data traffic.
- Achieving natural UX may be difficult.
- Much longer time to develop mobile applications.

Single-Page Application (SPA)

A Single-Page Application (SPA) is an app that runs under the browser and does not require page reloading during use. For instance, Gmail, Google Maps are typical SPAs.

SPA is just one web page and then loads all other content using JavaScript. SPA can serve an outstanding UX (User Experience) since there are no entire page reloads, no extra waiting period. Rather than re-loading each page entirely, a SPA application loads content dynamically. The fundamental code (HTML, CSS, and JavaScript) of the website is loaded just once.

In the client-side rendering, JavaScript renders the content in the browser. Instead of having the content inside the HTML file, we are getting an HTML document with a JavaScript file that will render the rest of the site using the browser. When we interact with the application, JavaScript intercepts the browser events. Instead of making a new request to the server for a new document, the client requests JSON or process on the server. Since the page that the user sees is not entirely updated, the users feel more like a desktop application.

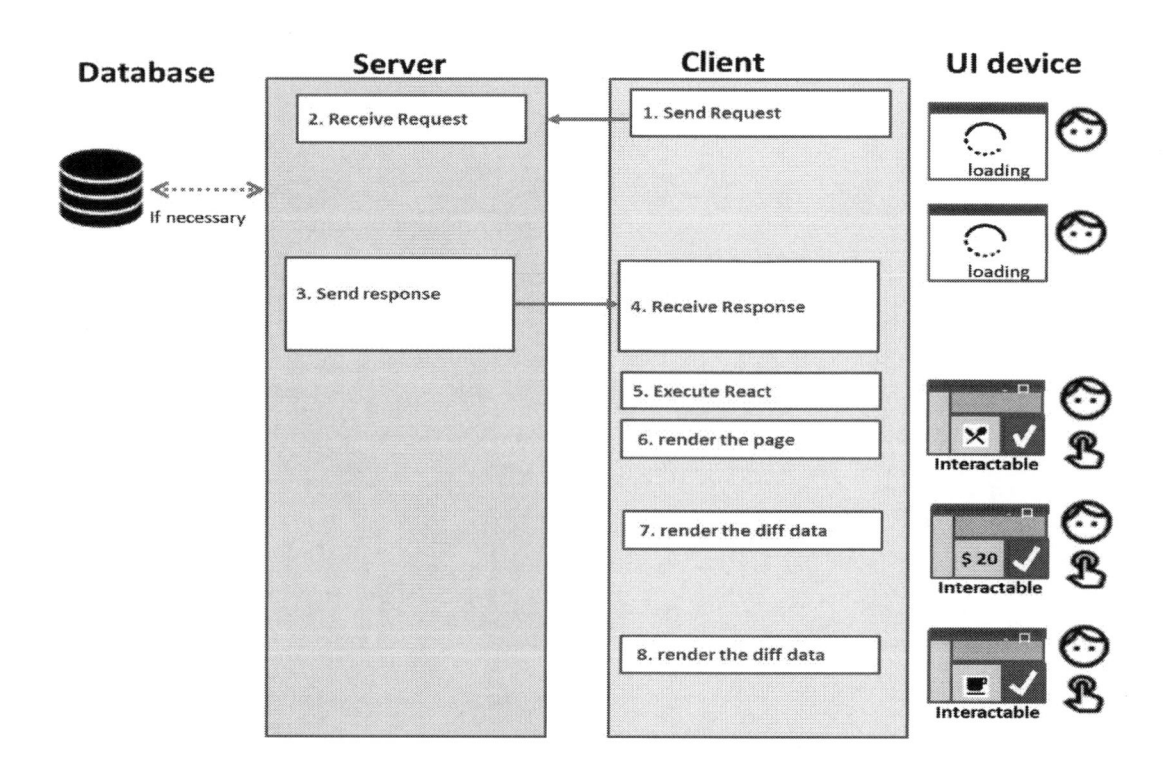

SPA has the following advantages and disadvantages.

PROS
- Handle heavy user interactions.
- Once the initial load is done, the second and further page loading duration is short.
- Partial real-time updates are possible.
- Asynchronous rendering that does not block other processes.
- Less server-client traffic.
- Excellent UX
- Mobile-friendliness
- Easy to transform into Progressive Web Apps with local caching and offline mode.

CONS
- Disadvantage in SEO (Search Engine Optimization).
- Long initial load duration.
- Performance issues on old mobile devices/slow networks.

Universal Server-Side Rendering (or simply referred to as SSR)

Server-Side Rendering (SSR) is not mandatory to build a React app. React is known as a client-side JavaScript library, but React supports server-side rendering as well. In the conventional SSR, every page is rendered and loaded from the server. However, with the introduction of Universal React SSR, things are different.

A typical pattern in Universal React SSR is that server renders a page and then (re)hydrates client-side DOM through a serialized version of a UI's dependencies. React SSR allows you to pre-render the initial state of your React components server-side. This speeds up initial page loads as users do not need to wait for all the JavaScript to load before seeing the web page.

Since the server renders the initial page and the subsequent pages load directly from the client, you have the best of both worlds — the power of the initial server-side content and the speedy subsequent loads, which requests just the content needed for subsequent requests. Your application becomes more visible for Google crawlers to find your page in addition to the above benefit.

The downside is that implementation can be very complicated. In many cases, you might end up creating systems having the worst of Server Side Rendering and Client-Side Rendering. Therefore, using a framework like Next.js is highly recommended. Next.js for React, Nuxt.js for Vue, Angular Universal for Angular are frameworks using Universal Rendering.

JAMstack and Static Rendering

JAMstack (JavaScript, APIs, and Markup stack) is the revolutionary architecture designed to make the web faster, more secure, and easier to scale. Its deployment doesn't run on a traditional setup of origin servers. Instead, automated deployments are used to push sites directly to CDNs (Content Delivery Network).

With various tools and workflows, pre-rendered content is served to a CDN and made dynamic pages through APIs and serverless functions. Technologies in the JAMstack include JavaScript frameworks, Static Site Generators, Headless CMSs, and CDNs.

The static site generators generate the content during build time. Then, once loaded, React takes over, and you have a single-page application. Static rendering achieves a consistently fast Time-to-First-Byte since the HTML for a page doesn't have to be generated on the fly. With HTML responses being generated in advance, static renders can be deployed to multiple CDNs.

Gatsby and Next.js (version 9.3 onwards) are the popular frameworks supporting the Static Site Generator.

JAMstack official docs: https://jamstack.org/

1.4 Mobile Apps

React Native

React Native is an open-source mobile application framework created by Facebook. It is for developing applications for Android and iOS. Developers can use React along with native platform capabilities.

The working principles of React Native are identical to React. The significant difference is that React Native does not manipulate the Browser DOM. React Native invokes Object-C APIs to render to iOS components or Java APIs to render to Android components instead of rendering to the Browser DOM. This is possible because of the bridge, which provides React with an interface into the host platform's native UI elements.

React components return markup from their render function, which describes how they should look. With React for the Web, this translates directly to the Browser DOM. As for React Native, this markup is translated to suit the host platform, so a <View> becomes an iOS-specific UI component or Android-specific UI component. React components wrap existing native code and interact with native APIs via React's declarative UI and JavaScript.

If you are comfortable with Web-based React, learning React Native is easy. Thousands of apps are using React Native.

React Native official site:
https://reactnative.dev/

PWA (Progressive Mobile Application)

PWA is considered to be the future of multi-platform development because of its application on several devices, improved speed, and requires no installation. It is intended to work on any platform that uses a standards-compliant browser, including both desktop and mobile devices.

PWA is delivered through a browser. It behaves like a native application, offering gestures and app-like style, but based on the Web. PWA is responsive and can be browsed on any mobile device, desktop, or tablet. Twitter, Uber, Instagram, Financial Times, Forbes, and many organizations use the PWAs.

PWA is not a specification but a design pattern. There is no official document.
There are three things you need to provide before your site turns into a valid PWA:

- **Service worker:** A service worker is a JavaScript file that runs in the background, separately from the main browser thread, intercepting network requests, caching or retrieving resources from the cache, and delivering push messages.
- **JSON manifest file:** The JSON file contains information on how your PWA should appear and function.
- **HTTPS:** PWAs only work on secured connections.

If your goal is to target mobile devices (Android and iOS) only via the app store, use React Native. If you want to reach a broader range of users and devices via the browser, go with PWAs. If you wish for the lowest-cost option for your development team, then PWAs wins.

1.5 Tools used in this book

CodeSandbox

CodeSandbox is a free Online editor/playground/Cloud IDE tool for JavaScript framework/library. CodeSandbox allows developers to focus on writing code while it handles all the necessary background processes and configurations. CodeSandbox focuses on building and sharing code demos that contain back-end components. The editor is optimized to analyze npm (Node Package Manager) dependencies, show custom error messages, and also make projects searchable by npm dependency.

CodeSandbox allows developers to go to a URL in their browser to start building. This makes it easier to get started and makes it easier to share with other developers. You can share your created work by sharing the URL. Others can then further develop on these sandboxes without downloading. You can also convert your repository (or its directories) to a CodeSandbox. Thanks to CodeSandbox, we can focus on the code without worrying about installation, build tooling, configuration.

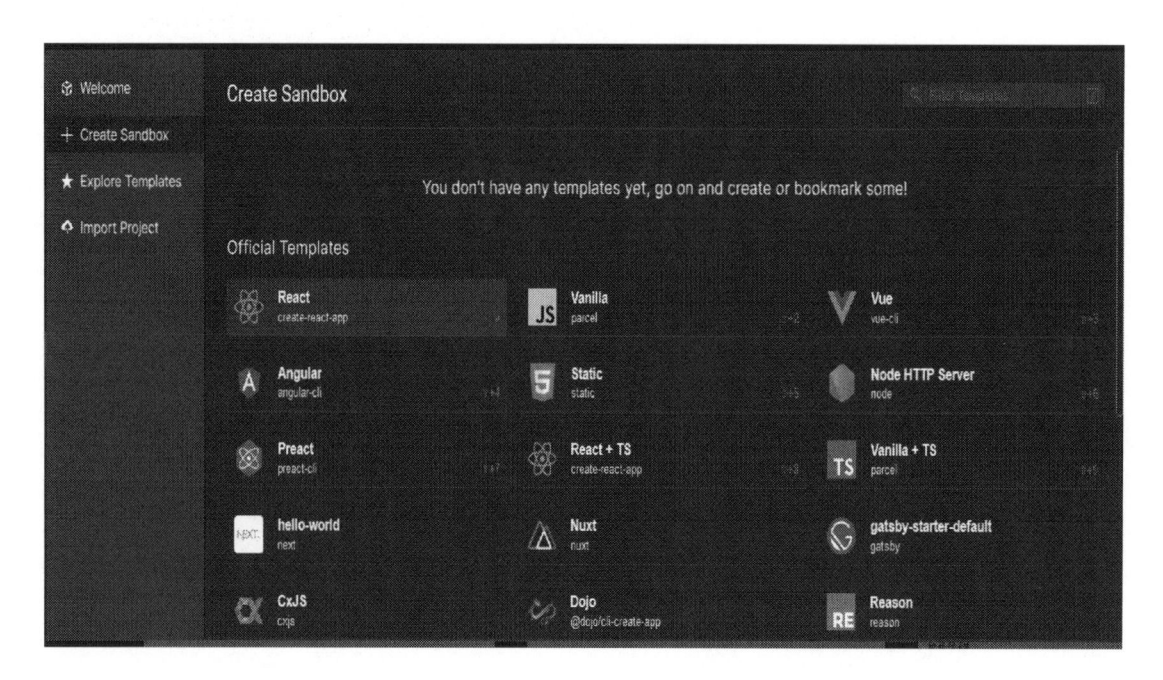

The following is an example of the "Hello CodeSandbox" with React. Please play around by modifying files - index.html, styles.css, index.js, and App.js.

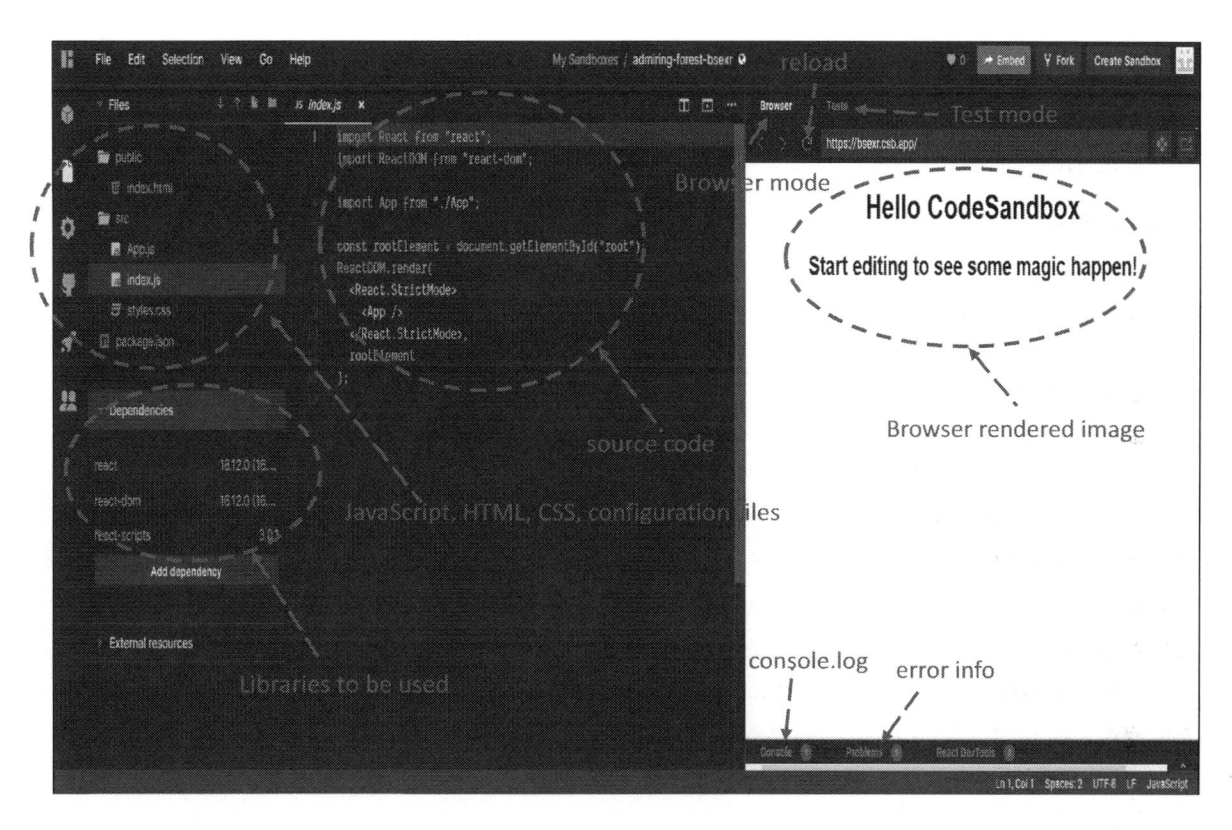

Code sample: https://codesandbox.io/s/react-template-h9y7w

Babel

Babel is a free and open-source JavaScript transpiler, mainly used to convert ES6+, JSX, or TypeScript code into a backward-compatible version of JavaScript that can be run by older JavaScript engines. You don't have to install Babel manually when using CodeSandbox.

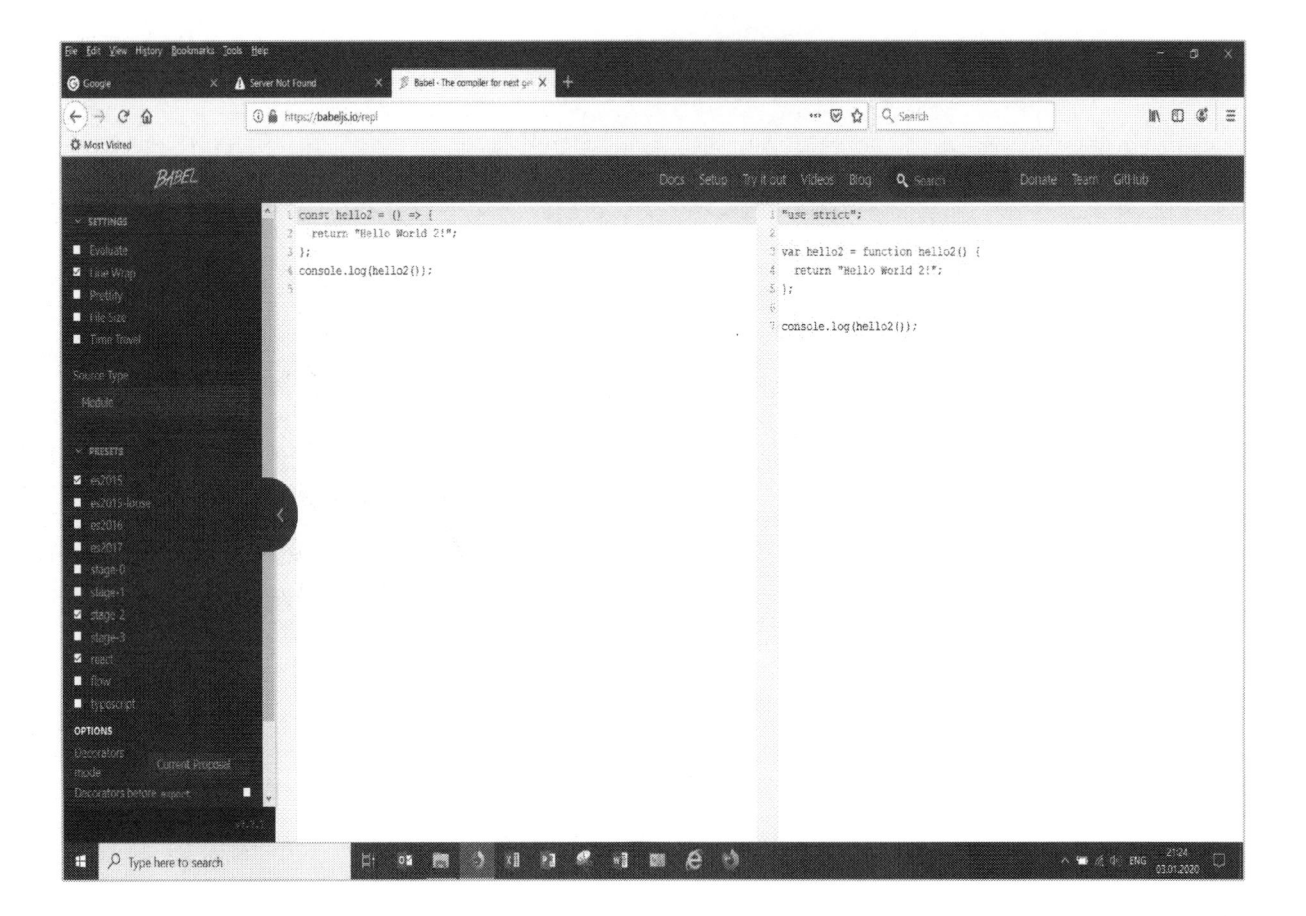

Webpack

Webpack is an open-source module bundler primarily for JavaScript, but it can transform front-end assets like HTML, CSS, and images if the corresponding loaders are included. Webpack takes modules with dependencies and generates static assets representing those modules. You don't have to install Webpack manually when using CodeSandbox.

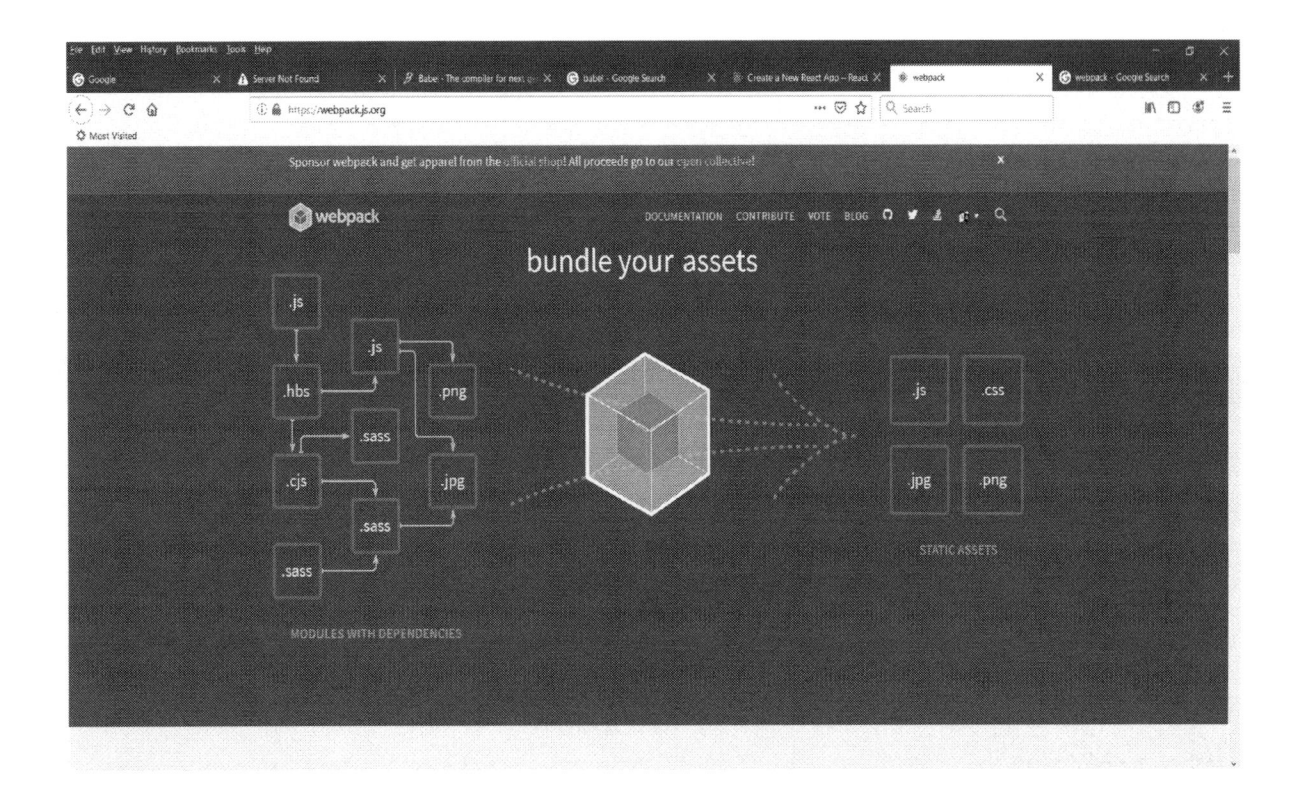

2. INTERMEDIATE JAVASCRIPT

(6 hours reading and exercise)

Common sense is not as common.

(Voltaire 1694-1778)

This chapter is not a complete tutorial on all features of the JavaScript language. Instead, it will outline a set of fundamental principal that require for understanding React ecosystems.

JavaScript is not a pleasant language by any standard. The good news is that you don't have to master the whole ECMAScript spec before learning React. You might as well focus on learning the minimum things, which are covered in this chapter.

If you don't know JavaScript at all, reading the following JavaScript tutorial is recommended.

https://developer.mozilla.org/en-US/docs/Learn/Getting_started_with_the_web/JavaScript_basics

We would also recommend "YOU DON'T KNOW JS series Up & Going " O'Reilly (Kyle Simpson). A free PDF version may be available depending on your area.

If you are comfortable with advanced JavaScript such as Closure, Currying, Higher-Order function, and ES6, you might as well skip this chapter.

2.1 Data Types

There are two kinds of JavaScript data types - primitive data type and reference data type.

Primitive data type

JavaScript has several data types passed by value: Boolean, String, Number, Null, Undefined, and Symbol. Those are referred to as **primitive data types**.

Primitive data Types	Descriptions	Examples
Boolean	true or false	var myBoolean = true
String	A character or sequence of characters placed inside quote marks (' ') or (" ")	var myString = 'hello world'
Number	Any integer or floating point numeric value.	var myNumber = 12345
Undefined	A declared variable has no assigned value.	var myUndefined = undefined
Null	A lack of identification, indicating that a variable points to no object.	var myNull = null
Symbol (ES6)	A symbol is a unique and immutable data type that is often used to identify object properties. Every symbol value returned from Symbol( ) is unique. A symbol value may be used as an identifier for object properties.	var mySymbol1 = Symbol(sym) var mySymbol2 = Symbol(sym)

In the primitive data type, the values themselves are stored in memory directly.

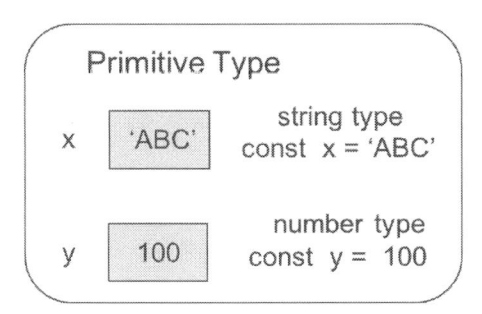

```
Primitive Type

x   [ 'ABC' ]     string type
                  const x = 'ABC'

y   [ 100 ]       number type
                  const y = 100
```

Reference data type (Complex data type or simply called Object)

Reference data types are passed by reference. The variables don't actually contain the value. **The variables store their reference values (memory locations that actually hold values) in memory.** In other words, the reference data type points to the object's location in memory. Many novice JavaScript programmers seem to misunderstand the Reference data type.

Reference data types	Descriptions	Examples
Object	An unordered list of properties consisting of a name and a value.	var myObject = {x:2, y:1, z:3}
Function	Enclosing a set of statements. Functions are the fundamental modular unit of JavaScript. They are used for code reuse, information hiding, and composition.	var myFunc = function (x, y){ return x +y}
Array	Type of structure representing block of data (numbers, strings, objects, functions, etc...) allocated in consecutive memory.	var myArray = ['USA', "India', 'UK', 'Russia']
Map (ES6)	A data collection type, in which data is stored in a form of pairs, which contains a unique key and value mapped to that key. Because of the uniqueness of each stored key, there is no duplicate pair stored.	new Map([iterable object])
Set (ES6)	An abstract data type which contains only distinct elements/objects without the need of being allocated orderly by index.	new Set([iterable object])
Error	A run time error	
Date	A date and time	var myDate = new Date()
RegExp	Regular expression	var myPattern = /pattern/i

In the reference data type, the values point to the object's location (address) in memory. In this diagram below, *x* contains address 1100, and *y* contains address 1300. These are only examples to understand the reference data type.

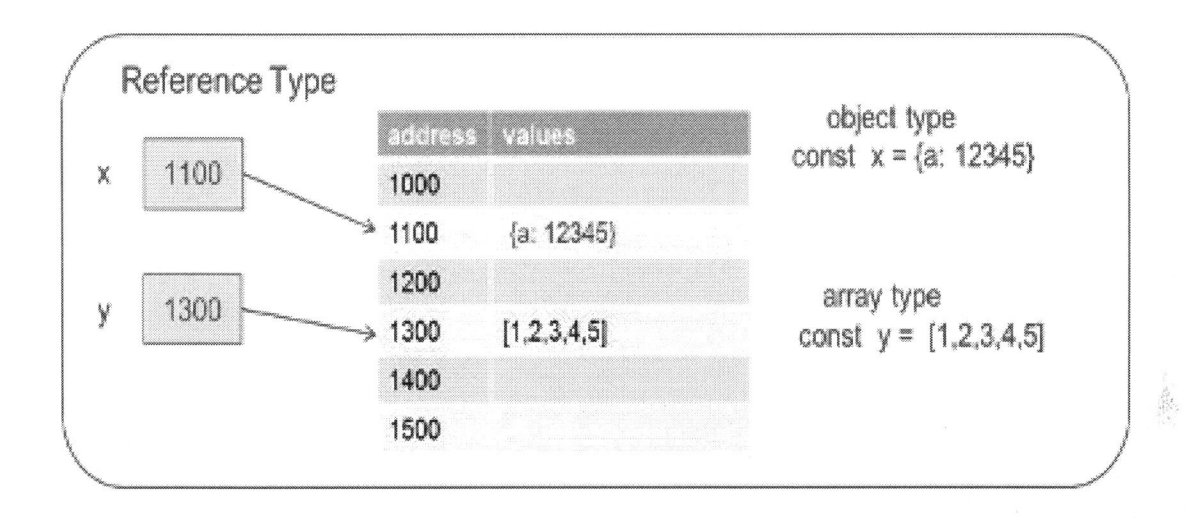

Reference Type

address	values
1000	
1100	{a: 12345}
1200	
1300	[1,2,3,4,5]
1400	
1500	

x → 1100
y → 1300

object type
const x = {a: 12345}

array type
const y = [1,2,3,4,5]

Note: Reference data types are all technically "object," and we refer to them collectively as "object". In a broader sense, all reference data types are considered as "object". However, depending on the context, Function, Array, Map, Set....are not "Object". In this narrow context, an "Object" indicates a reference data type with an unordered list of properties consisting of a name and a value.

Strings & Literals

When writing strings in JavaScript, we normally use single (') or double (") quotes:

var str1 = 'hello string';
var str2 = "hello string";

Template Literal (ES6)

Template literals are indicated by enclosing strings in backtick characters (`) and provide syntactic sugar for concatenating strings, multi-line strings, and line breaks. Template literals are still a string. Template literals improve readability.

```
let a = {
  title: "Dr.",
  name: "Ada Lovelace",
  amount: "100"
};

console.log(`
Dear ${a.title} ${a.name},

I am apologetic about the bad service that you have experienced at our restaurant last week.
I would like to gift you a $${a.amount} check for your continued association with us, and as a way to make an apology.

Sincerely,
`);
```

Code sample: https://codesandbox.io/s/js-tmp-literal-jmxl2

Variables and constant

Variables are used in programming languages to refer to a value stored in memory. Variables in JavaScript do not have any specific type. Therefore, JavaScript is referred to as an untyped language or dynamic language. Once you assign a specific literal type to a variable, you can later reassign the variable to use for any other data type.

Interestingly, *var* declarations are globally scoped or function scoped. On the other hand, *let* and *const* are block-scoped.

var

var is a variable that can be updated and redeclared within its scope. Surprisingly there is no block scope. You can duplicate *var* with the same variables name. However, in ES5 strict mode, duplication is not allowed.

```
var myage = 10;
var myage = 20;   //duplication allowed. The last var is valid.
```

let (ES6)

let variables can be updated but not redeclared. It is block-scoped and cannot be used until declared. You cannot duplicate *let* with the same variables name.

```
let myage = 10;
let myage = 20;   //error ! duplication not allowed
```

If data is a reference data type, such as an array, an object, or a function, you can still change its contents.

```
let myarray = [1,2,3,4,5]
  myarray[2] = 100;   //[1,2,100,4,5]
```

const (ES6)
const behaves in a very similar way to *let*. It is also block-scoped and cannot be used until declared. Just Like *let*, you cannot duplicate *let* with the same variables name.

```
const myage = 10;
const myage = 20;   //error!  duplication not allowed
```

Just like *let*, if data is a reference data type, such as array, object, or function, you can still change its contents.

```
const myarray = [1,2,3,4,5]
  myarray[2] = 100;   //[1,2,100,4,5]
```

If data is a primitive type, *const* variables can neither be updated nor re-declared.
On the other hand, *let* variables can be updated but not re-declared.

```
let myage1 = 10;
myage1 = 20;       // updating primitive type variable allowed

const myage2 = 10;
myage2 = 20;       // error!  updating primitive type variable not allowed
```

Block scope of var, let, and const

Block scope controls the visibility and lifetime of variables and parameters. Variables declared using *var* do not have block scope, while variables declared using *let* and *const* have block scope. Anything within curly braces { } is a block. A variable declared in a block with *let* or *const* is only available for use within { }.

```
//===== no block scope with var ===========
var myage = 1;

if (myage === 1) {
  var myage = 2;

  console.log(myage);
  // expected output: 2
}
console.log(myage); //expected value: 2

//=========block scope created by let ===========
var myage1 = 10;

if (myage1 === 10) {
  let myage1 = 20;

  console.log(myage1);
  // expected output: 20
}
console.log(myage1); // expected output: 10
```

2.2 Expressions and Statements

Any unit of code that can be evaluated to a value is referred to as an expression. Since they produce values, expressions can appear anywhere in a program where JavaScript expects a value, such as the arguments of a function invocation.

A statement is an instruction to perform a specific action that includes creating a variable or a function, looping through an array of elements, evaluating code based on a specific condition, etc. A statement is a standalone unit of execution. It does not return anything. For example, if / if-else / while/ do-while/for/switch/for-in are statements.

2.3 Shorthand expression

Instead of *if / if-else / while/ do-while/for* switch statements, shorthand expression can be used. The ternary expression takes three operands: a condition followed by a (?), then an expression to execute if the condition is truth followed by a (:), and finally the expression to execute if the condition is false.

```
let msg1 = undefined;
msg1 = msg1 === undefined ? "hello world 1" : msg1;
console.log(msg1);      //hello world 1
```

Logical AND operator can replace *if-else* statement. When *x is false*, right expression is not executed. When *x* is *true*, right expression is executed.

```
let x = 1;
if (x === 1) {console.log("hello world 2");} //hello world 2
   //using && expression – the result same as above
x === 1 && console.log("hello world 3");   //hello world 3
```

Logical OR operator can be used to assign the default value. When msg2 is empty, the right value is assigned.

```
let msg2 = "";
msg2 = msg2 || "hello world 4";
console.log(msg2);      //hello world 4
```

Code sample: https://codesandbox.io/s/js-shorthand-gl10b

2.4 Iterators

Iterator is a way to loop over any collection or lists in JavaScript. It is an object with a mechanism for enumerating the contents of an object. For example, built-in objects such as Array, String, Map, and Set have an iterator by default so that the elements can be enumerated by the ***for ... of iterator***.

for…of iterator (ES6)

The ***for...of statement*** loops/iterates through the collection, providing the ability to modify specific items. It replaces the conventional way of doing a *for-loop*. It leads to a clean and readable code.

```
const cities = ['London', 'Paris', 'Rome']
for (const name of cities) {
  console.log(name)}          //Paris London Rome
```

Code sample: https://codesandbox.io/s/js-iterator-zuj5n

Symbol.iterator (ES6)

Symbol.iterator will return an iterator object. The iterator has a method **next()**, which will return an object with keys value and done.

```
const iterable = ['Tokyo', ' Bangalore', 'New York'];

// generate iterator
const it = iterable[Symbol.iterator]()

while (true) {
 // get current status
 const result = it.next()

 // check condition
 if (result.done) {
   break
 }

 // aquire value
 const item = result.value
 console.log(item).      //Tokyo, Bangalore, New York
}
```

Code sample: https://codesandbox.io/s/js-iterator-zuj5n

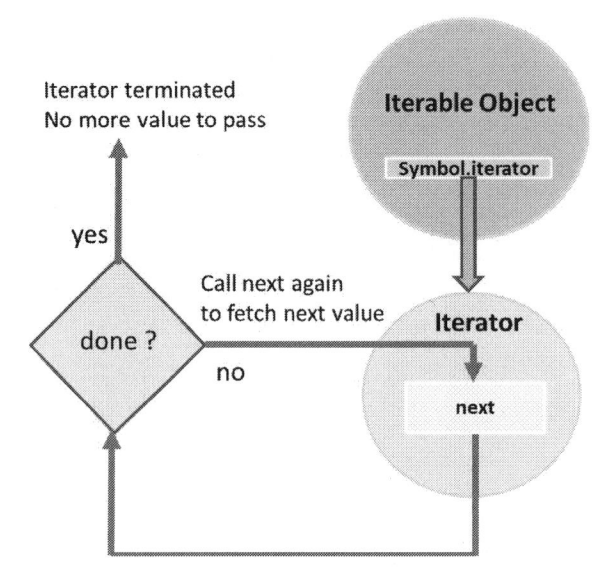

The comparison between classic **for...in** and ES6 **for ...of** is as follows:

	for...in	for...of (ES6)
Applicable to	Enumerable Properties of an Object	Objects that have a [Symbol.iterator] property
Objects	Yes	No
Arrays	Not recommended	Yes
Strings	Not recommended	Yes

2.5 Functions

If you only consider functions as a collection of reusable processes, JavaScript functions may be weird to you. A JavaScript function is a first-class object. It is not the only syntax but also values. The function itself can be set as an argument and return as a value (call back or higher-order function). Functions can be executed with the ( ) operator. There are two literal forms of functions: function declaration and function expression.

When a function is invoked, it begins execution with the first statement and ends when it hits the curly **bracket }** that closes the function body. This causes the function to return control to the part of the program that invoked the function. The return statement can be used to cause the function to return early. When the return is executed, the function returns immediately without executing the remaining statements.

When a function is invoked, the JavaScript interpreter creates an **execution context**. This record contains information about where the function was called from (the call-stack), how the function was invoked, what parameters were passed, etc. One of this record's properties is this reference, which will be used for the duration of that function's execution.

Functions in JavaScript can be used like below:

- Store functions as variables
- Use functions in arrays
- Assign functions as object properties (methods)
- Pass functions as arguments
- Return functions from other functions

Function Declaration (Function Statement)

The function declaration starts with the function keyword and includes the name of the function following it. The contents of function are enclosed in { }.

```
function foo() {//do something }
foo()            //calling above function
```

Function declaration

```
function func1() {
  console.log("dog1");
}
func1();              // dog1

function func2(a) {
  console.log(a);
}
func2("dog2");        // dog2
```

Code sample: https://codesandbox.io/s/js-function-twvy4

Function Expression

The function expression does not require a name after the function. This is referred to as an **anonymous function**. Function expressions are referenced through variables or property. *let,* and *const* can be used as well as *var*.

```
var foo = function () {//do something}
    foo()
```

functional expression – assignment to variable

```
//===== functional expression - assignment to variable=====
let func3 = function() {
  console.log("dog3");
};
func3();                        // dog3

let func4 = function(b) {
  console.log(b);
};
func4("dog4");                  // dog4

//===== functional expression return a value =====
let add3 = function(x, y) {
  return x + y;
};
console.log(add3(3, 7));        //10
```

Code sample: https://codesandbox.io/s/js-function-twvy4

The function expression can add a name after the function. This can be useful in debugging.

```
var foo = function foo() {//do something}
foo()
```

IIFE (Immediately Invoked Function Expression)

The anonymous functions cannot invoke by themselves. The anonymous function can be an expression if we use it where JavaScript expecting a value. That means if we can tell JavaScript to expect a value with parentheses, we can pass an anonymous function as that value.

The main usage is to create a closed scope that protects internal identifiers from undesired external access. In other words, it's a method of encapsulation.

IIFE examples

```
//========= IIFE without arguments ===========

(function() {
  console.log("dog5");
})();                        // dog5

//========= IIFE with arguments ============
(function(a, b) {
  console.log(a + b);
})("dog6", " dog7");         // dog6 dog7
```

Code sample: https://codesandbox.io/s/js-function-twvy4

Arrow function (ES6)

Arrow functions, which are often referred to as Lambda functions, are a concise way of writing functions. Their short syntax is further enhanced by their ability to return values implicitly in one line, single return functions. Arrow functions are always considered anonymous functions.

```
const myFunction = function( ) { //...}
```

is shortened to:

```
const myFunction = ( ) => { //...}
```

If the function body contains just a single statement, you can omit the brackets and write all on a single line:

```
const myFunction = ( ) => doSomething()
```

```
const myFunction = (param1, param2) => doProcess(param1, param2)
```

Parameters are passed in the parentheses. If you have only one parameter, you could omit the parentheses completely:

```
const myFunction = param => doSomething(param)
```

Arrow Function Return

Arrow functions have a built-in way to shorten a return syntax. **When you use curly brackets { }, you need to return the state explicitly. However, when you don't use curly brackets in the arrow function, the return is implied, and you can omit the return.**

```
const name = function(parameter){ return something}
```

is shortened to:

```
const name = (parameter) => { return something}
```

is shortened to:

```
const name = parameter => something
```

```
//conventional function expression
const hello1 = function() {
  return "Hello World 1!";
};
console.log(hello1());

//the syntax of an Arrow Function
const hello2 = () => {
  return "Hello World 2!";
};
console.log(hello2());

//Arrow Function without the brackets or the return keyword
//This works only if the function has only one statement.
const hello3 = () => "Hello World 3!";
console.log(hello3());

//Arrow Function with parameters
//if only one parameter, the parentheses can be omitted.
const hello4 = val => `Hello ${val}`;
console.log(hello4("World 4!"));
```

Code sample: https://codesandbox.io/s/js-arrow-function-b1sq3

Methods

JavaScript methods are actions that can be performed on Object. It is a property containing a function definition. In ES6, the colon and function keywords can be eliminated for simplicity. This coding pattern is used in the Hooks section in this book.

```
//method in ES5 and earlier
const person1 = {
  name: "Alonzo Church",
  sayName: function(name) {
    console.log(person1.name);
  }
};
person1.sayName();

//ES6 method - the colon and function can be eliminated
const person2 = {
  name: "Haskell Curry",
  sayName(name) {
    console.log(person2.name);
  }
};
person2.sayName();
```

Code sample: https://codesandbox.io/s/js-method-6tkd1

Arguments

Surprisingly there is no strict checking of arguments. If a function is called with missing arguments (less than the argument declared), the missing values are set as: undefined. If a function is called with extra arguments, it will be ignored.

```
function func(a, b, c) {
    console.log(a, b, c)
}
//less arguments passed
func(' a')                        // output:  a undefined undefined

//more arguments passed
func(' a', 'b', 'c', 'd')         //output:  a b c

// no arguments
func()                            // output: undefined undefined undefined
```

Code sample: https://codesandbox.io/s/js-arguments-qh9f6

Arguments Object

The Arguments Object is an object that manages the arguments passed by the caller and is available within the scope of the function body. Whether or not arguments are defined in the function, the Arguments Object manages all the arguments passed to the functions.

```
function func1(a, b, c) {
    for (let p of arguments) {
      console.log(p)
    }
}
func1('a', 'b', 'c', 'd')           // a b c d
func1('a')                          // a
func1()                             // nothing happens

function func2() {
    // structure similar to array object
    console.log(arguments.length, arguments[0]);
}
func2(' x', 'y', 'z')               // 3 x
```

Code sample: https://codesandbox.io/s/js-arguments-qh9f6

Function Rest parameter (ES6)

The function Rest parameters (...), indicated by three consecutive dot characters, allow your functions to have a variable number of arguments without using the **Arguments** Object. The **Rest** parameter is an instance of **Array,** so all array methods work.

Function Rest Parameter (ES6)

```
let nameCity = (arg1, arg2, ...moreArgs) => {
  console.log(arg1); // Logs arg1
  console.log(arg2); // Logs arg2
  console.log(moreArgs);
  // Logs an array of any other arguments you pass in after arg2
};
nameCity("Seattle", "Montreal", "Berlin", "Rome", " Bangalore", " Sydney", "Prague");
```

Code sample: https://codesandbox.io/s/js-func-rest-default-param-3686r

Default parameter values and optional parameters (ES6)

Default parameters allow your functions to have optional arguments without checking **arguments.length** or checking for **undefined**.

Default parameter values and optional parameters(ES6)

```
let sayHi = (msg = "hello", name = "world") => { console.log(msg, name);};
sayHi();                              //hello world
sayHi("goodbye");                     //goodbye world
sayHi("Hi", "Mars");                  //Hi Mars

let sum = function(a, b = 10, c) { return a + b + c;};
console.log(sum(1, 2, 3));            // 6
console.log(sum(1, undefined, 200));  // 211
```

Code sample: https://codesandbox.io/s/js-func-rest-default-param-3686r

Functions as Values

JavaScript functions are first-class objects. It is one of the most important concepts in JavaScript. You can use functions like other objects. You can assign functions to variables, pass them to other functions as arguments, return them from functions, add them to objects, or remove them from objects.

Functions as values

```
function sayHello() {
  console.log("Hello World");
}
sayHello();                    //output: Hello World

const sayHello2 = sayHello;
sayHello2();                   //output: Hello World
```

Code sample: https://codesandbox.io/s/js-function-as-value-rjyxy

Note: In the CodeSandbox console, instead of "Hello World   Hello World", " ② Hello World" will be displayed. It is a CodeSandBox log format.

Passing Anonymous functions as values (callback)

Anonymous functions are used for passing functions as a parameter to another function. Anonymous functions can be executed later. It is referred to as a callback, which is like leaving a message in the voice message to be called later. One example of a callback is the event listener. In the event listener, the callback function registered in advance is called when the expected event occurs. You can get used to the callback concept through several exercises below:

callback example 1

```javascript
//Passing Anonymous functions as values
// function expression that can invoke an anonymous function
const sayHi = function(myFunc) {
  myFunc();
};

//pass an anonymous function as parameter
sayHi(function() {
  console.log("Hi anonymous");
});                              // output: Hi anonymous
```

Code sample: https://codesandbox.io/s/js-function-as-value-rjyxy

callback example 2

```javascript
//=====Passing Anonymous functions as values
const add1 = x => x + 1;

//this is not a callback.
console.log(add1(100));                  //101

//callback function example
const setupCallback = callback => arg => {
  return callback(arg);
};
const myCallback = setupCallback(add1);
const result = myCallback(200);
console.log(result);                     //201
```

Code sample: https://codesandbox.io/s/js-function-as-value-rjyxy

callback example 3

```
// functions declaration that can invoke an anonymous function
function myFunc(callback) {
  console.log("hello");
  callback();              //hello
}

// pass an anonymous function as parameter
myFunc(function() {
  console.log("USA");
});                        //USA
```

Code sample: https://codesandbox.io/s/js-function-as-value-rjyxy

callback example 4

```
//**********callback example 4 ********************
//display latitude and longitude by calling Geolocation API
//which is supported by browsers.

navigator.geolocation.getCurrentPosition(success);
function success(pos) {
  console.log(`my latitude: ${pos.coords.latitude}`);
  console.log(`my longitude: ${pos.coords.longitude}`);
}
```

Code sample: https://codesandbox.io/s/js-function-as-value-rjyxy

Use cases of callbacks

Although JavaScript runs code sequentially in top-down order, there are some cases that code runs after something else happens and also not sequentially. This is called asynchronous programming. Callbacks ensure that a function will not run before a task is completed but will run right after the task has been completed. It helps us develop asynchronous JavaScript code and keeps us safe from problems and errors.

For details, refer to 2.8 Asynchronous Systems.

Higher-Order Functions

Functions that take and/or return other functions are called *Higher-Order Functions*. Below, we pass an anonymous function to the *myFunc* function, which we then immediately return from the *myFunc* function.

Higher Order functions

```javascript
// functions can be sent to another function and return from the function
const myHOF = function(myFunc) {
  return myFunc;
};
const sayHi2 = myHOF(function() {
  console.log("Hello world");
});
sayHi2();                        // 'Hello world'
```

Code sample: https://codesandbox.io/s/js-function-as-value-rjyxy

Function declaration hoisting

Function declarations in JavaScript are hoisted to the top of the execution context - enclosing function or global scope. You can use the function before you declared it. However, Function expressions are not hoisting.

```javascript
//functional declaration hoisted to top
myFunc() // logs "function hoisted"

function myFunc() {
  console.log('function hoisted')
}

//functional expression cannot be hoisted.
myFunc2() // this does not work

var myFunc2 = function() {
  console.log('function not hoisted')
}
```

Constructors

A constructor is simply a function that is used with a *new* keyword to create an object. The advantage of constructors is that constructors contain the same properties and methods. When you create many identical objects, you can create a constructor with reference types. After the constructor is defined, you can create instances by using a *new* keyword.

Instances are runtime instances of Component Class. These are represented as JavaScript objects in memory. If the functions are intended to be used as constructors, the first letter is capitalized by convention to avoid confusion. There is no syntactic difference between constructors and normal functions.

```
// define City constructor function in order to create custom instances later
let City = function(name) {
  this.name = name;
};
// instantiate a City object and store it in the city1,city2 variable
let city1 = new City("Paris");     //create instance
let city2 = new City("Tokyo");     //create instance

console.log(city1);      //City {name:"Paris", constructor: Object}
console.log(city2);      // City{name:"Tokyo", constructor: Object}
```

Code sample: https://codesandbox.io/s/js-constructor-d9tko

Many React projects have been using ES6 Class base components to handles states. However, starting with React version 16.8.0, new projects can use Hooks, which do not require Classes any longer. Although there are no plans to remove Classes from React, Class base components have been replaced by Hooks in many projects. It is far cleaner than using Classes in React. But you still need to understand the JavaScript class to maintain and support many existing projects.

'this' keyword in function

A function's *this* keyword behaves differently in JavaScript compared to other languages. It also has some differences between strict mode and non-strict mode. JavaScript function context is defined when running the function, not while defining it. This can surprise many programmers from different fields. Such late binding can be a powerful mechanism that allows us to re-use loosely coupled functions in various contexts. On the other hand, it could lead to sloppy code.

If a function has *this* reference inside, *this* reference usually points to an object. But which object it points to is depending on how the function was called.

'this' location	Location where 'this' refers to
Outside of functions	Global object
Inside of function	Global object
Inside of function (strict mode)	undefined
Inside of ES6 arrow function	The location where the allow function declared
Function being called using call/apply	Object specified by the argument
.bind(this)	Calling bind(this) on a function will return a new (bound) function that has the value of this already defined.
Inside of constructer	Instance generated by the constructer
Inside of method	Receiver object (object calling the method)
Inside of event listener	Event origin

this behavior is very confusing in JavaScript. Fortunately, in React, *this* keyword can be avoided by using functional components like React Hooks. However, as many existing React projects still use Class, understanding *this* may still be necessary.

If you would like to practice *this* behavior, we would suggest the following link.
https://developer.mozilla.org/en-US/docs/Web/JavaScript/Reference/Operators/this

'this' behavior in ES6 Arrow function

An arrow function does not have its own *this*, but it has *this* value of the enclosing execution context. Arrow Functions lexically bind their context, so *this* actually refers to the originating context (defined when you write the code). The following example is ES5 function with bind(this) and Arrow function without bind(this).

```javascript
//ES5  with bind(this), this points to obj1. Without bind(this), it is undefined.
let obj1 = {
  msg: 'obj1 timeout',
  counter: function counter() {
    setTimeout(function() {
      console.log(this.msg)        //obj1 timeout
    }.bind(this), 1000);           //if bind(this) is removed, undefined is displayed
  }
}
obj1.counter()

// ES6 Arrow function points to obj2 without bind(this)
let obj2 = {
  msg: 'obj2 timeout',
  counter: function counter() {
    setTimeout(() => {
      console.log(this.msg)        //ob2 timeout
    }, 2000)
  }
}
obj2.counter()
```

Code example: https://codesandbox.io/s/js-arrow-bind-u0nxl

call & apply

Both *call* and a*pply* are similar in usage. They execute a function in the context or scope of the first argument that you pass. They are functions that can only be called on other functions. With *call*, subsequent arguments are passed into the function as they are, while *apply* expects the second argument to be an array that it unpacks as arguments for the called function.

```
function sum(val1, val2) {
  console.log(this.val + val1 + val2)
}

let obj1 = {val: 1}
let obj2 = {val: 2}

sum.call(obj1, 1, 1)         // 3  ( 1 + 1 + 1 )
sum.call(obj2, 1, 1)         // 4  ( 2 + 1 + 1)
sum.apply(obj1, [1, 1])      // 3  ( 1 + 1 + 1)
sum.apply(obj2, [1, 1])      // 4  ( 2 + 1 + 1)
```

Code sample: https://codesandbox.io/s/js-call-appply-bind-isqqn

Bind

bind( ) can be used by every single function. *bind( )* returns a bound function with the correct context *this* for calling the original function when executed later. *bind( )* can be used when the function needs to be called later in certain events.

```
function sum(val1, val2) {
  console.log(this.val + val1 + val2)
}

let obj1 = { val: 100}
let obj2 = { val: 200}

let obj1Sum = sum.bind(obj1)
let obj2Sum = sum.bind(obj2, 1, 2)

obj1Sum(1, 2)                    // 103  ( 10 + 1 + 2 )
obj2Sum()                        // 203  ( 200 + 1 + 2 )
```

```
function sum(val1, val2, val3) {
  console.log(val1 + val2 + val3)
}

let sumA = sum.bind(null, 1, 2, 3)          // bind all arguments
let sumB = sum.bind(null, 1)                // bind partial arguments

sumA()                                       // 6  ( 1 + 2 + 3 )
sumB(2, 3)                                   // 6  ( 1 + 2 + 3 )
sumB(4, 5)                                   // 10  ( 1 + 4 + 5 )
```

Code sample: https://codesandbox.io/s/js-call-appply-bind-isqqn

calling from arrow function

```
const obj = {
  val: 'dog',
  show: function() {
    console.log(this)                // Object {val: 'dog'}

    let fncA = function() {
      console.log(this)              // undefined   (no bind)
    }
    fncA()

    let fncB = () => {
      console.log(this)              // Object {val: 'dog'}
    }
    fncB()
  }
}

obj.show()
```

Code sample: https://codesandbox.io/s/js-call-appply-bind-isqqn

Recursive function

A recursive function is a coding pattern that invokes itself until a condition is met. In functional programming, recursion is often used instead of loop/while. The downside of the recursion is that it consumes the stack area. It is a trade-off between simplicity and higher memory usage.

In the code below, we start the *countDown* function, which then calls itself via the function name *countDown*. This counts down from 5 to 0.

```
const countDown = function countDown(value) {
   console.log(value)
   value--;    // decrement
   return (value >= 0) ? countDown(value) : false
}

countDown(5)                    // output: 5,4,3,2,1,0
```

Code sample: https://codesandbox.io/s/js-memoize-ktwo5

Memoization

Memoization is an optimization technique that increases a function's performance by remembering its previously computed results. Because JavaScript objects behave like associative arrays, they can act as caches. Each time a memoized function is called, its parameters are used to index the cache. If the data is present, then it can be returned without executing the entire function. However, if the data is not cached, then the function is executed, and the result is added to the cache. This method of optimization is not unique to JavaScript. It is useful in recursive functions as calls are more likely to call with the same arguments.

In the below example, *memoizedAdd* returns a function that is invoked later. This is possible because, in JavaScript, functions are first-class objects which let us use them as higher-order functions and return another function. A cache can remember its values since the returned function has a closure over it.

The memoized function must be pure. A pure function will return the same output for a particular input, no matter how many times being called, which makes the cache work as expected.

```javascript
// a simple memoized function to add something
const memoizedAdd = () => {
  let cache = {};
  return n => {
    if (n in cache) {
      console.log("Fetching from cache");
      return cache[n];
    } else {
      console.log("Calculating result");
      let result = n * (n - 1);
      cache[n] = result;
      return result;
    }
  };
};

// returned function from memoizedAdd
const newAdd = memoizedAdd();
console.log(newAdd(6)); // calculated result 30
console.log(newAdd(6)); // cached  result 30
```

Code sample: https://codesandbox.io/s/js-memoize-ktwo5

Enhanced Object Properties

Property shorthand

ES6 syntax for creating an object literal is simple and clean.

Enhanced Object Properties

```js
let first = "Ada";
let last = "Lovelace";

//ES5 and earlier
let obj1 = {
  first: first,
  last: last
};
console.log(obj1);    // Object {first: "Ada", last: "Lovelace"}

//ES6 Shorthand
let obj2 = {
  first,
  last
};
console.log(obj2);    // Object {first: "Ada", last: "Lovelace"}
```

Code sample: https://codesandbox.io/s/js-enhanced-obj-props-vfq24

ES6 Shorthand for Function Declarations

In ES5, we must state the property name, then define it as a function. ES6 added a shorthand for declaring function methods inside objects. We can omit the property name and the function keyword. ES6 syntax for methods is used throughout this book.

ES6 method syntax example

```
//==================ES5 and earlier method==================
let mathES5 = {
  add: function(a, b) {
    return a + b;
  },
  subtract: function(a, b) {
    return a - b;
  }
};
console.log(mathES5.add(1, 2));           //3
console.log(mathES5.subtract(9, 7));      //2

//==================ES6 method==================
let mathES6 = {
  add(a, b) {
    return a + b;
  },
  subtract(a, b) {
    return a - b;
  }
};
console.log(mathES6.subtract(10, 2));     //8
console.log(mathES6.add(4, 5));           //9
```

Code sample: https://codesandbox.io/s/js-enhanced-obj-props-vfq24

Object.assign (ES6)

The **Object.assign( )** method is used to copy property values from one or more source objects to a given target object. It will return the target object.

In the following example, Object.assign( ) method is used to create the new object by specifying { } as the first parameter:

ES6 Object.assign(example 1)

```
let obj = {
  firstname: "Ada",
  lastname: "Lovelace"
};
let copy = Object.assign({}, obj);
console.log(copy);

// output:   Object {firstname="Ada",  lastname="Lovelace"}
```

Code sample: https://codesandbox.io/s/js-obj-assign-r9evy

The next example is to provide multiple sources as well as a target with values. The target will receive the values from the sources and return with the values merged. The original target variable is also changed as well, *o1* being the target with *o2* and *o3* the two sources:

ES6 Object.assign (example 2)

```
let o1 = { a: 1 };
let o2 = { b: 2 };
let o3 = { c: 3 };

let obj1 = Object.assign(o1, o2, o3);

console.log(obj1);        //output:  Object {a=1, b=2, c=3}
console.log(o1);          //output:  Object {a=1, b=2, c=3}
```

Code sample: https://codesandbox.io/s/js-obj-assign-r9evy

Destructuring Assignment (ES6)

Destructuring assignment syntax is an ES6 expression that unpacks values from arrays, or properties from objects, into named variables. It is a widely used syntax in React/Redux.

Array destructuring examples

```
let numbers = ['one', 'two']   //Basic array destructuring
let [one, two] = numbers
console.log(one)               // "one"
console.log(two)               // "two"

let a, b                       //Assignment separate from declaration
[a, b] = [10, 20]
console.log(a)                 // expected output: 10
console.log(b)                 // expected output: 20

let [c, d, ...rest] = [1, 2, 3, 4, 5]     // Assigning the rest of an array to a variable
console.log(c)                 //expected output: 1
console.log(d)                 //expected output: 2
console.log(rest)              // expected output: [3,4,5]

let [x, , y] = [10, 20, 30]    //Ignoring some returned values
console.log(x)                 //expected output: 10
console.log(y)                 //expected output: 30

let [e = 100, f = 200] = [10]  //default values
console.log(e)                 // 10
console.log(f)                 // 200

let g = 1;
let h = 2;                     //swapping variables
[g, h] = [h, g]
console.log(g)                 // 2
console.log(h)                 // 1
```

Code sample: https://codesandbox.io/s/js-destructure-assign-ychh4

Object destructuring examples

```
let o = { p: 10, q: 20}   //Basic Object destructuring
let {p, q} = o
console.log(p)                    // 10
console.log(q)                    // 20

let a, b   // Assignment without declaration
({a, b} = { a: 30, b: 40})
console.log(a)                    // 30
console.log(b)                    // 40

let x = {c: 50, d: 60}    //Assigning to new variable names
let {c: foo, d: bar} = x
console.log(foo)                  // 50
console.log(bar)                  // 60

let {e = 70, f = 80} = {e: 1}     //default values
console.log(e)                    //1
console.log(f)                    // 80
```

Code sample: https://codesandbox.io/s/js-destructure-assign-ychh4

Functions can return multiple values in array.

```
let [i,j] =(function f(){return [50,60]})()
console.log(i)                    // 50
console.log(j)                    // 60
```

Code sample: https://codesandbox.io/s/js-destructure-assign-ychh4

Spread Operator (ES6)

The Spread Operator expands an array into multiple parameters. It is like a reverse operation of function rest parameters. It can also be used for object literals. It is a simple and intuitive way to pass arguments. The Spread Operator operator makes copying and merging arrays a lot simpler. Rather than calling the *concat( )* or *slice( )* method, you could use the Spread Operator. Spread Operator is a syntax commonly used in React/ Redux.

```
// showing elements of array without creating a loop function.
const city = ["Paris", "London", "Rome"]
console.log(...city)                              //Paris London Rome

// if you do not use the Spread Operator, it is like this
// or create loop if there are many element in the array.
console.log(city[0], city[1], city[2])            //Paris London Rome

//combing two arrays.
let myArray1 = ['two', 'three', 'four']
let myArray2 = ['zero', 'one', ...myArray1, 'five']

console.log(myArray2)        // output: ['zero', "one", "two", "three", "four", "five"]
```

Code sample: https://codesandbox.io/s/js-spread-operator-k12ov

Using Spread Operator, functions can be called without using apply

```
function sum(x, y, z) {
  return x + y + z
}
var myArray = [1, 2, 3]

// Call the function with apply
console.log(sum.apply(null, myArray))             //output: 6

// Call the function using Spread operator
console.log(sum(...myArray))                      //output: 6
```

Code sample: https://codesandbox.io/s/js-spread-operator-k12ov

2.6 Arrays Methods

In JavaScript, arrays are basically a data structure that holds a list of values. These values can be strings, integers, objects, or even functions. Arrays don't have fixed types or restricted lengths.

Includes( ) method

The **includes( )** method is used to check if a specific string exists in an array, returning true or false. It is case-sensitive.

array includes examples

```
const cities1 = ["London", "Paris", "Rome"];
const findcity1 = cities1.includes("Paris");
console.log(findcity1);                  //true
const findcity2 = cities1.includes("NYC");
console.log(findcity2);                  //false
```

Code sample: https://codesandbox.io/s/js-array-method1-50lhi

Some( ) method

The *some( )* method checks if some elements exist in an array, returning true or false. It is similar to the concept of the *includes( )* method, except the argument is a function and not a string. (logical OR)

array some( ) examples

```
const cities2 = ["London", "Paris", "Rome"];
let result1 = cities2.some(name => name === "Paris");
console.log(result1);                    //true
let result2 = cities2.some(name => name === "Berlin");
console.log(result2);                    //false
```

Code sample: https://codesandbox.io/s/js-array-method1-50lhi

every( ) method

The *every( )* method loops through the array, checks every item, returning true or false. Same concept as *some( )*. Except every item must satisfy the conditional statement. Otherwise, it will return false. (logical AND)

array every( ) examples

```
const age = [85, 25, 36];
result1 = age.every(person => person >= 20);
console.log(result1);                              // true
result2 = age.every(person => person >= 30);
console.log(result2);                              // false
```

Code sample: https://codesandbox.io/s/js-array-method1-50lhi

forEach( ) method

The *forEach( )* method executes a provided function once for each array element. The *forEach( )* method doesn't actually return anything (undefined). It simply calls a provided function on each element in your array. The *forEach()* method allows a callback function to mutate the current array.

array forEach( ) examples

```
const array1 = ["1", "2", "3"];
array1.forEach(function(element) {
  console.log(element);                            // 1  2  3
});
console.log(array1);                               //["1", "2", "3"];
```

Code sample: https://codesandbox.io/s/js-array-method1-50lhi

map( ) method

The *map( )* method creates a new array by calling a provided function on every element in the calling array. The *map( )* method is used to modify each element. The original array is unchanged.

Array Map( )

```js
const myArray = [50, 10, 3, 1, 2];

//using Anonymous function
const myArray1 = myArray.map(function(x) {
  return x * 2;
});
console.log(myArray1);              //[100,20,6,2,4];

//using ES6 arrow function
const myArray2 = myArray.map(x => x * 2);
console.log(myArray2);              //[100,20,6,2,4];


console.log(myArray);               //[50,10,3,1,2]
```

Code sample: https://codesandbox.io/s/js-array-method2-wzp3b

Filter( ) method

The *filter( )* method creates a new array with all elements that pass the test.
It lets you filter out items you do not need. The original array remains the same.

Array Filter( )

```
const age = [85, 25, 6, 100, 17];

//using Anonymous function
const result1 = age.filter(function(legalAge) {
  return legalAge >= 18;
});
console.log(result1);                              //[85, 25, 100]

//using ES6 arrow function
const result2 = age.filter(legalAge => legalAge >= 18);
console.log(result2);                              //[85, 25, 100]
```

Code sample: https://codesandbox.io/s/js-array-method2-wzp3b

reduce( ) method

The *reduce( )* method is used to apply a function to each element in the array to reduce the array to a single value. The *reduce( )* transforms an array into something else, which could be an integer, and another array, an object, a chain of promises, etc. In short, it reduces the whole array into one value. It is used for calculating value, grouping objects by the property, executing promises sequentially. The original array remains the same.

Array Reduce( ) example 1

```
const array1 = [5, 4, 3, 2, 1];
const myReducer = (accumulator, currentValue) => accumulator + currentValue;
   // 5+4+3+2+1
const array2 = array1.reduce(myReducer);
console.log(array2);                            // output: 15    //accumulated value

   // 100+5+4+3+2+1
const initialValue = 100;       //set initial value
const array3 = array1.reduce(myReducer, initialValue);
console.log(array3);                            // output: 115
```

Code sample: https://codesandbox.io/s/js-array-method2-wzp3b

Array Reduce( ) example 2

```
const data = [
  { area: "Paris", population: 11 },
  { area: "London", population: 13 },
  { area: "Rome", population: 4 },
  { area: "Berlin", population: 6 }
];

let sum = data.reduce((acc, val) => { return val.area === "London" ? acc : acc + val.population;}, 0);
console.log(sum);                 // 21   (Million) metropolitan population
```

Code sample: https://codesandbox.io/s/js-array-method2-wzp3b

Array Reduce( ) example 3

```
const array4 = [["A", "B", "C"], ["x", "y"], ["1", "2"]];

const array4x = array4.reduce((acc, val) => {return acc.concat(val); }, []);
console.log(array4);
console.log(array4x);
```

Code sample: https://codesandbox.io/s/js-array-method2-wzp3b

map.filter.reduce chaining example

map method, *filter* method, and *reduce* method can be combined together. This pattern is often used in functional programming.

array map filter

```javascript
let a = [1, 2, 3, 4, 5];
const result = a
  .map(function(i) {
    return i + 1;
  })
  .filter(function(i) {
    return i % 2 === 0;
  })
  .reduce(function(total, current) {
    return (total += current);
  });
console.log(result);            //12
console.log(a);                 //1, 2, 3, 4, 5];
```

Code sample: https://codesandbox.io/s/js-array-map-filter-reduce-fxyey

array map filter using Arrow function

```javascript
let b = [1, 2, 3, 4, 5];
const result2 = b
  .map(i => i + 1)
  .filter(i => i % 2 === 0)
  .reduce((total, current) => {
    return (total += current);
  });

console.log(result2);           //12
console.log(b);                 //1, 2, 3, 4, 5];
```

Code sample: https://codesandbox.io/s/js-array-map-filter-reduce-fxyey

If we visualize this code, it is like this.

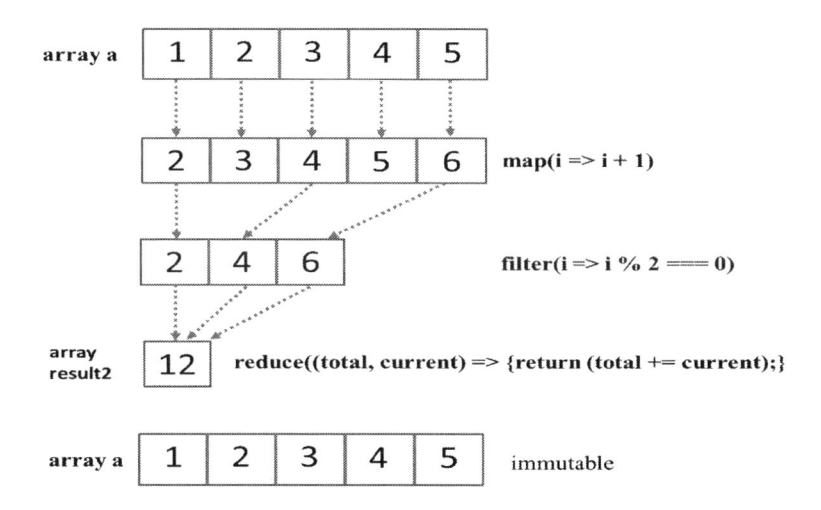

```
array a    | 1 | 2 | 3 | 4 | 5 |

           | 2 | 3 | 4 | 5 | 6 |   map(i => i + 1)

           | 2 | 4 | 6 |             filter(i => i % 2 === 0)

array
result2    | 12 |   reduce((total, current) => {return (total += current);}

array a    | 1 | 2 | 3 | 4 | 5 |   immutable
```

In React, it is recommended to use immutable array methods. Mutable array methods should be avoided.

Immutable array methods (recommended to use with React/Redux)

Length	isArray(obj)	toString( )
toLocaleString( )	indexOf(elm [,index])	lastIndexOf(elm [,index])
entries( )	keys( )	values( )
concat(ary)	join(del)	slice(start [,end])
from(alike [,map [,othis]]	of(el ,…)	
map(fnc [,that])	every(fnc [,that])	some(fnc [,that])
filter(fnc [,that])	find(fnc [,that])	findIndex(fnc [,that])
reduce(fnc [,init])	reduceRight(fnc [,init])	

Destructive array methods (not recommended to use with React/Redux)

splice(,start, cnt [,rep [,…]])	copyWithin(target ,start [,end])	fill(val [,start [,end]])
pop( )	push(data)	shift( )
Unshift(data1 [,data2 ,…])	reverse( )	sort([fnc])
forEach(fnc [,that])		

If you really prefer to use methods mutating original arrays, you can use Immer library. We will learn it later.

2.7 Function Scope & Closure

A closure is an important concept for React/Redux. To comprehend closure, understanding the concept of lexical scope and functional scope is mandatory.

A lexical scope or scope chain in JavaScript refers to the accessibility of the variables, functions, and objects based on their physical location in the source code. **The lexical scope is defined when you write the code.** No matter where the function is invoked from or how it is invoked, its lexical scope is defined by where the function was declared.

The function scope is created for a function call execution, not for the function itself. Every function call creates a new function scope dynamically at run time. When the function has completed the execution, the scope is usually destroyed. The function scope is garbage collected. (JavaScript has memory management)

In the following example, there are two variables: outside is accessible throughout the program and inside is only accessible inside the function:

```
const outside = 'I live in the global scope'

function myFunc() {
  const inside = 'I live in the function scope'
}
console.log(outside)          //I live in the global scope
console.log(inside)           //(cannot access)
```

Execution Context

An execution context is an abstract environment where the JavaScript code is evaluated and executed. When the global code is executed, it is executed inside the global execution context, and the function code is executed inside the function execution context.

JavaScript is a single-threaded language. There is only one currently running execution context managed by a stack data structure known as Execution Stack or Call Stack.

An execution stack uses LIFO (Last-In, First-Out) buffer structure in which items can only be added or removed from the top of the stack only. The current running execution context will always be on the top of the stack. When the currently running function completes the execution, its execution context is popped off from the stack, and the control reaches the execution context below it in the stack.

Lexical Environment

In JavaScript, scopes are implemented via lexical environments. Every time the JavaScript engine creates an execution context, it also creates a new lexical environment to store the variable defined in that function during the execution of that function.

A lexical environment is a data structure that holds an identifier-variable mapping. Identifier refers to the name of variables/functions, and the variable is the reference to the actual complex type object or primitive value.

A Lexical Environment has two components:

1. An **environment record**: the actual place where the variable and function declarations are stored.
2. A **reference to the outer environment**: access to its outer (parent) lexical environment. This concept is the most important to understand how closures work.

Closure

Most JavaScript Developers use closure consciously or unconsciously. Even if you use it unconsciously, it may work fine in many cases. But understanding closure will provide you better control over the code. After React Hooks had been released in 2019, React gradually moved towards functional programming. That means understanding the closure is one of the most important knowledge for studying React.

In JavaScript, every running function, code block, and script has an associated object known as the Lexical Environment. A new Lexical Environment is created each time a function is executed.

If the function has more than two-level nested inner functions, the innermost Lexical Environment is searched first, then the more outer one, and so on until the end of the chain.

For example, we write a two-level nested function like a Closure example 2b. When this function is called multiple times, each invocation will have its own Lexical Environment, with local variables and parameters specific for that very run. When the code wants to access a variable – the inner Lexical Environment is searched first, then the outer one.

In plain English, **a closure is a function with access to its outer function scope even after the outer function has returned. This means a closure can remember and access variables and arguments of its outer function even after the function has been completed.**

Typically, a function has local variables in its code body, including any parameters, and it also might have valuables that are not defined locally nor global valuables. These valuables are called free valuables. Closures are functions that refer to free variables. In other words, **the function defined in the closure remembers the environment in which it was created.**

Learning Closure through code examples

One of the key principles in creating closures is that an "inner" function, which is declared inside another function, has full access to all of the variables declared inside the scope of the function in which it's declared (the "outer" function). In other words, the inner function preserves the scope chain of the enclosing function at the time the enclosing function was executed. Therefore, it can access the enclosing function's variables.

Closure examples 1 – Function scope

The following example shows the scope of the inner function and the outer function. The *outer( )* function has access to the variable outside only, which is declared in its scope. On the other hand, the *inner( )* function has access to the variable inside and the variable outside.

```javascript
function outer() {
  const outside = 'I live outside!';

  function inner() {
    const inside = 'I live inside!';
    console.log(outside);    //I live outside!
    console.log(inside);     //I live inside!
  }
  return inner;
}
const myclosure = outer();
myclosure();
```

Code sample: https://codesandbox.io/s/js-closure1-oo30c

Closure examples 2a – counter without closure

The following example is a counter without closure. The problem is that each time *xcounter* is called, the global variable *xcount* is incremented. Global variables could clash with the names of other variables.

```
let xcount = 0;     //global variable !

function xcounter() {
  return ++xcount;
}

console.log(xcounter()); //1
console.log(xcounter()); //2
console.log(xcounter()); //3
```

Closure examples 2b –closure remains even after the function returned

The following example is a counter with local and protected variable i. The inner function creates an independent execution context containing variable i. The returned function can refer to the variable i, even after the outer function is terminated. Therefore each time *count* is invoked, the variable i is incremented from the previous value. The closure keeps the execution context.

```
function counter(init) {
  let i = init
  return function() {
    return ++i
  }
}
const count = counter(100)
console.log(count())        //101
console.log(count())        //102
console.log(count())        //103
```

Code sample: https://codesandbox.io/s/js-closure1-oo30c

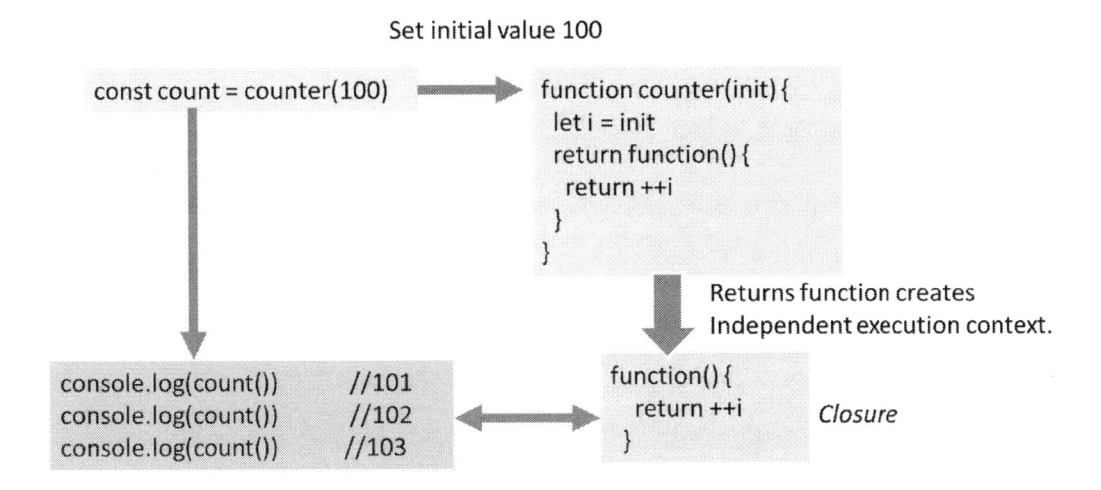

Set initial value 100

const count = counter(100) → function counter(init) {
　　　　　　　　　　　　　　　　let i = init
　　　　　　　　　　　　　　　　return function() {
　　　　　　　　　　　　　　　　　return ++i
　　　　　　　　　　　　　　　　}
　　　　　　　　　　　　　　　}

Returns function creates Independent execution context.

console.log(count())   //101
console.log(count())   //102   function() {
console.log(count())   //103　　　　　return ++i   *Closure*
　　　　　　　　　　　　　　　　　　　}

Execution context contains variable *i*.
Returned function can refer to variable *i*
even after the outer function have returned.

Closure examples 3 – two independent closures created

In the following example, *count10* and *count100* maintain their independence from the other. Each closure references a different version of the private counter variable through its own closure. Each time one of the counters is called, its lexical environment is updated by changing the value of this variable. However, changes to the variable value in one closure do not affect the value in the other closure. We have access to variables defined in the enclosing function(s) even after the enclosing function, which defines these variables, has returned.

```
function counter(init) {
  let i = init
  return function() {
    return i++
  }
}
const count10 = counter(10)
const count100 = counter(100)
console.log(count10())        //10
console.log(count100())       //100
console.log(count10())        //11
console.log(count100())       //101
```

Code sample: https://codesandbox.io/s/js-closure2-r564h

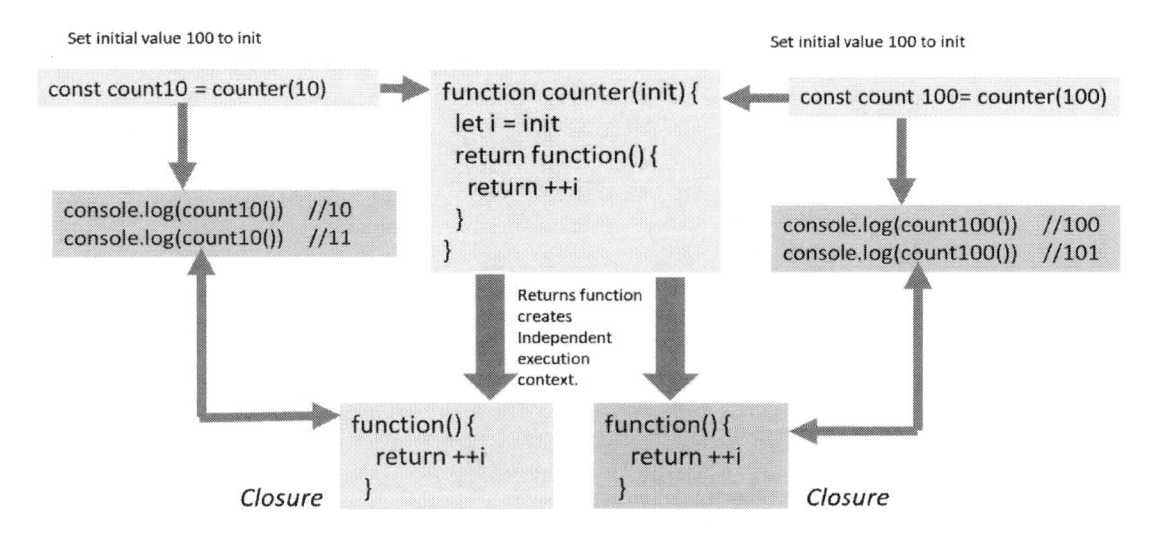

Set initial value 100 to init

const count10 = counter(10) → function counter(init) { let i = init return function() { return ++i } } ← const count 100= counter(100)

Set initial value 100 to init

console.log(count10()) //10
console.log(count10()) //11

console.log(count100()) //100
console.log(count100()) //101

Returns function creates Independent execution context.

function() { return ++i }   *Closure*

function() { return ++i }   *Closure*

Execution context contains variable *i*.
Returned function keeps accessing variable *i*.

Closure examples 4 – Adder using closures

In the following example, we define a function *adder(x)*, which takes a single argument *x*, and returns another function. The returning function **takes a single argument *y* and returns the sum of *x* and *y*.** *adder(x)* creates functions that can add a specific value to their argument.

We use *adder(x)* to create two new functions — *add10 for* adding 10 and *add100* for adding 100. *add10* and *add100* share the same function body definition but store different lexical scope environments. In the lexical scope environment for *add10*, *x* is 10, while in the lexical scope environment for *add100*, *x* is 100.

Using a closure, a function can remember and access its lexical scope even when that function is executing outside its lexical scope.

```
function adder(x) {
  return function(y) {
    return x + y
  }
}

const add10 = adder(10)
const add100 = adder(100)

console.log(add10(5))       // 15
console.log(add100(5))      // 105
```

Code sample: https://codesandbox.io/s/js-closure2-r564h

Closure examples 5 – Methods create closures

JavaScript Methods can be used as well to create closures. This example produces an object containing two closures: inc and reset properties. Each closure shares access to the n variable. The *inc* closure updates the value of *n*, and *reset* closure clears the values of *n*.

```javascript
function xcounter() {
  var n = 0;

  return {
    inc: function() {
      return ++n;
    },
    reset: function() {
      n = 0;
    }
  };
}

let xcounter1 = xcounter(); //create xcounter1
let xcounter2 = xcounter(); //create xcounter2

//two counters count independently
console.log(xcounter1.inc());            //1
console.log(xcounter2.inc());            //1
xcounter2.reset();                       //reset xcounter2
console.log(xcounter1.inc());            //2
console.log(xcounter2.inc());            //1
```

Code sample: https://codesandbox.io/s/js-closure2-r564h

Curry

Named after Haskell Curry, Curry is the process of breaking down **a function into a series of functions that take a single argument**. A curried function is a function that takes multiple arguments one at a time. A curried function will be split into many chained functions, all taking exactly one argument. A curried function works by creating a closure that holds the original function and the arguments. With Curry, functions become more predictable and reusable. For example, Redux middleware uses Curry. The below examples un-curried and curried functions.

```
//================un-curried divider =================
//calling function with two arguments x,y.

const div = (x, y) => x / y;
console.log(div(10, 2));          //5

//==============curried divider =====================
//invoking function with the first argument x.
//The result is a function which will be called
//with the second argument y to produce the result.

const divCurry1 = function(x) {
  return function(y) {
    return x / y; // first x=20,  second y=2
  };
};
console.log(divCurry1(20)(2));         //10

//=============curried divider using arrow function======
//syntax is simpler
const divCurry2 = x => y => x / y;  // first x=30,  second y=2
console.log(divCurry2(30)(2));       // 15
```

Code sample: https://codesandbox.io/s/js-curry-partialapplication-08zi5

Partial Application

Partial application is a technique used to transform functions with multiple arguments into multiple functions that take fewer arguments. A function can be called with fewer arguments than it expects. And the function returns a function that takes the remaining arguments. And this is called the Partial Application of functions. A curried function will be split into many chained functions, all taking exactly one argument, but a partially applied function does not have that limitation.

Partial Application

```
//call a function with fewer arguments than it expects.
//And the function returns a function that takes the remaining arguments.

const add = (a, b) => a + b;
let add1 = add.bind(null, 1);
let add2 = add.bind(null, 2);

console.log(add1(10));      //11
console.log(add2(10));      //12
```

Code sample: https://codesandbox.io/s/js-curry-partialapplication-08zi5

Prototypes and ES6 Classes

A prototype is a mechanism provided by JavaScript for inheritance implementation. It is the basis for code reuse. While most Object-Oriented languages use class-based inheritance, JavaScript utilizes prototypal inheritance. Every function has a prototype property that defines any properties shared by objects created with a particular constructor.

Prototypes with Constructors

```javascript
// define City constructor function in order to create custom instances later
let City = function(name) {
  this.name = name;
};
// sayName() is a prototype property instead of an own property.
City.prototype.sayName = function() {
  console.log(this.name);
};

// instantiate a City object and store it in the city1,city2 variable
let city1 = new City("Kyoto");
let city2 = new City("Tokyo");

city1.sayName();
city2.sayName();
```

Code sample: https://codesandbox.io/s/js-prototype-95x48

ES6 Classes

JavaScript does not have Classes. JavaScript uses Prototypes, singleton objects from which other objects inherit. In fact, all objects in JavaScript have a prototype from which they inherit. This means that JavaScript Classes do not behave exactly like conventional Classes. You can actually add a new method to an array, and suddenly all arrays can use it. This can be done in runtime, affecting an already instanced object.

ES6 Class is merely syntax sugar of the prototypes with constructers. JavaScript developers who want to implement classical inheritance can use ES6 Classes and avoid explicit use of prototypes:

ES6 class
```
class Point1 {
  constructor(x, y) {
    this.x = x;
    this.y = y;
  }
  toString() {
    return this.x + ", " + this.y;
  }
}

let p = new Point1(25, 8);
console.log(p.toString());         // 25, 8
```

Code sample: https://codesandbox.io/s/js-prototype-95x48

Subclassing

The *extends* clause lets you create a subclass of an existing constructor (which may or may not have been defined via a class):

ES6 subclass

```
class Point {
  constructor(x, y) {
    this.x = x;
    this.y = y;
  }
  toString() {
    return this.x + ", " + this.y;
  }
}

class ColorPoint extends Point {
  constructor(x, y, color) {
    super(x, y);                               // (A)
    this.color = color;
  }
  toString() {
    return super.toString() + " in " + this.color;   // (B)
  }
}
let cp = new ColorPoint(25, 8, "green");
console.log(cp.toString());                    //'(25, 8) in green'
```

Code sample: https://codesandbox.io/s/js-prototype-95x48

2.8 Asynchronous systems

Computers are synchronous systems from digital circuits point of view. Generally, all internal logic gates are synchronized with the system clock. However, computers are asynchronous from a high-level systems point of view. Normally, programming languages are synchronous, and some provide a way to manage the asynchronous operation, using the language or through libraries. C, Java, C#, PHP, Go, Ruby, Swift, Python are all synchronous by default. Some of them handle async by using threads, spawning a new process. Unlike most languages, JavaScript is asynchronous by default and is single-threaded. This means that code cannot create new threads and run in parallel. However, commands which can take any amount of time do not halt the execution. That includes operations such as requesting a URL, reading a file, or updating a database. The asynchronous event handling of JavaScript is similar to the event driven RTOS (Real Time Operation System) in low-level software.

The below picture is a comparison between the synchronous process and the asynchronous process. The synchronous process executes task 1a →1b → 1c → 2a →2b →2c sequentially. If one of the tasks blocks the execution, it would add the total system delay. On the other hand, the asynchronous process does not block the process. Even if one of the tasks blocks the execution, it would not add to the total system delay.

time

1b and 2b below are external event delay, such as timer delay, external resources access.

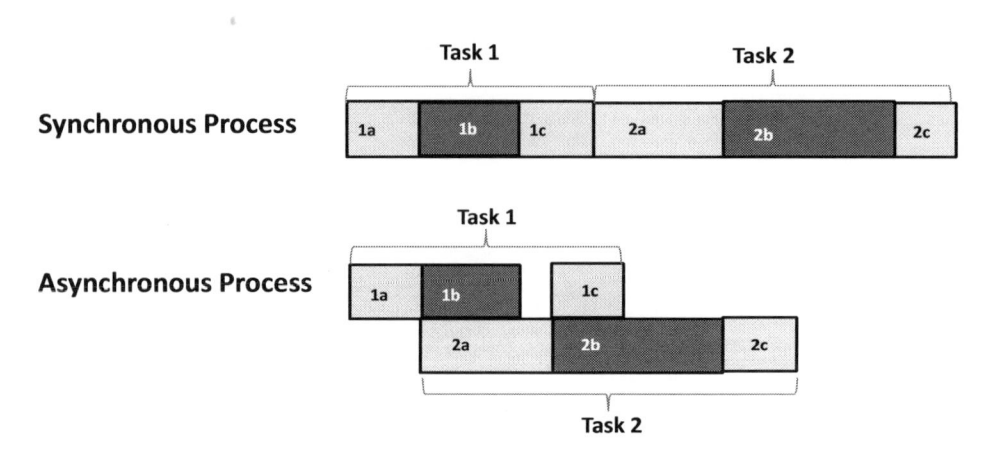

The following example and diagram could help you understand the asynchronous process with a timer event. The setTimeout() method calls a function that evaluates an expression after a specified number of milliseconds. As the setTimeout() method does not block the next processing, "test point 3" is displayed before displaying "test point 2".

Asynchronous (non-blocking) example

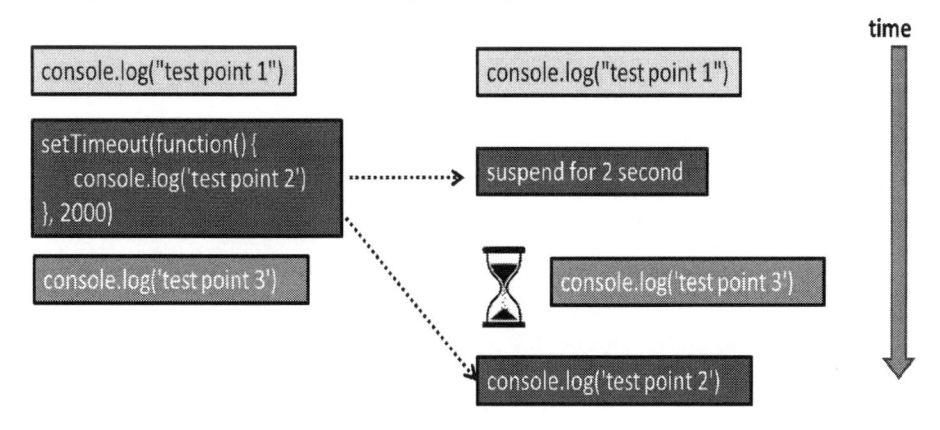

```
console.log("test point 1");

setTimeout(function() {
  //setTimeout triggers an asynchronous operation.
  console.log("test point 2");
}, 2000);

console.log("test point 3");   //this runs while waiting for the 2 sec. timeout.

//expect result
// test point 1
// test point 3
// test point 2
```

Code sample: https://codesandbox.io/s/js-async-n19gm

Nested callbacks - Callback hell

A callback can lead to callback hell when a series of nested asynchronous functions are executed in order. While the concept of callbacks is great in theory, it can lead to some really confusing and difficult-to-read code. For example:

```
function doSomething() {
  doSomething1((response1) => {
   doSomething2(response1, (response2) => {
    doSomething3(response2, (response3) => {
     // etc...
    };
   });
  });
}
```

Promise

ES6 introduced Promises, which provided a cleaner way to express the same functionality. A promise represents a value that we can handle at some point in the future. A promise is an object which can be returned synchronously from an asynchronous function. Promises give us advantages over callbacks:

- No other registered handlers of that value can change it. A promise contract is immutable.
- We are guaranteed to receive the value, regardless of when we register a handler for it, even if it's already resolved. This contrasts with conventional events - once an event is fired, you can't access its value at a later time.
- The promise can handle multiple asynchronous operations easily and provide better error handling than callbacks and events.

A Promise has four states:
1. **pending:** Promise is pending. i.e., not fulfilled or rejected yet
2. **fulfilled:** Action related to the promise succeeded
3. **rejected:** Action related to the promise failed
4. **settled:** Promise has fulfilled or rejected

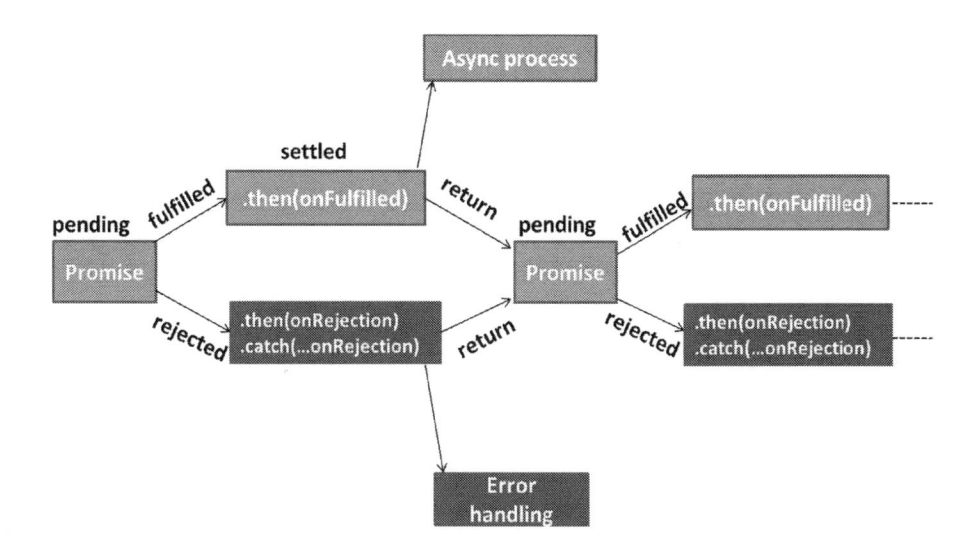

Creating Promise

new promise(function (resolve, reject) {.....}) return promise

Promise constructor takes only one argument, which is a callback function.
The callback function has two arguments, resolve and reject. It performs operations inside the callback function and if everything went well, then call a resolve. If the expected operations fail, then call a reject.

Promise Consumer - Promise.then

Promise.then ([onFulfilled], [OnRejected]) return promise

```js
//========immediately resolved promise=================
let myPromise1 = Promise.resolve("my promise 1");
myPromise1.then(res => console.log(res));          //my promise 1

//========Promise constructor and then resolve=========
/*After 1 sec, a Promise will be resolved.*/

let myPromise2 = new Promise(function(resolve, reject) {
  setTimeout(() => resolve("my promise 2"), 1000);
});

myPromise2.then(res => {
  console.log(res);                //my promise 2
});
```

Code sample: https://codesandbox.io/s/js-promise-xekte

In the below example we are calling *reject* after 2 sec delay. *then( )* can also take in a second handler for errors.

Promise constructor and then reject

```js
/*reject with time out error */
let myPromise3 = new Promise(function(resolve, reject) {
  setTimeout(() => reject("timedout 1"), 2000);
});
myPromise3.then(res => console.log(res), err => console.log(err));
                                                                    //time out 1
```

Code sample: https://codesandbox.io/s/js-promise-xekte

For example, we can integrate resolve and reject like this.

A function returns a Promise object and then reject

```js
function asyncProcess(value) {
  return new Promise((resolve, reject) => {
    setTimeout(() => {
      if (value) {
        resolve(`input value: ${value}`);
      } else {
        reject("no input");
      }
    }, 4000);
  });
}
asyncProcess().then(
  response => {
    console.log(response);
  },
  error => {
    console.log(`error: ${error}`);          //error: no input
  }
);
```

Code sample: https://codesandbox.io/s/js-promise-xekte

Promise consumer - Promise.catch

Promise.catch (OnRejected) return promise.

The Promise.catch method returns a Promise and deals with rejected cases only. So you have to provide an onRejected function even if you want to fall back to an undefined result value.

Promise constructor and then Promise.catch

```js
let myPromise4 = new Promise(function(resolve, reject) {
  setTimeout(() => reject("Timeout 2"), 3000);
});
myPromise4
  .then(res => console.log("Response:", res))
  .catch(err => console.log("error:", err));        //error: Timeout2
```

Code sample: https://codesandbox.io/s/js-promise-xekte

Promise consumer - Promise.all

Promise.all(iterable) return promise.

Promise.all will return a promise once all the promises are resolved. If one of the promises is failed, it will reject immediately with the error value of the promise that is rejected regardless of whether the remaining promises are resolved or not.

Promise.all

```js
function delay(ms) {
  return new Promise((resolve, reject) => {
    setTimeout(resolve, ms);
  });
}
Promise.all([
  delay(2000).then(() => "second."),
  delay(1000).then(() => "first.")
])
  .then(function(txt) {
    console.log(txt);              //["second", "first"]
  })
  .catch(function(err) {
    console.log("error:", err);
  });
```

Code sample: https://codesandbox.io/s/js-promiseall-promiserace-e3lx0

Promise consumer - Promise.race

Promise.race(iterable) return promise.

Like *Promise.all,* it takes an iterable of promises, but instead of waiting for all of them to finish, it waits for the first result (or error) and returns a promise.

Promise.race

```
function delay1(ms) {
  return new Promise((resolve, reject) => {
    setTimeout(resolve, ms);
  });
}
Promise.race([
  delay1(4000).then(() => "second."),
  delay1(3000).then(() => "first.")
])
  .then(function(txt) {
    console.log(txt);              //first
  })
  .catch(function(err) {
    console.log("error:", err);
  });
```

Code sample: https://codesandbox.io/s/js-promiseall-promiserace-e3lx0

Function	Syntax	Description
Promise	new Promise(function (resolve, reject) {...} return promise	The promise global creates promise objects that have the two methods - then and catch.
promise.then	promise.then ([onFulfilled], [onRejected]) returns promise	The promise.then() method accepts an onFulfilled and onRejected callback. The function returns a promise that is resolved by the return value of the onFulfilled or onRejected callback. Any errors thrown inside the callback rejects the new promise with that error.
promise.catch	promise.catch (onRejected) returns promise	The catch() method returns a Promise and deals with rejected cases only if the callback throws an error. You must explicitly re-throw an error inside a catch callback.
Promise.resolve	Promise.resolve ([value|promise]) returns promise	The Promise.resolve() function is a for creating a promise with a given value. Passed a promise as the argument to Promise.resolve(), the new promise is bound to the promise and will be fulfilled or rejected accordingly.
Promise.reject	Promise.reject([reason]) returns promise	The Promise.reject() function is a function for creating a rejected promise with a given reason.
Promise.all	Promise.all(iterable) returns promise	The Promise.all() function accepts a single argument, which is an iterable (such as array) and returns a promise that is resolved only when every promise in the iterable is resolved. The returned promise is fulfilled when every promise in the iterable is fulfilled.
Promise.race	Promise.race(iterable) returns promise	This method also accepts an iterable of promises to monitor and returns a promise, but the returned promise is settled as soon as the first promise is settled.

Generators (ES6)

Generators are functions that can be paused and resumed instead of executing all the statements of the function in one shot. They simplify iterator-authoring using the *function** and *yield* keywords. A function declared as *function** returns a *Generator* object.

The Generator function can be implemented in ES3/ES5 through the closures, returning an iterator object that will remember its own state. However, it is more complicated to implement to be adapted to each use case. We recommend using ES6 generator syntax.

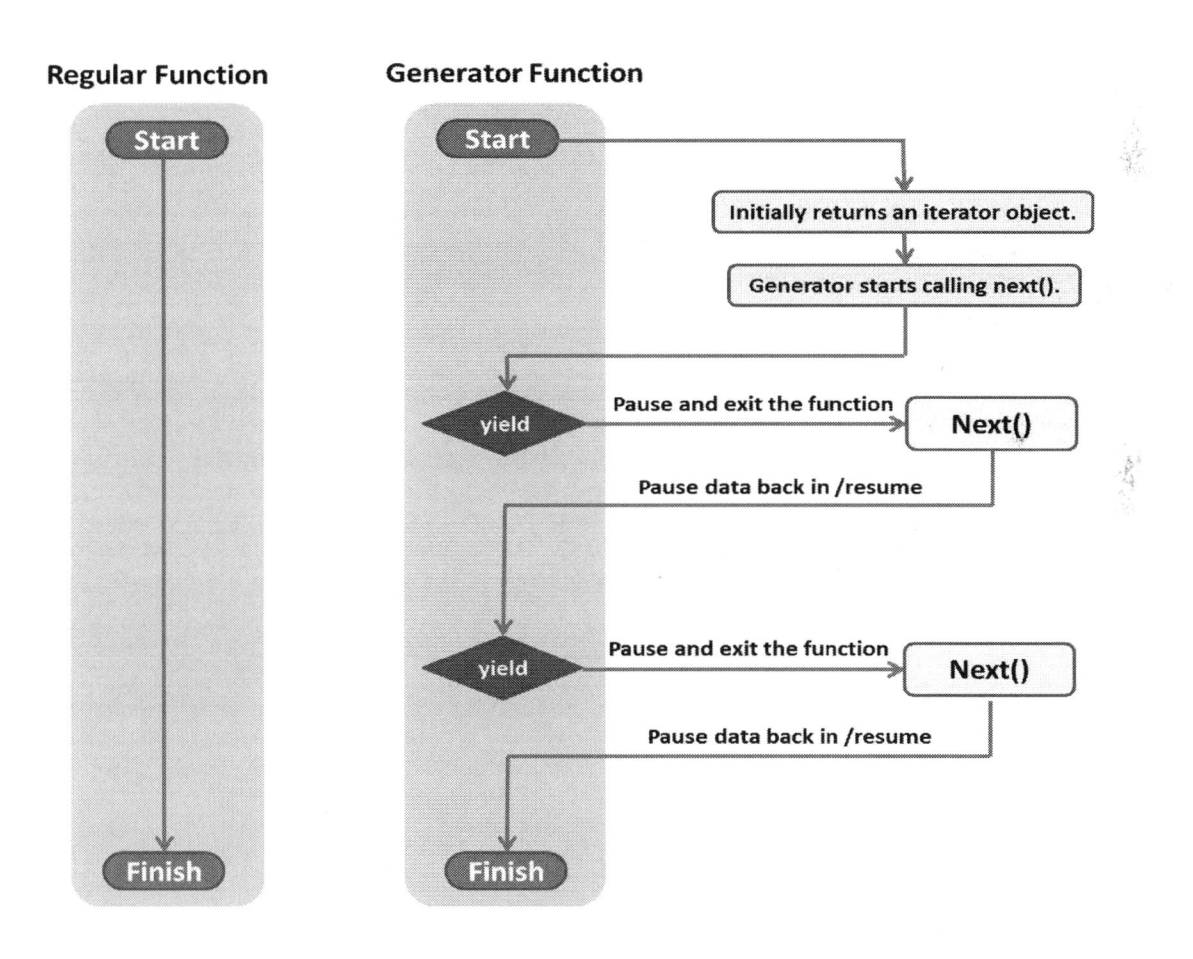

In the following example, we will create a generator named genFunc. We are pausing in the middle of the function using the *yield* keyword. When we call the function, it won't be executed until we iterate over the function, and so here, we iterate over it using the *next* function. The *next* function will run until it reaches a *yield* statement. Here it will pause until another *next* function is called. This, in turn, will resume and continue executing until the end of the function.

```
function* genFunc() {
  console.log("First");        // First
  yield;
  console.log("Second");       //Second
  yield;
  console.log("Third");        //Third
}
let gen1 = genFunc();
console.log(gen1.next());      //{ value=undefined   done=false}
console.log(gen1.next());      //{ value=undefined   done=false}
console.log(gen1.next());      //{ value=undefined   done=true }
```

Code sample: https://codesandbox.io/s/js-generator-nq18f

generator example 2

```
function* foodGenerator() {
  console.log("First"); //output: First
  yield "Sushi"; //return "Sushi" to caller

  console.log("Second"); //output: Second
  yield "Hamburger"; //return "Hamburger" to caller

  console.log("Third"); //output: Third
  return "Pizza"; //return "Pizza" to caller
}

let gen2 = foodGenerator();
console.log(gen2.next()); // {value="Sushi", done=false}
console.log(gen2.next()); // {value="Hamburger", done=false}
console.log(gen2.next()); // {value="Pizza", done=true}
```

Code sample: https://codesandbox.io/s/js-generator-nq18f

Redux-Saga is based on the ES6 generator. It is mandatory to understand the generator concept to use the Redux-Saga library.

async/await (ES8)

async/await functions expand on Promises+Generators to make asynchronous calls even cleaner. The *async* function declaration defines an asynchronous function, which returns an asynchronous function object. An asynchronous function operates asynchronously via the event loop, using an implicit Promise to return its result. But the syntax and structure of your code using *async* functions are still like using conventional synchronous functions:

```
async function doSomething() {
  const   response1 = await doSomething1(),
  const   response2 = await doSomething2(response1),
  const   response3 = await doSomething3(response2);
}
```

await effectively makes each call appear as if it's a synchronous operation while not holding up JavaScript's single processing thread.

async

We will start with the *async* keyword. It is placed before function, like below:

```
async function f(){ return "promise 1 done";}    f().then(alert);
                                                 // "promise 1 done!"
```

Code sample: https://codesandbox.io/s/js-async-await-z26x3

The keyword *async* before a function means that a function always returns a Promise. If the code has return <non-promise> in it, then JavaScript automatically wraps it into a resolved promise with that value. For instance, the code above returns a resolved Promise with the result "promise 1 done".

We could explicitly return a Promise that would result in the same:

```
async function f() { return Promise.resolve("promise 2 done");}   f().then(alert);
                                                                  // "promise 2 done!"
```

Code sample: https://codesandbox.io/s/js-async-await-z26x3

async ensures that the function returns a *Promise*, wraps non-promises in it. And there is another keyword *await* that works only inside *async* functions.

await

The *await* syntax works only inside *async* functions:
let value = await promise;

The keyword *await* makes JavaScript wait until that Promise settles and returns its result. Below is an example with a Promise that resolves in 2 seconds:

```
async function myFunc() {
  let promise = new Promise((resolve, reject) => {
    setTimeout(() => resolve("promise 3 done!"), 2000)
  })
  let result = await promise; // wait till the promise resolves (*)
  console.log(result)                                    // "promise 3 done!"
}

myFunc()
console.log("Please wait")              //while waiting, this is executed
```

Code sample: https://codesandbox.io/s/js-async-await-z26x3

The function execution "pauses" at the line (*) and resumes when the Promise settles. So the code above shows "promise 3 done!" in 2 seconds. *await* literally makes JavaScript wait until the Promise settles and then go on with the result. However, that doesn't cost any CPU resources because the JavaScript engine can execute other tasks while waiting.

Solution	Description	Pros	Cons
Native Javascipt with callback	Uses native Javascript callback and clousure to handle async events.	Highest performance	Difficult to track in case of nested callbacks.
Promise (ES6)	The Promise object represents the eventual completion (or failure) of an asynchronous operation, and its resulting value.	It can handle multiple async operations easily and provide better error handling than callbacks and events. Being able to wait for multiple promises at the same time.	A bit difficult API syntax.
Generators (ES6)	halting function execution and yielding values . Generator function are executed yield by yield.	Easy to test. A generator function is similar to a state machine.	Generators are one-time access only. To generate the values again, a new generator object has to be made.
Async/Await (ES8)	built on top of promises + generatos. Functions with the async keyword will always return a promise.	It allows applications to retain a logical structure that resembles synchronous but handles asynchronous. It doesn't use callbacks	It makes asynchronous code less obvious. The await keyword can only wait for promises one at a time, not several at once.

Asynchronous process summary

2.9 Making HTTP requests

Fetch and Axios are promise-based JavaScript APIs that lets us use Ajax requests without using complicated XMLHttpRequest API.

Fetch API

The Fetch API provides an interface for accessing and manipulating parts of the HTTP sequence, such as requests and responses. It also provides a global fetch( ) method that provides a simple, logical way to fetch resources asynchronously across the network.

The fetch( ) method takes one mandatory argument that indicates the path to the resource you want to fetch, and it returns a Promise that resolves with an object of the built-in Response class as soon as the server responds with headers.

The code below shows a basic fetch request in which we are fetching a JSON file across the network.

```
fetch("https://examples/example.json")            // make the request
  .then(response => response.json())              // json method on the response
  .then(data => {console.log(data)}).             // handle success
  .catch(error => console.error(error)).          //handle error
```

When receiving data without errors and assuming that we expect a JSON response, we first need to call the json( ) method to transform the Response object into an object that we can interact with.

There are a number of methods available to define the body content in various formats: *response.json(), response.text(), response.formData(), response.blob(), response.arrayBuffer()*

For more details Fetch API information:
https://developers.google.com/web/updates/2015/03/introduction-to-fetch
https://developer.mozilla.org/en-US/docs/Web/API/Fetch_API/Using_Fetch

Axios library

Axios is a JavaScript library that helps us make HTTP requests to external resources and supports the Promise API.

Unlike Fetch API, Axios does not come as a native JavaScript API, but there are many advantages over fetch API.

- It automatically transforms request and response data.
- It has built-in support for download progress.
- It has the ability to cancel requests.
- It can be used to intercept HTTP requests and responses.
- It enables client-side protection against CSRF(Cross-Site Request Forgery).

On the other hand, Fetch API supports lower-level operations and more flexible than Axios.

The code below shows a basic fetch request in which we are fetching JSON data across the network. With Fetch API, we need to deal with two promises. With Axios, we can directly access the JSON result inside of the response object data property.

```
axios.get('https://examples/example.json')        //make the request expecting JSON
  .then((response) => {console.log(response);})   //handle success
  .catch((error) => {console.log(error);}).       // handle error
```

Axios also provides functions to make other network requests as well, matching the HTTP verbs that you wish to execute:

axios.request, axios.get, axios.delete, axios.head, axios.options, axios.post, axios.put, axios.patch

The response from a request contains the following information:

response.data, response.status, response.statusText, response.headers, response.config, response.request

For details, refer to the official information:
https://github.com/axios/axios

2.10 Modules

ES6 supports modules using *import/export* syntax. You can use the *export* keyword to export parts of code to other modules. And when you have a module with *exports*, you can access the functionality in another module by using the *import* keyword.

Named exports

Named exports are useful to export several values. During the import, you can use the same name to refer to the corresponding value. Exported functions can be used by other modules by using import syntax. It is also possible to export all the variables in one area by using this syntax for listing. You can import all of the module's functionality by using import * as <Namespace> syntax.

(File name: test.js)

```javascript
// export an array
export let months = ["Jan","Feb","Mar","Apr","Aug","Sep","Oct","Nov","Dec"];

// export a constant
export const year = 2050;

// export function
export const hello1 = function() {console.log("Hello World 1");};

// export arrow function
export const hello2 = () => console.log("Hello World 2");
```

(File name: index.js)

```javascript
import { months, year } from "./test.js";
import { hello1, hello2 } from "./test.js";

console.log(months);        //{"Jan","Feb","Mar".....}
console.log(year);          //2050

console.log(hello1);        //function hello1() {}
hello1();                   //hello World 1

console.log(hello2);        //function hello2() {}
hello2();                   //hello World 2
```

Code sample: https://codesandbox.io/s/js-module1-l34x3

Default export

The other type of export is a default export. A module can contain only one default export. A default export can be a function, a class, an object, or anything else. This value is considered as the "main" exported value since it will be the simplest to import.
This is a common pattern for libraries because you can import the library without specifying each library.

(File name: test.js)

```javascript
export default function sum(x, y) {
  return x + y;
}
```

(File name: index.js)

```javascript
import sum from "./test.js";

console.log("10 + 20 = " + sum(10, 20));
```

It is common for a module using mixing of both named exports and default exports.

```
import ReactDOM from 'react-dom';

ReactDOM .render(
    // ...
);
```

In case of using only *render( )* function , the named render( ) function can be imported like this.

```
import {render} from 'react-dom';

render(
    // ...
);
```

The export implementation to achieve above is like this.

```
export const render = (component ,target) => {
    // ...
};

const ReactDom = {
render,
    // ... other functions
};

export default ReactDOM;
```

3. REACT FUNDAMENTALS

(10 hours reading and exercise)

Each problem that I solved became a rule, which served afterward to solve other problems.

(René Descartes 1596-1650)

React official site: https://reactjs.org/

3.1 JSX

JSX is a JavaScript syntax extension that allows us to write HTML like JavaScript. JSX produces React "elements". JSX is converted into browser-compatible JavaScript using transpilers (i.e., Babel). Although it is not mandatory to use JSX, there are many advantages.

- JSX is faster because it performs optimization when compiling code to JavaScript.
- JSX is also type-safe, and most of the errors can be detected during compilation.
- JSX makes it easier and faster to write templates if you are familiar with HTML.
- JSX is a declarative style language that is more readable when describing hierarchy structure. (DOM's structure is hierarchy)

In the following example, component App returns a React element <div> ....</div> using JSX that looks like a regular HTML.

(index.js)
```
import React from "react";
import ReactDOM from "react-dom";
import "./styles.css";

const App = () => {
 return (
  <div>
    <h1>Hello world!</h1>
    {/*Multi line comment*/}
  </div>
 );
};
ReactDOM.render(<App />, document.getElementById("root"));
```

Code sample: https://codesandbox.io/s/react-hello-world-qjgq9

Even though it's similar to HTML, we need to keep in mind a couple of things when working with JSX.

Naming Convention

All DOM properties and attributes (including event handlers) must be camelCase. For example, *onclick* must be *onClick*.

```
const element = <input type="text" onClick{( ) => { }} />;
```

Since JSX is a JavaScript extension, identifiers such as *class* and *for* are discouraged. Instead, React DOM components expect to use DOM property names such as *className* and *htmlFor,* respectively.

```
const element = (<label htmlFor="…….." className="label" > do something …..</label>);
```

Multiple Elements

If we want to return more elements, we need to wrap them with one container element. The following code shows how we are using *div* as a wrapper for *h1, h2,* and *p* elements. Modify the index.js file used for the Hello world example in the CodeSandbox.

```
const App =() => {

  return (
    <div>
      <h1>Heading</h1>
      <h2>Content</h2>
      <p>This is the paragraph</p>
    </div>
  );
}
```

Attributes

We can use our own custom attributes in addition to regular HTML properties and attributes. When we want to add a custom attribute, we could use a custom data prefix. In the following example, we added *data-myattribute* as an attribute of the *p* element. Modify the index.js file used for the Hello World example in the CodeSandbox.

```
const App =()=> {

  return (
    <div>
      <h1>Heading</h1>
      <h2>Content</h2>
      <p data-myattribute = "somevalue">My paragraph</p>
    </div>
  );
}
```

JavaScript Expressions

JavaScript expressions can be used inside of JSX. We just need to wrap it with curly brackets { }. The following example will render *3*. In order to use a JavaScript expression in a component's attribute, we wrap it in *curly brackets { }*.

```
const App =()=> {
  return (
    <div>
      <h1>{1+2}</h1>
    </div>
  );
}
```

We cannot use *if-else* statements inside JSX. Instead, we could use *conditional ternary expressions*. The conditional expression is the JavaScript operator that takes three operands: a condition followed by a question mark (?), then an expression to execute if the condition is truth followed by a colon (:), and finally the expression to execute if the condition is false.

In the following example, if the variable *age* is higher than 18, the browser will render *'You can join'*. If we change it to 15, it will render *'We need your parent's permission'*.

```
const App =()=> {
  const age = 20;
  return (
    <div>
      <h1>{age > 18 ? 'You can join.' : 'We need your parent's permission'}</h1>
    </div>
  );
}
```

We can also use logical AND (&&) instead of *if-else* statements. In JavaScript, true && expression always evaluates to expression, and false && expression always evaluates to false.

In the below example, if the condition is true, the element right after && will appear in the output. If it is false, React will ignore and skip it.

```
const App = () => {
  const messages = ["Alan", "Ada", "Haskel"];
  return (
    <div>
      <h1>inbox</h1>
      {messages.length > 0 && <h2>You have {messages.length} new messages.</h2>}
    </div>
  );
};
```

Styling

You can use inline styling. React implements a browser-independent DOM system for performance and cross-browser compatibility. React will also automatically append *px* after the number value on specific elements. The following example shows how to add *myStyle* inline to the *h1* element.

```
const App =()=> {
  return (
    <div>
      <h1 style = {{color: "green", fontSize: 100}}>Heading</h1>
    </div>
  );
}
```

In JSX, JavaScript expressions are written inside curly braces, and JavaScript also uses curly braces, the styling in the example above is written inside two sets of curly braces{{ }}.

Like the below example, you can also create an object with styling information and refer to it in the style attribute.

```
const App =()=> {
  const myStyle = {color: "green" , fontSize: 100}

  return (
    <div>
      <h1 style = {myStyle}>Heading</h1>
    </div>
  );
}
```

There are many different ways to style React with CSS. You can also use a standard *CSS* style module that can be imported into each application. The CSS module is available only for the component that is imported, and you do not have to worry about name conflicts.

While React encourages you to think of your application in terms of components, stylesheets force you to think of it the conventional way. Various other approaches are being practiced to merge the CSS and the JS code into a single file. The Inline Style is probably the most popular among them. However, in this book, we won't cover the design aspect in detail.

Comments

When writing comments, you need to put curly brackets { } within the children section of a tag.

```
const App =()=> {
  return(
    <div>
      <h1>Header</h1>
        { /*Multi line comment*/}
    </div>
  );
}
```

3.2 Props and State

Props is data passed from a parent component to a child component, and *state* is data managed within the component itself.

Props is used when components talk to each other. *Props* flows from parent component to child components. This is why React is considered to have unidirectional data flow architecture. A component can access all its *props* through the object *this.props* (in case of the ES6 Class component). The children can read their *props* but cannot modify them. The parent component owns *props* of the child components. In other words, the parent components can control their child components through *props*.

If child components need some way to signal events to the parent, **callback functions can be passed down from the parent to child components as props because functions are the first-class object in JavaScript. The child components can receive callback functions in the props from their parent component. These callback functions can be used to change the local state of the parent component.**

While *props* is immutable and owned by a component's parent, the *state* is mutable and owned by the component. The *state* is used within components to keep track of UI information. Anytime there is data that is going to change within a component, *state* can be used. Therefore, the container parent component should update/change the *state*, while the child components should only receive data from the *state* using *props*.

Components that do not have a *state* are referred to as **stateless components**. A component using *state* is known as **stateful components**.

props and state comparison summary

Description	Props	State
Mutable?	No	Yes
Can get initial value from parent Component?	Yes	Yes
Can be changed by parent Component?	Yes	No
Can set default values inside Component?	Yes	Yes
Can change inside Component?	No	Yes
Can set initial value for child Components?	Yes	Yes
Can change in child Components?	No	No

3.3 Components

In this chapter, we will learn how to combine components to make the app easier to maintain. This approach allows you to update and change your components without affecting the rest of the page.

Functional Components and Class Components

The simplest way to define a component is to write a JavaScript function:

```
function App(props) {
  return <div>Hello, {props.name}</div>;
}
```

This function is a valid React component because it accepts props. Object argument with data and returns a React element. We call such component **Functional Component** because they are literally JavaScript functions.

You can also use the ES6 arrow function like the below example.

```
const  App = (props) => {
return <div>Hello, {props.name}</div>;
};
```

You can also use an ES6 class to define a component. ES6 Class components have a **render( )** method that takes input data and returns what to display. Keep in mind *this.props* must be used instead of *props*.

```
class App extends React.Component {
  render() {
    return <div>Hello, {this.props.name}</div>;
  }
}
```

Note: No matter functional component or ES6 Class component, the component name must start with a capital letter.

The difference between Functional component and ES6 Class component are:

- A class component can handle *state* which keeps track of the component status.
- A class component can use the component Lifecycle method.
- A class component requires *this.props* when receiving *props*.
- A class component inherits *React.Component* explicitly.

Classes have some additional features that we will discuss in the next sections. Until then, we will use functional components for consistency.

Rendering a component

When React detects an element representing a user-defined component, it passes JSX attributes to this component as a single object as *props*. The JSX components being returned is not the classic HTML element that gets rendered but is the presentation that React renders in the DOM.

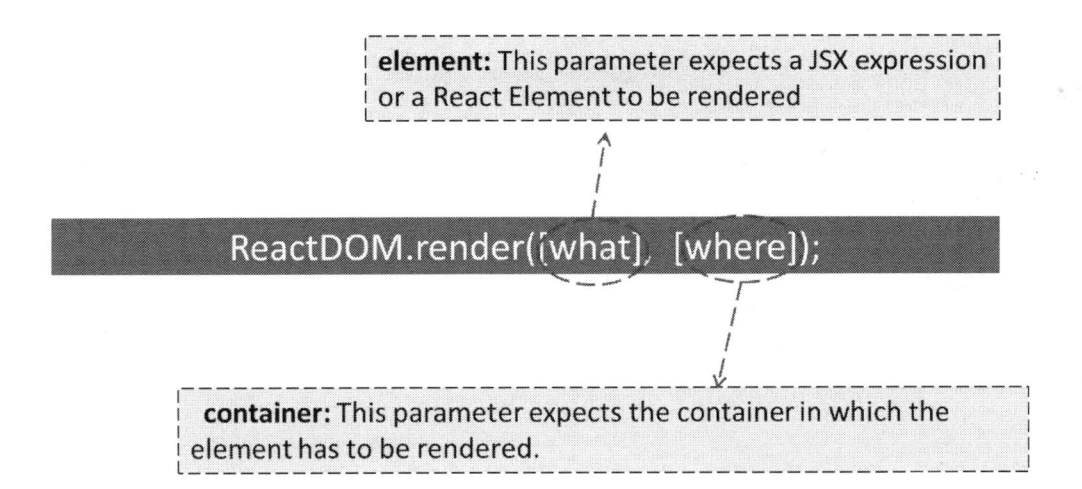

element: This parameter expects a JSX expression or a React Element to be rendered

```
ReactDOM.render([what], [where]);
```

container: This parameter expects the container in which the element has to be rendered.

For example, this code renders "Hello Ada Lovelace" :

```
function App(props) {
  return <h1>Hello {props.name}</h1>;
}
ReactDOM.render(
  <App name="Ada Lovelace " />,
  document.getElementById("root"));
```

Code sample: https://codesandbox.io/s/react-component1-rojgp

Component reuse

Components can call other components multiple times.
For example, we can create an App component that renders Hello world multiple times:

```
const App =() => {
  return <div>Hello world!</div>;
};

ReactDOM.render(
  <div>
    <App />
    <App />
    <App />
  </div>,
  document.getElementById("root")
);
```

Code sample: https://codesandbox.io/s/react-component-reuse1-ygd3n

Components can call other components with props:

```
const Welcome = props => {
 return <h1>Hello {props.name}</h1>;
};

const App = () => {
 return (
  <div>
   <Welcome name="Ada Lovelace" />
   <Welcome name="Alan Turing" />
   <Welcome name="Haskell Curry" />
  </div>
 );
};
ReactDOM.render(<App />, document.getElementById("root"));
```

Code sample: https://codesandbox.io/s/react-component-reuse2-963p8

Typically, React apps have a single App component at the very top. However, if you integrate React components into an existing app, it is likely that you start bottom-up with a small component and gradually work your way to the top of the view hierarchy.

React Element

An element is a plain object that describes a component instance or DOM node and its properties. It contains information about the component type (for example, Button), its properties (for example, its color), and any child elements inside it. It is a way to tell React what you want to see on the screen. React elements can also be stored in variables like JavaScript regular values. Handling with JSX is exactly the same as the normal JavaScript value:

```
const Hello = () => {
 return <div> Hello world</div>;
};
const HelloElement = <Hello />;

ReactDOM.render(<div>{HelloElement}</div>, document.getElementById("root"));
```

Code sample: https://codesandbox.io/s/react-element1-8f3md

Fragment Component

React V16.2 onwards supports fragment components. When you need to wrap the content of a component and don't want to add an extra *div* or other wrapping elements to the DOM, you could use <React.fragment> ……</React.fragment>. The content of the component will render as expected without the wrapping elements.

```
const App =()=> {

  return (
    <React.Fragment>
      <h1>Heading</h1>
      <h2>Content</h2>
      <p>This is the paragraph</p>
    </React.Fragment>
  );
}

ReactDOM.render(
 <div>
  <App/>
 </div>,
 document.getElementById("root"));
```

Code sample: https://codesandbox.io/s/react-fragment-component-y23we

Instead of **<React.Fragment>……………..</React.Fragent>**, you could use shorthand. **< >…………….. </ >**

Passing data using props

Props can be passed as the argument of the function that defines the component. Although any variable name can be used, it is common to name it as *props* by convention. The variable received as *props* is an object. When we need immutable data in our component, we can add *props* to **reactDOM.render( )** function and use it inside our component:

```jsx
const App = props => {

  return (
    <div>
      <h1>{props.headerProp}</h1>
      <h2>{props.contentProp}</h2>
    </div>
  );
}

ReactDOM.render(
  <App headerProp = "Prop from Header"  contentProp = "Prop from Content"/>,
  document.getElementById("root")
);
```

Code sample: https://codesandbox.io/s/react-props-fchz7

Values that can be passed as props

Values such as strings, numbers, arrays, objects, and functions can be passed as props. As a general rule, surround it with { } to pass the value.

String

When passing a string, you can only use a single quote ('), double quote ("). A backquote (`) cannot be used.

```
<MyComponent stringValue ="Alan Turing" />
<MyComponent stringValue = {"Alan Turing"} />
```

Numeric value, Boolean value

Numeric value and Boolean value can be passed using { }.
However, if they are surrounded by quote (')("), they are interpreted as a string.

```
<MyComponent numberValue ={100} />
<MyComponent numberValue = {true} />
```

Object, Array, Function

Object, Array, Function can be passed using { }.

```
<MyComponent objectValue={{ name: 'Ada' , birthday: '10/12/1815' }} />
<MyComponent arrayValue={['Ada' , 'Alan' , 'Haskell']} />
<MyComponent functionValue={( name) => console.log(name)} />
```

Variable

Defined variable can be passed by using { }.

```
const name = 'Ada' ;
<MyComponent value = {name} />
```

Children

Children are special props. *props.children* property allows you to inject components inside from other components. Child elements of the React component are passed as children. In the example below, the string Haskell enclosed in Hello is passed as *props.children*:

```
const Hello = (props) => {
  return ( <div> hello, {props.children} </div> )
}

ReactDOM.render(
<div>
   <Hello> Haskell </Hello>
</div>,
document.getElementById('root')
)
```

Code sample: https://codesandbox.io/s/react-children1-wtkfr

Nested example

In the following example, two Hello elements are passed to the Greeting *props.children*:

```
const Hello = (props) => {
 return ( <div> hello, {props.children} </div> )
}

const Greeting = (props) => {
 return (
  <div>
    <div> GREETING </div>
      {props.children}
   </div>
 )
}

ReactDOM.render(
 <Greeting>
  <Hello>Ada</Hello>
  <Hello>Alan</Hello>
 </Greeting>,
 document.getElementById('root'))
```

Code sample: https://codesandbox.io/s/react-children2-151dk

HTML is rendered like this:

```
<div>

<div> GREETING</div>
 <div> hello, Ada</div>
 <div> hello, Alan</div>
</div>
```

Passing multiple values

If you want to pass multiple values to a component, you can do it by enumerating attributes like in regular HTML.

```
const Profile = (props) => {
  return (
   <ul>
    <li> name: {props.name}</li>
    <li> birthday: {props.birthday}</li>
   </ul>
   )
}
ReactDOM.render(<Profile name= 'Ada Lovelace' birthday='10.12. 1815'/>,
 document.getElementById('root'))
```

Code sample: https://codesandbox.io/s/react-multi-value1-23vs1

The following code is similar to above, but we use {myProfile.name} to pass name, {myProfile.birthday} to pass birthday.

```
const Profile = (props) => {
  return (
   <ul>
    <li>  name:{props.name}</li>
    <li>  birthday:{props.birthday}</li>
   </ul>
   )
}
const myProfile = {
    name:'Alan Turing',
    birthday:'23.06. 1912'
}
ReactDOM.render( <Profile name={myProfile.name} birthday ={myProfile.birthday} />,
 document.getElementById('root'))
```

Code sample: https://codesandbox.io/s/react-multi-value2-f142n

You could also use ES6 spread operator (...) to expand the contents of the object and pass the value.

Pre-ES6 style

```
ReactDOM.render( <Profile name={myProfile.name} birthday ={myProfile.birthday} />,
document.getElementById('root'))
```

using ES6 spread operator

```
ReactDOM.render( <Profile {...myProfile} />,
document.getElementById('root'))
```

```
const Profile = props => {
  return (
    <ul>
      <li> name:{props.name}</li>
      <li> birthday:{props.birthday}</li>
    </ul>
  );
};
const myProfile = {
  name: "Alan Turing",
  birthday: "23.06. 1912"
};
ReactDOM.render(<Profile {...myProfile} />, document.getElementById("root"));
```

Code sample: https://codesandbox.io/s/react-multi-value3-hnefw

Default Props

With default props, props are set even if a parent component does not pass props down to the child component:

```jsx
const App =(props)=> {

  return (
    <div>
      <h1>{props.headerProp}</h1>
      <h2>{props.contentProp}</h2>
    </div>
  )
}
App.defaultProps = {
 headerProp: "Hi from header props",
 contentProp:"Hi from content props"
}
ReactDOM.render(<App/>, document.getElementById('root'))
```

Code sample: https://codesandbox.io/s/react-default-props-8y6q8

You can also set default property values directly on the component constructor instead of adding it to the **ReactDOM.render( )** element.

Conditional Rendering

Conditional rendering in React works the same way conditions work in JavaScript. Using JavaScript statements such as *if-else* or the conditional operator to create elements representing the current state so that React updates the UI to match them.

```
import React from "react";
import ReactDOM from "react-dom";
import "./styles.css";

const UserCart = (props) => {
  return <h1>Your Shopping Cart is empty</h1>;
};

const GuestLogin = (props) => {
  return <h1>Please login </h1>;
};

const App = (props) => {
  const isLoggedIn = props.isLoggedIn;
  if (isLoggedIn) {
    return <UserCart />;
  }
  return <GuestLogin />;
};
// Try changing to isLoggedIn={true}:
ReactDOM.render(<App isLoggedIn={false} />, document.getElementById("root"));
```

Code sample: https://codesandbox.io/s/react-conditional-render1-z9ytl

Instead of if-else statement, conditional ternary expression can be used like this:

```
const App = (props) => {
  const isLoggedIn = props.isLoggedIn;
  return isLoggedIn ? <UserCart /> : <GuestLogin />;
};
```

Code sample: https://codesandbox.io/s/react-conditional-render2-wqjhw

Instead of if-else statement, shorthand using logical AND expression can be used as well:

```jsx
import React from "react";
import ReactDOM from "react-dom";
import "./styles.css";

const App = () => {
  const messages = ["Alan", "Ada", "Haskel"];
  return (
    <div>
      <h1>inbox</h1>
      {/*if there are messages, render the message. if not, skip the rendering*/}
      {messages.length > 0 && <h2>You have {messages.length} new messages.</h2>}
    </div>
  );
};

ReactDOM.render(<App />, document.getElementById("root"));
```

Code sample: https://codesandbox.io/s/react-eonditional-render3-5xnn8

Stateless Component

So far, we have used components without *state*. All logic revolves around the props they receive. Stateless components are functions that take in props and return a DOM element without side effects. Since stateless components are functions, not Objects (in narrow terms), they do not have *this* scope. It improves readability and testability. In general, it is recommended to start with a stateless functional component.

The downside is that the state is the real world, and components generally rely on external systems (databases, message queues, external applications) that can't act like pure functions themselves, pushing complexity to a different location.

When you find out you need lifecycle methods or component level state, it's trivial to refactor to a class component or adding Hooks.

Stateful Component

The internal component state, also known as the local state, allows you to save, modify, and delete properties in your component. The ES6 Class component can use a constructor to initialize the internal component state.

The constructor is invoked only once when the component is initialized. *State* is used for mutable data, such as user inputs. We should always try to make our *state* as simple as possible and minimize the number of stateful components. For example, if we have many components that need data from the *state*, we could create one container component to keep the *state*.

Keep in mind not to update the *state* directly using *this.state*. In the Class component, always use this.setState( ) method to update the state objects. Using this.setState( ) re-renders the component and all the child components.

In the constructor function, you can inherit from the parent component by including the *super( )* statement, which executes the parent component's constructor function. Your component has access to all the functions of the parent component. If your component has a constructor function, *props* should always be passed to the constructor.

The complicated Stateful Class Components are hard to maintain, difficult to decouple logic from UI. The good news is that Hooks APIs were released in 2019. Hooks are special functions that let you hook onto React state and lifecycle methods inside functional components. You can use state without writing a class component. We will learn Hooks API in Chapter 4. For the time being, we focus on the Stateful Class Components to understand the React basic concept.

The following is the simple Stateful Class Component example.

```
class App extends React.Component {
  constructor(props) {
    super(props);

    this.state = {
      header: "Breaking News",
      content: "Physicists Find Strong Evidence of Four-Top Quark Production."
    };
  }
  render() {
    return (
      <>
        <h1>{this.state.header}</h1>
        <h2>{this.state.content}</h2>
      </>
    );
  }
}
ReactDOM.render(<App />, document.getElementById("root"));
```

Code sample: https://codesandbox.io/s/react-stateful1-s14i3

Both *props* and *state* can be used in the Stateful Class Component. Stateful Class Components are in charge of client-server communication (XHR, web sockets, etc.), processing data, and responding to user events. These logics should be encapsulated in a moderate number of Stateful Class Components, while all visualization and formatting logic should move into as many Stateless Function Components as possible.

Functional Component vs Class Component

Description	Function Component	Class Component
Props usage	Props	this.props
render( ) function	No	Yes
Destructuring	argument list in the function	Top of render
Default props declaration	Default arguments	Below the components or via class properties
State	No (but with Hooks API, state is possible)	Yes

Inter Components Communication

React is a component-based UI library. When the UI is split into small, focused components, they can handle one job well. But in order to build up a system into something that can accomplish a useful task, multiple components are needed. These components often need to work in coordination together. Therefore, they must be able to communicate with each other.

React components are composed in a hierarchy that mimics the DOM tree structure. Some components are parents (higher hierarchy), and those components may have children (lower hierarchy) in the tree hierarchy.

From Parent to Child with Props

The simplest data flow direction is from parent to child direction. A React component is a function that receives props. Props are a collection of data, an object that can contain any number of fields. If a parent component wants to send data to a child component, it simply passes it via props. When we update input data to a parent component, a child component should reflect the change.

From Child to Parent with Callbacks

On the other hand, children don't have the same right as parents. When a child wants to talk to a parent, it must first receive a mechanism to communicate with its parent: Parents pass down data to children through props, which is a special type of callback function. At the time of a relevant event, the child can then call this function as a callback.

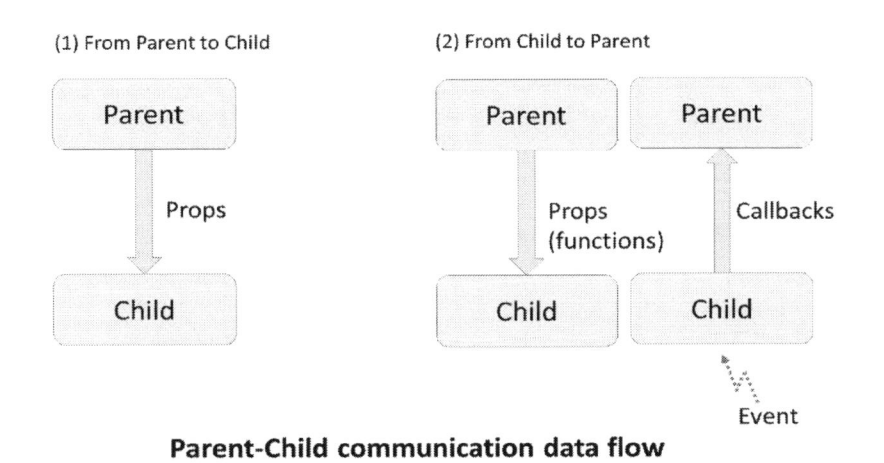

Parent-Child communication data flow

Unidirectional Data Flow in components tree

In general, unidirectional data flow means that data has only one way to be transferred to other parts of the application. Unidirectional data flow makes state management predictable. In React, a unidirectional data flow is recommended, and bidirectional data flow is not encouraged.

- actions can be triggered by the view
- actions can update the state
- the state/props change can be passed to the view and child components
- The view is a result of the application state. The state can only change when actions happen. When actions happen, the state will be updated.

Passing props down components tree

For example, we have deeply nested components and their hierarchy, which look like below. When you want to pass props from component-1 all the way down to component-7, component-1 cannot pass its props to component-7 directly. The props have to be passed to the direct descendent.

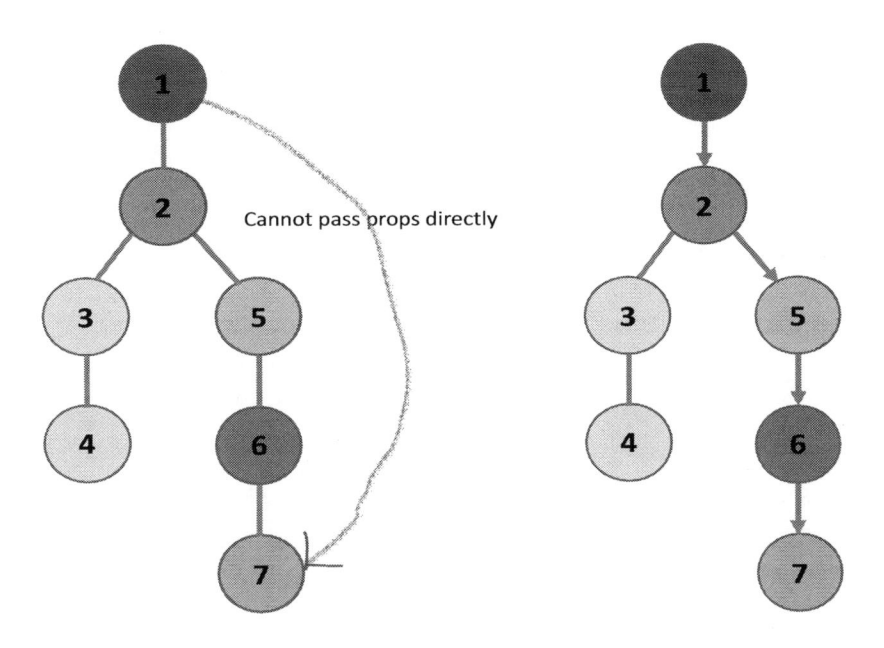

It is fine if you only need to pass the props down one or two levels into the subcomponents, but beyond that, it can be confusing. In this case, it is much easier to store the state in Redux and use a container component to access the desired data from the store. If Redux is overkill for your apps, Context API or useContext API can be used. We will study these patterns later.

Talking to siblings - lifting state in components tree

When siblings need to communicate with each other, they do not pass state to each other directly. The state should pass through a parent. **In order to share a state between two components, the most common operation is to move it up to their closest common ancestor.** It is referred to as "lifting state up". (i.e., removing the local state from the descendant component and move it into its ancestor instead.)

There should be a single "source of truth" for any data that changes in a React application. Usually, the state is first added to the component that needs it for rendering. Then, if other components also need it, you can lift it up to their closest common ancestor. Instead of trying to synchronize the state between different components, you should rely on the top-down data flow. Lifting state involves writing more "boilerplate" code than two-way binding approaches, but it takes less work to find and isolate bugs as a benefit.

Combining state and props examples

Both state and props hold model information. The props are immutable, while the state is mutable. Typically, state variables are passed down to child components as props because the children do not maintain or modify them. They take in read-only copy and use it only to render the view of the component.

The following example shows combining state and props in an app. We are setting our state in the parent component and passing it down the component tree using props. Every time the state changes, the component render method is called, and the App is updated. Inside the render function, we are passing *headerProp*, *contentProp* used in child components:

```
class App extends React.Component {
  constructor() {
    super();
    this.state = {
      header: "Breaking News",
      content: "Physicists find strong evidence of four-top Quark production"
    };
  }
  render() {
    return (
      <>
        <Header headerProp={this.state.header} />
        <Content contentProp={this.state.content} />
      </>
    );
  }
}
const Header = (props) => {
  return (
    <>
      <h2>{props.headerProp}</h2>
    </>
  );
};
const Content = (props) => {
  return (
    <>
      <p>{props.contentProp}</p>
    </>
  );
};
ReactDOM.render(<App />, document.getElementById("root"));
```

Code sample: https://codesandbox.io/s/react-state-props2-pltki

The following example uses the ES6 Class for the child components. *this.prop* is used instead of *props*. Since React's recent trend is functional programming, ES6 Class should not be overused. However, if you still prefer ES6 classes over functions, then you could use it like below:

```jsx
class App extends React.Component {
  constructor(props) {
    super(props);
    this.state = {
      header: "Breaking News",
      content: "Physicists find strong evidence of four-top Quark production."
    }
  }
  render() {
    return (
      <>
        <Header headerProp = {this.state.header}/>
        <Content contentProp = {this.state.content}/>
      </>
    )
  }
}
class Header extends React.Component {
  render() {
    return (
      <>
        <h2>{this.props.headerProp}</h2>
      </>
    )
  }}
class Content extends React.Component {
  render() {
    return (
      <>
        <p>{this.props.contentProp}</p>
      </>
    )
  }
}
ReactDOM.render(<App/>, document.getElementById('root'))
```

Code sample: https://codesandbox.io/s/react-state-props1-fumk2

Events - Working with DOM events in React

In the native DOM/JavaScript environment, when you attach an event handler function to a DOM element using the native addEventListener() function, the callback will get an event argument passed to it.

In the React environment, event handler functions are also passed an event argument, but it's not the standard event instance. It is called **SyntheticEvent**, which is a simple wrapper to native event instances. Your event handlers don't get native event arguments of MouseEvent, KeyboardEvent, etc. They always get event arguments of **SyntheticEvent** that wraps your browser's native event instead.

SyntheticEvent brings consistency and high performance to React applications and interfaces. It achieves consistency by normalizing events so that they have the same properties across different browsers and platforms. React uses "top-level delegation". React listens for all the required events on the DOM.

SyntheticEvent is commonly used both in React browser and React Native. React browser is basically a cross-browser wrapper object on top of the native event (browser event) object. If required, we can still access the native event by reading the value of "nativeEvent" key inside the synthetic event object.

Each SyntheticEvent contains the following common generic properties:

boolean	bubbles
boolean	cancelable
DOMEventTarget	currentTarget
boolean	defaultPrevented
number	eventPhase
boolean	isTrusted
DOMEvent	nativeEvent
void	preventDefault()
boolean	isDefaultPrevented()
void	stopPropagation()
Boolean	isPropagationStopped()
DOMEventTarget	target
number	timeStamp
string	type

The non-generic properties depend on what type of native event our SyntheticEvent is wrapping. For example, a SyntheticEvent that wraps a MouseEvent will have access to mouse-specific properties are as follows:

boolean	altKey
number	button
number	buttons
number	clientX
number	clientY
boolean	ctrlKey
boolean	getModifierState(key)
boolean	metaKey
number	pageX
number	pageY
DOMEventTarget	relatedTarget
number	screenX
number	screenY
boolean	shiftKey

Similarly, a SyntheticEvent that wraps a KeyboardEvent will have access to these additional keyboard-related properties are like this:

boolean	altKey
number	charCode
boolean	ctrlKey
boolean	getModifierState(key)
string	key
number	keyCode
string	locale
number	location
boolean	metaKey
boolean	repeat
boolean	shiftKey
number	which

In the end, you still get the same functionality in the SyntheticEvent that you had in the vanilla DOM.

For other events, please refer to the React reference guide.

https://reactjs.org/docs/events.html

onClick event example

React events use **camelCase** syntax.
For example, **onClick** is used instead of onclick.

React event handlers must be inside curly braces:
onClick = {doSomething} instead of onClick = doSomething( ).

```
onClick or onMouseOver, as in
onClick={function() {...}}
or
onClick={() => {...}}
```

You can define an event listener that is triggered when you click the button. In the event listener, you are logging *this* context. The event object is an enhanced version of a native DOM event object - **SyntheticEvent.**

```
<button onClick={(function(event) {
console.log(this, event)
}).bind(this)}>
Save
</button>
```

In the ES6 Class components, **bind(this)** is needed in the event-handler function in order to get a reference to the instance of the class. If you don't bind, *this* will be null (in the case of ES5 strict mode).

initializing state

There are two ways to initialize state in a React class component: inside the constructor and directly inside the class definition using a class property. We focus on the constructor for the time being. When the component class is created, the constructor is the first method called, so it's the right place to initialize everything. The class instance has already been created in memory, so you can use it to set properties.

updating state

State can be updated in response to event handlers, server responses, or prop changes. setState( ) is the only legitimate way to update state of the class components after the initial state setup. There are several things we must understand when updating states:

1. Do not modify state directly

Directly accessing *this.state* to update our component is not a reliable way to update our component's next state because *this.props* and *this.state* can be updated asynchronously. You should not rely on their values for calculating the next state:

this.state.comment = 'Hello';   //wrong

(The only place where you can assign *this.state* is the constructor for the initialization.)

2. Component state update should be done using setState()

setState() enqueues changes to the component state and tells React that this component and its children need to be re-rendered with the updated state. The correct way to update state is like this:

this.setState({comment: 'Hello'});   //correct

3. State updates are merged.

this.setState( ) method performs a shallow merge between the new state you provide and the previous state. In the example below, we are updating the variable *instock* independently of the other state variables. The merging is partial, so this.setState({ instock:false }) leaves the other variables intact, replacing only the value of *instock*.

```
state = {
    bookID: 765,
    title: "Master React in 10 minutes",
    instock: true,
}

this.setState({ instock:false });
```

4. You can pass an object or a function to setState()

setState( ) method full syntax is as follows:

setState( ): tells React that this component and its children need to be re-rendered with the updated state.

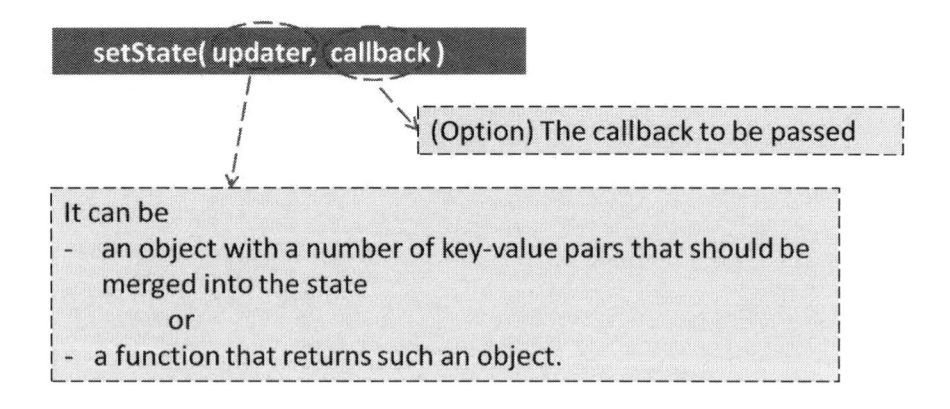

setState(updater, callback)

(Option) The callback to be passed

It can be
- an object with a number of key-value pairs that should be merged into the state
    or
- a function that returns such an object.

5. **Do not depend on this.state immediately after calling setState() and make use of the updater function instead.**

We will talk about the timing issues in the section 3.4 Component Life Cycle.

Component initialization/updating example

The following example is updating our component's state using the previous state of the component.

```
class App extends React.Component {
  constructor() {
    super();
    this.state = {
      data: []
    };
    this.updateState = this.updateState.bind(this);
  }
  updateState() {
    const item = " Data updated ";
    this.setState(prevState => ({ data: prevState.data + item }));
  }
  render() {
    return (
      <>
        <button onClick={this.updateState}>CLICK</button>
        <h1>State Array: {this.state.data}</h1>
      </>
    );
  }
}
ReactDOM.render(<App />, document.getElementById("root"));
```

Code sample: https://codesandbox.io/s/react-setstate1-xlr16

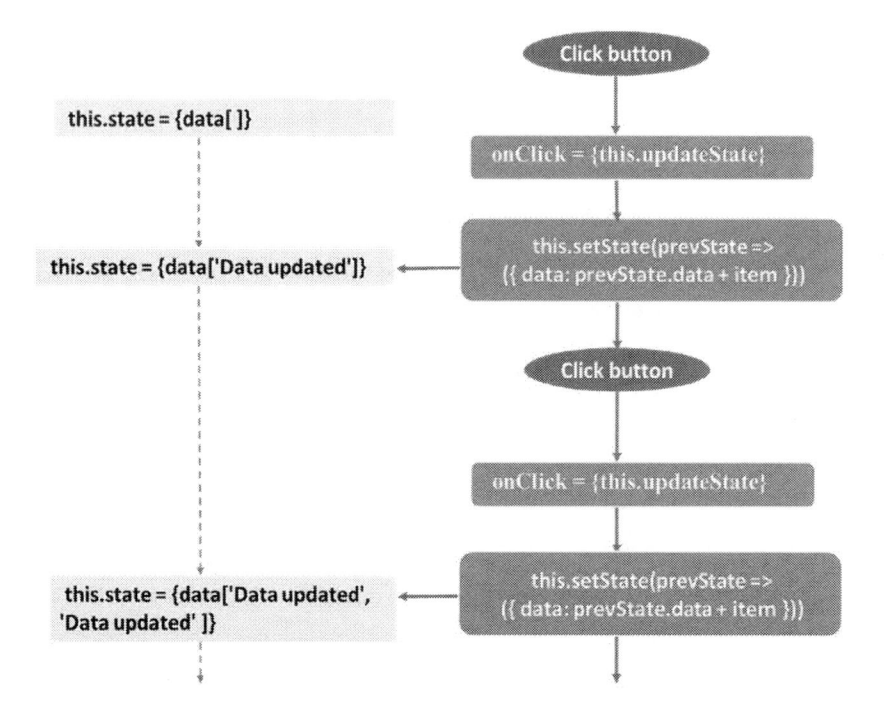

```
                                    ┌─────────────┐
                                    │ Click button│
                                    └──────┬──────┘
                                           │
  this.state = {data[ ]}                   ▼
  ─ ─ ─ ─ ─ ─ ─ ─ ─ ─ ─ ─ ─ ─ ┐   ┌──────────────────────┐
                              │   │ onClick = {this.updateState} │
                              │   └──────┬──────────────┘
                              │          │
                              │          ▼
  this.state = {data['Data updated']}  ┌──────────────────────────────┐
  ◄─────────────────────────────────── │ this.setState(prevState =>   │
                                       │ ({ data: prevState.data + item })) │
                                       └──────┬───────────────────────┘
                                              │
                                              ▼
                                       ┌─────────────┐
                                       │ Click button│
                                       └──────┬──────┘
                                              │
                                              ▼
                                       ┌──────────────────────┐
                                       │ onClick = {this.updateState} │
                                       └──────┬───────────────┘
                                              │
                                              ▼
  this.state = {data['Data updated',    ┌──────────────────────────────┐
  'Data updated' ]}                     │ this.setState(prevState =>   │
  ◄──────────────────────────────────── │ ({ data: prevState.data + item })) │
                                        └──────┬───────────────────────┘
                                               │
                                               ▼
```

setState() confusing part

The usage of setState( ) is a bit tricky.

1. Objects being used as setState updater parameter

These calls will be batched together by React. React uses Object.assign() internally, resulting in the counter being incremented by 1 while you might expect 3.

```
this.setState({ counter: this.state.counter + 1 });   //1
this.setState({ counter: this.state.counter + 1 });   //1
this.setState({ counter: this.state.counter + 1 });   //1
```

2. Functions being used as setState updater parameter

If you pass a function as the first argument of setState, React will call it with the previous state (or at-call-time-current state) and expect you to return an Object to merge into the state. So the example below counter increments by 3.

```
this.setState(prevState => ({ count: prevState.count + 1 }));   //1
this.setState(prevState => ({ count: prevState.count + 1 }));   //2
this.setState(prevState => ({ count: prevState.count + 1 }));   //3
```

The following example shows different between object parameter and function parameter.

```jsx
import React from "react";
import ReactDOM from "react-dom";

class App extends React.Component {
  state = { count: 0 };
  // use an object as setState parameter. Incremented only 1.
  handleObject = () => {
    this.setState({ count: this.state.count + 1 });
    this.setState({ count: this.state.count + 1 });
    this.setState({ count: this.state.count + 1 });
  };
  // use a function as setState parameter. Incremented as you expected.
  handleFunction = () => {
    this.setState(prevState => ({ count: prevState.count + 1 }));
    this.setState(prevState => ({ count: prevState.count + 1 }));
    this.setState(prevState => ({ count: prevState.count + 1 }));
  };
  render() {
    return (
      <div>
        <div>{this.state.count}</div>
        <button onClick={this.handleObject}>Increment by 1</button>
        <button onClick={this.handleFunction}>Increment by 3</button>
      </div>
    );
  }
}
ReactDOM.render(<App />, document.getElementById("root"));
```

Code sample: https://codesandbox.io/s/react-setstate2-8jfjx

Stateful Class Component Design Patterns

1. Bind in constructor

When you create a class component that extends from **React.Component**, any custom methods you create are not bound to the component by default. You need to bind your custom methods so that *this* refers to the component instance.

In the following example, we add an **onClick** event that triggers the **updateState** function when the button is clicked. Binding callbacks is necessary because you have to tell your callback what its context is. *this* in React is a reference to the current component. Usually, *this* in React is bound to its built-in methods.

In JavaScript, functions can be passed as variables. But normally, the context is not passed. (The context here means what *this* points to). By binding a **updateState** function, you can set the value of *this* for later, so it doesn't matter where exactly your callback function is called. You can achieve *this* by calling **bind(this)** for your function.

The binding step is necessary because class methods don't automatically **bind(this)** to the class instance. Calling **bind(this)** on a function returns a new (bound) function with the value of *this* already defined. This way, if you pass it to another object or down a prop inside a React component, the value of *this* inside the component will not change anymore.

```
class App extends React.Component {
  constructor(props) {
    super(props);
      this.state = {data: 'Initial data'}
      this.updateState = this.updateState.bind(this);
  }
  updateState() {
    this.setState({data: 'Data updated'})
  }
  render() {
    return (
      <div>
        <button onClick = {this.updateState}>CLICK</button>
        <h2>{this.state.data}</h2></div>); }}

ReactDOM.render(<App/>, document.getElementById("root"))
```

Code sample: https://codesandbox.io/s/react-event1-8krzc

```
class App extends React.Component {
  constructor(props) {                          Initialization
    super(props);
    this.state = { data: "Initial data" };
    this.updateState = this.updateState.bind(this);   ←-- The value of 'this' does not change
  }                                                       by binding, no matter where it is called.
  updateState() {                               Event handler
    this.setState({ data: "Data updated" });
  }
  render() {
    return (                                    Rendering
      <div>
        <button onClick={this.updateState}>CLICK</button>
        <h2>{this.state.data}</h2>
      </div>
    );
  }
}

ReactDOM.render(<App />, document.getElementById("root"));
```

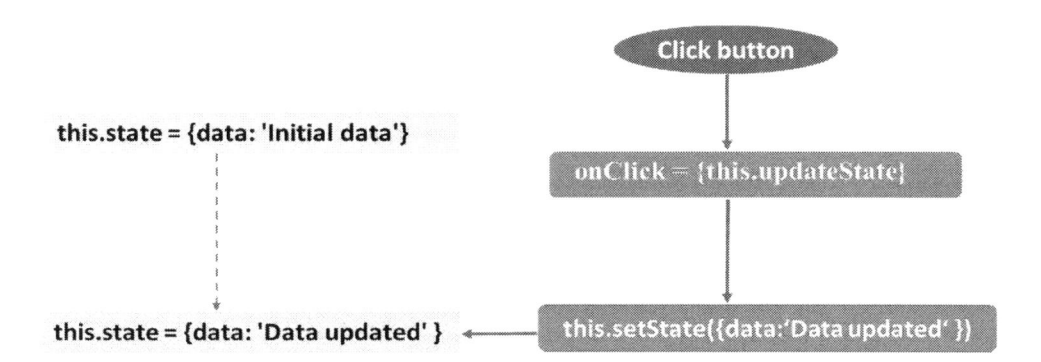

```
                                    Click button
                                         │
                                         ▼
this.state = {data: 'Initial data'}   onClick = {this.updateState}
            ┊                            │
            ┊                            ▼
            ▼
this.state = {data: 'Data updated'} ← this.setState({data:'Data updated'})
```

2. Using arrow function in render

This method is less verbose than binding in the constructor. On the other hand, child components are re-rendered because they are passing new functions. The performance can be reduced. Not recommended to use this style.

3. Using arrow function as a class property

This pattern is based on the ECMAScript class property. There is no performance concern like the arrow function in the render. Not all browsers support this feature, but it is possible with Babel. This design pattern will be used throughout this chapter.

```javascript
import React from "react";
import ReactDOM from "react-dom";

class App extends React.Component {
  constructor(props) {
    super(props);
    this.state = { data: "Initial data" };

  }
  updateState = () => {
    this.setState({ data: "Data updated" });
  }
  render() {
    return (
      <div>
        <button onClick={this.updateState}>CLICK</button>
        <h2>{this.state.data}</h2>
      </div>
    );
  }
}

ReactDOM.render(<App />, document.getElementById("root"));
```

Code sample: https://codesandbox.io/s/react-event1a-s0fwk

```
class App extends React.Component {
  constructor(props) {                    Initialization
    super(props);
    this.state = { data: "Initial data" };
  }

  updateState = () => {                   Event handler
    this.setState({ data: "Data updated" });
  }

  render() {                              Rendering
    return (
      <div>
        <button onClick={this.updateState}>CLICK</button>
        <h2>{this.state.data}</h2>
      </div>
    );
  }
}

ReactDOM.render(<App />, document.getElementById("root"));
```

With the new ECMAscript TC39 proposal, using arrow function as a class property is feasible.

Child Events update the states of the parent component

When we need to update the state of the parent component from its child, we create an event handler in the parent component and pass it as a prop to the child component. If any event in the child affects the parent's state, the child calls a method defined in the parent.

In the following example, we create an event handler (*updateState*) in the parent component and pass it as a prop (*updateStateProp*) to the child component.

```jsx
class App extends React.Component {
  constructor() {
    super();
    this.state = { data: "Initial data" };
  }

  updateState = () => {
    this.setState({ data: "Data updated from the child component" });
  };

  render() {
    return (
      <div>
        <MyChild
          myDataProp={this.state.data}
          updateStateProp={this.updateState}
        />{" "}
      </div>
    );
  }
}

const MyChild = props => {
  return (
    <div>
      <button onClick={props.updateStateProp}>CLICK</button>
      <h3>{props.myDataProp}</h3>
    </div>
  );
};

ReactDOM.render(<App />, document.getElementById("root"));
```

Code sample: https://codesandbox.io/s/react-event2-b2fhl

3.4 Component Life Cycle

After being generated for the first time, the component changes state upon the change of props/state. The component is discarded when it is finally removed from the document tree. The flow from generation to destruction is called the component lifecycle.

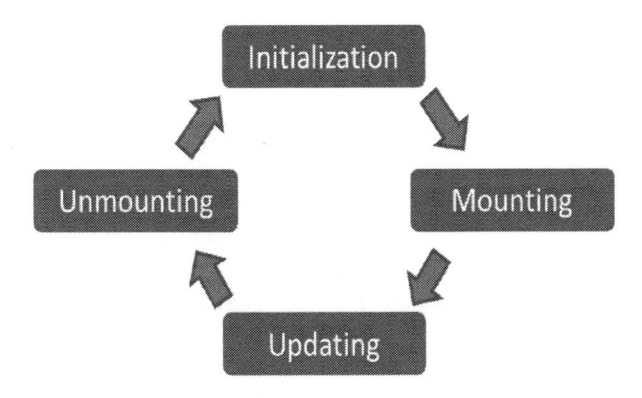

Lifecycle Methods

Various methods are called according to this lifecycle change. Such methods are called lifecycle methods. With the life cycle method, you can execute application-specific processing at the timing of component mounting /updating /unmounting.

- **Constructor( )** is called before it is mounted. When you are implementing the constructor for a React.Component subclass, you should call **super(props)** before any other statement. Otherwise, **this.props** will be undefined in the constructor, which can lead to bugs.

  Typically, constructors are used for two purposes:
  - (1) Initializing local state by assigning an object to **this.state**.
  - (2) Binding event handler methods to an instance.

- **render( )** method is the only required method in a class component. It renders a React element into the DOM in the supplied container and returns a reference to the component. The render( ) function should be pure, so it does not modify the component state, it returns the same result each time it is invoked, and it does not directly interact with the browser. If you need to interact with the browser, perform your code in **componentDidMount( )** or the other lifecycle methods instead.

- **componentDidMount( )** is invoked immediately after a component is mounted (inserted into the tree). Initialization that requires DOM nodes should be here. If you need to load data from a remote endpoint, this is a good place to instantiate the network request. This is where AJAX requests and DOM or state updates should occur. This method is also used for integration with other JavaScript libraries/frameworks and any functions with delayed execution, such as setTimeout or setInterval. We are using it to update the state so we can trigger the other lifecycle methods.

- **componentDidUpdate( )** is called just after rendering. This method is not called for the initial render. You can use this as an opportunity to operate on the DOM when the component has been updated. This is also the right place to make network requests as long as you compare the current props to previous props (e.g., a network request may not be necessary if the props have not changed).

- **componentWillUnmount( )** is invoked immediately before a component is unmounted and destroyed. Perform any necessary cleanup in this method, such as invalidating timers, canceling network requests, or cleaning up any subscriptions created in componentDidMount( ).

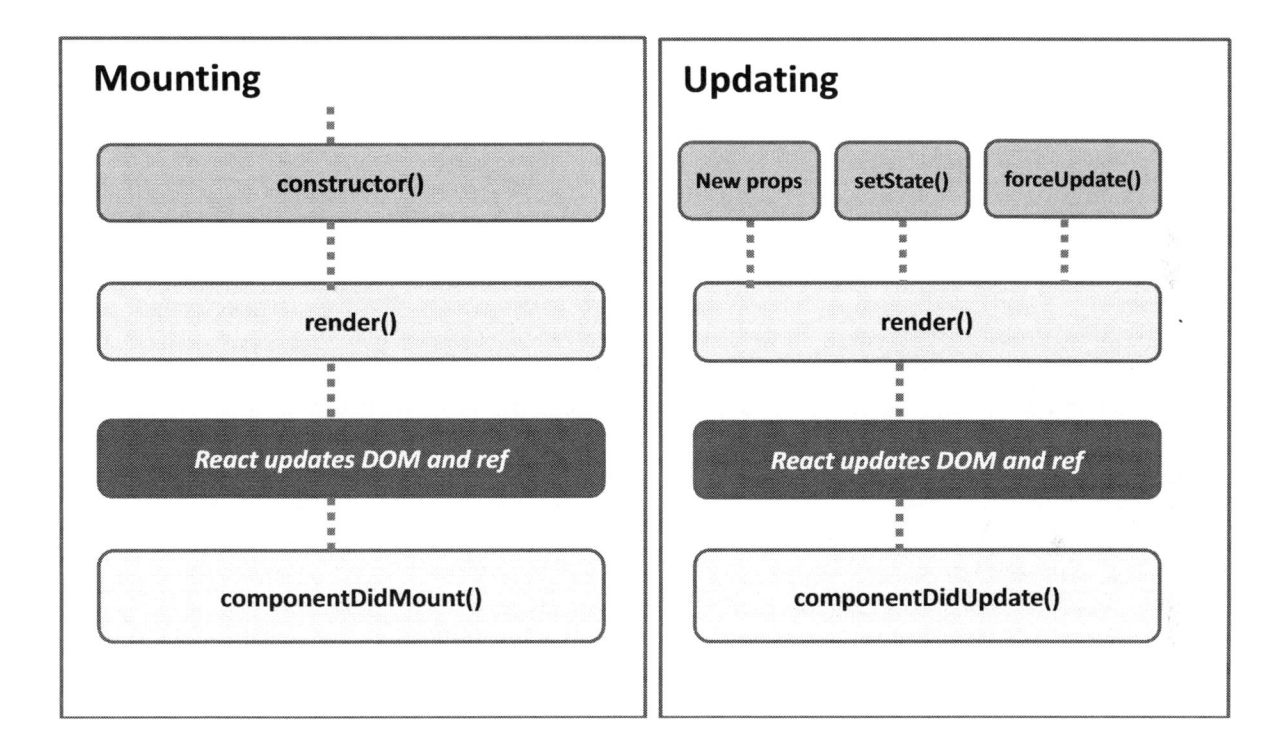

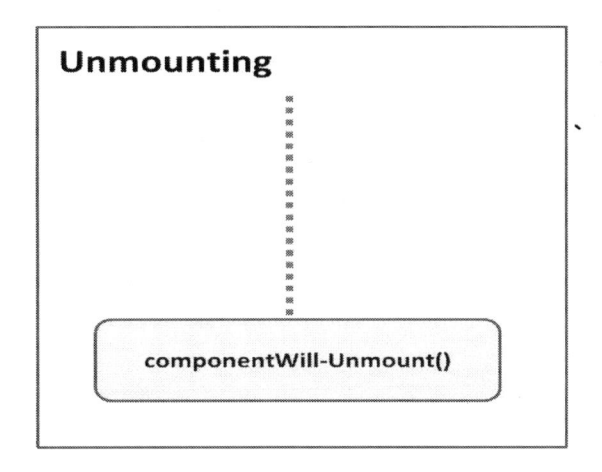

Mounting

- constructor()
- render()
- *React updates DOM and ref*
- componentDidMount()

Updating

- New props / setState() / forceUpdate()
- render()
- *React updates DOM and ref*
- componentDidUpdate()

Unmounting

- componentWill-Unmount()

In the following example, we will set the initial state in the constructor function. All the lifecycle methods are inside the Child component.

```jsx
class App extends React.Component {
  constructor(props) {
    super(props);
    this.state = { count: 0 };
  }
  setCount = () => {
    this.setState({ count: this.state.count + 1 });
  };
  render() {
    return (
      <>
        <button onClick={this.setCount}>+1</button>
        <Child myCount={this.state.count} />
      </>
    );
  }
}

class Child extends React.Component {
  componentDidMount() {
    console.log("Component Did Mount");
  }
  shouldComponentUpdate(newProps, newState) {
    return true;
  }
  componentDidUpdate(prevProps, prevState) {
    console.log("Component Did Update");
  }
  componentWillUnmount() {
    console.log("Component Will Unmount after 15 secW");
  }
  render() {
    return (
      <>
        <h2>{this.props.myCount}</h2>
      </>
    );
  }
}
ReactDOM.render(<App />, document.getElementById("root"));
//removes a mounted React component from the DOM and clean up its event handlers.
setTimeout(() => {
  ReactDOM.unmountComponentAtNode(document.getElementById("root"));
}, 15000);
```

Code sample: https://codesandbox.io/s/react-lifecycle-6lz9z

In the above example, **componentDidMount** is invoked and displayed in the console. When you click the +1 button, the update will occur, and **componentDidUpdate** will be invoked and logged. After 15 seconds, **unmountComponentAtNode** will remove a mounted React component from the DOM and clean up its event handlers. The **componentWillUnmount** will be logged in the console.

Note: Lifecycle methods will always be invoked in the same order, so it is good practice to write it in the correct order, as shown in the example. unmountComponentAtNode is used for a demo purpose only in this code. Normally you do not have to use it.

3.5 Form

In the conventional HTML, the browser keeps track of its values and serializes them for the server when you submit the form. The form data is handled by the DOM, and the form elements such as **<button>**, **<input>**, **<textarea>**, and **<select>** maintain their own state and update it based on user input.

On the other hand, in React, form data is usually handled by the components. The React component controls what happens in that form upon user input. There are two categories of components handling the form elements in React:

- **Controlled component:** input form element, whose value is controlled by React. The React components handle data, and all data is stored in the component state. You can handle changes by using event handlers.

- **Uncontrolled component:** form data is handled by the DOM. To write an uncontrolled component in React, instead of using an event handler for every state update, you can use a *ref* to get form values from the DOM. We will introduce a *ref* in the next sections.

React form's structure is similar to those of conventional HTML forms. However, each React input element does not keep any internal state. It is often referred to as a dumb input component.

The React container component is responsible for maintaining the state. A callback function is used to process form events and then use the container's state to store the form data. This gives our React component better control over the form's control elements and the data.

The callback function is triggered by events, including changes of form control values or form submission. The component then pushes the form values into the component's local state, and the component will control the data. Since we are using the value attribute on the form element, the value displayed will be the value of *this.state.value* in the ES6 Class component.

Container components　　　　**Dumb Input components**

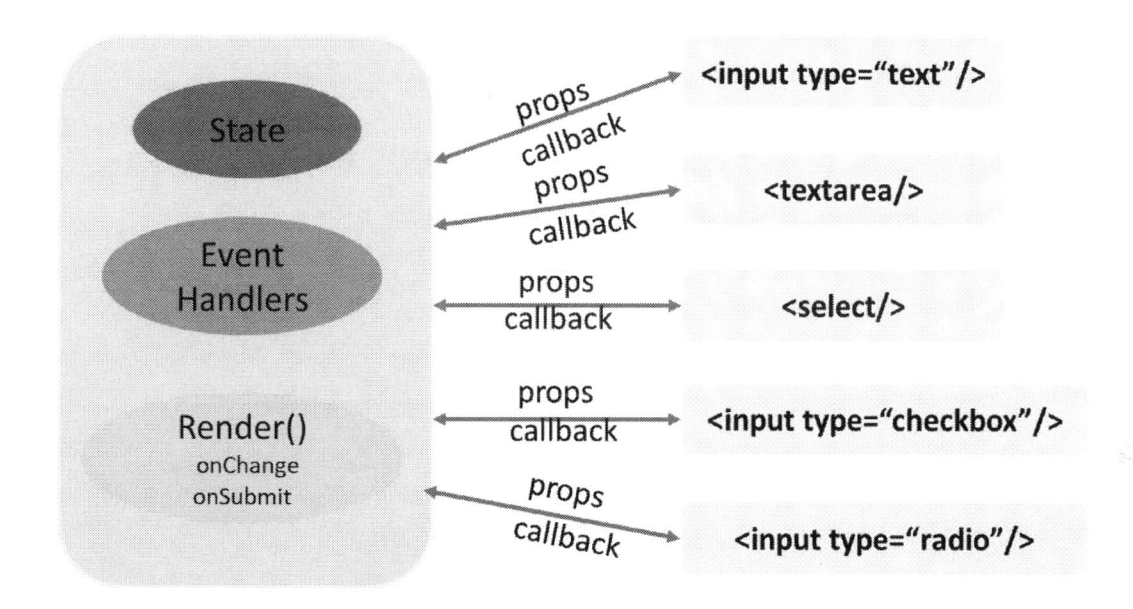

- State → props / callback → `<input type="text"/>`
- Event Handlers → props / callback → `<textarea/>`
- props / callback → `<select/>`
- Render() onChange onSubmit → props / callback → `<input type="checkbox"/>`
- props / callback → `<input type="radio"/>`

React form input is similar to the conventional HTML, except for target callback values.

Description	Element	Value property	New value in the callback
Text input	`<input type="text"/>`	value="string"	e.target.value
Text area	`<textarea />`	value="string"	e.target.value
Select options	`<select />`	value="option value"	e.target.value
Checkbox	`<input type="checkbox" />`	checked={boolean}	e.target.checked
Radio button	`<input type="radio" />`	checked={boolean}	e.target.checked

HTML Form and React Form example

React form input is a bit like conventional HTML. In traditional HTML, the user can edit text with HTML input. On the other hand, in React, input text cannot be changed, although the same input type is used. That is why it is called a dumb component:

(index.html)

```html
<div> HTML input: <input type='text' value = "initial data" /> </div>     <!-- pure HTML input -->
<div id="app"></div>                                                      <!-- REACT input placeholder-->
```

(index.js)

```js
class App extends React.Component {
  render() {
    return (
      <div> REACT dumb input: <input type='text' value = "initial data" /> </div>
    )
  }
}
ReactDOM.render(<App/>, document.getElementById("root"))
```

Code sample: https://codesandbox.io/s/react-form0-3qyhg

You will get a warning if you use Firefox or Chrome.

> Warning: Failed prop type: You provided a 'value' prop to a form field without an 'onChange' handler. This will render a read-only field. If the field should be mutable use 'defaultValue'. Otherwise, set either 'onChange' or 'read-only'.

In order to make a React dumb input usable, you have to add an onChange handler so that a React component can handle the form data.

The alternative is to use uncontrolled components, where form data is handled by the DOM itself. An uncontrolled component stores its own state internally, so you have to get the value (using *refs*) directly from the field when you need it.

React Controlled component example without <form> element

In the following example, an input form with *value = {this.state.data}* updates the state whenever the input value changes. We are using the *onChange* event that will monitor the input changes and update the state accordingly. When the input text value changes, the state will be updated.

```
class App extends React.Component {
  constructor() {
    super();
    this.state = {
      data: "Jupiter "
    };
  }
  updateState = (e) => {
    this.setState({ data: e.target.value });
  };

  render() {
    return (
      <>
        <h2> Destination: {this.state.data}</h2>
        <input
          type="text"
          value={this.state.data}
          onChange={this.updateState}
        />
      </>
    );
  }
}
ReactDOM.render(<App />, document.getElementById("root"));
```

Code sample: https://codesandbox.io/s/react-form1-cm7wj

React Controlled component example with <form> element

A Controlled Component takes its current value through props and notifies changes through callbacks like *onChange*. The input fields can be enclosed within an *<form>* element. The main purpose of the <form> is to ask the application user for certain pieces of information. React keeps track of data within a component state. We will have a state attribute for every field, and we will pass the current field values to the input components in the render. You can control the submit action by adding an event handler in the *onSubmit* attribute. *e.preventDefault* is used to discard default behaviors of the *onSubmit* event.

```
class App extends React.Component {
  constructor() {
    super()
    this.state = {
      data: ' '
    }
  }
  updateState = (e) => {
    this.setState({data: e.target.value})
  }
  handleSubmit = (e) => {
    e.preventDefault();
    alert(`your destination: ${this.state.data}`)
  }
  render() {
    return (
      <form onSubmit={this.handleSubmit}>
        <p> Destination: </p>
        <input type = "text"
          placeholder="enter your destination"
          value = {this.state.data}
          onChange = {this.updateState} />
        <button>Confirm{this.state.data}</button>
      </form>
    )
  }
}
ReactDOM.render(<App/>, document.getElementById('root'))
```

Code sample: https://codesandbox.io/s/react-form2-nr4fo

3.6 Refs Attribute

In the typical React dataflow, props are the only way that parent components interact with their children. Re-rendering with new props modifies a child. However, there are a few cases where you need to modify a child outside of the typical dataflow imperatively. We can use the *refs* attribute for these cases, which gives you direct access to a DOM node in your elements. Usually, this is an escape hatch and anti-pattern in React.

According to the React official docs, there are a few good use cases for *refs*:

- Managing focus, text selection, or media playback.
- Triggering imperative animations.
- Integrating with third-party DOM libraries.

React team recommends using controlled components over *refs* to implement forms. *Refs* offer a backdoor to the DOM, which might tempt you to use it to do things the jQuery way.

The following example shows how to use *refs* to access the input field directly. *Refs* are created using React.createRef() and attached to React elements via the *ref* attribute.

```
import React from "react";
import ReactDOM from "react-dom";

class App extends React.Component {
  constructor() {
    super();
    // create a ref to store the textInput DOM element
    this.textInput = React.createRef();
  }
  // focus the text input
  handleSubmit = (e) => {
    e.preventDefault();
    console.log(this.textInput.current.value);
  };
  render() {
    return (
      // associate the <input> ref with the `textInput`
      // that we created in the constructor
      <div>
        <input type="text" ref={this.textInput} />
        <input type="button" value="SUBMIT" onClick={this.handleSubmit} />
      </div>
    );
  }
}
ReactDOM.render(
  <div>
    <App />
  </div>,
  document.getElementById("root")
);
```

Code sample: https://codesandbox.io/s/react-refs-v70lm

3.7 Keys

React needs to identify each item in the list uniquely. If the state of an element of the list changes in Reacts Virtual DOM, React needs to figure out which element got changed and where to change in the DOM. This way, browser DOM will be in sync with the Reacts Virtual DOM.

React keys are necessary when working with dynamically created components or when the lists are modified by the users. Setting the key value will keep your components uniquely identified after the change. The key attribute must be a stable identifier. For example, using the index of the item in the array should be avoided. If the elements of the arrays get reordered in the future, it will be confusing as the key corresponding to the elements will also change. Keys do not have to be globally unique. The same keys can be used for different arrays.

In the following example, we create Content elements with a unique index i. The map function will create three elements from our data array. Since the key value needs to be unique for every element, we will assign i as a key for each created element. When we add or remove some elements in the future or change the order of the dynamically created elements, React will use the *key* values to keep track of each element.

We are using ES6 arrow syntax ($\Rightarrow$), which looks much cleaner than the old JavaScript syntax. The Arrow function is handy when we need to create a list with a lot of items:

```
class App extends React.Component {
  constructor() {
    super();
    this.state = {
      data: [
        { name: "Ada Lovelace", id: 100 },
        { name: "Alan Turing", id: 50 },
        { name: "Haskell Curry", id: 201 }
      ]
    };
  }
  render() {
    return (
      <>
        <ul>
          {this.state.data.map((myData, i) => (
            <Content key={i} scientistData={myData} />
          ))}
        </ul>
      </>
    );
  }
}

const Content = (props) => {
  return (
    <div>
      <div>{props.scientistData.name}</div>
      <div>{props.scientistData.id}</div>
    </div>
  );
};
ReactDOM.render(<App />, document.getElementById("root"));
```

Code sample: https://codesandbox.io/s/react-keys1-cdvky

Try removing keys generation from the above code.
this.state.data.map((myData) => (<Content scientistData={myData} />

It works, but the following warning message will be logged.
Warning: Each child in a list should have a unique "key" prop.

In the following example, we will set the state for the parent component (App). The Header and Row components are added. We create *table* and *tbody* elements, where we will dynamically insert objects from the data array. We are using *key = {i}* inside map( ) function. This will help React update the necessary elements only instead of re-rendering the entire list when something changes.

```
import React from "react";
import ReactDOM from "react-dom";

class App extends React.Component {
  constructor() {
    super();
    this.state = {
      data: [
        { id: 1, city: "Paris", country: "France" },
        { id: 2, city: "Tokyo", country: "Japan" },
        { id: 3, city: "Madrid", country: "Spain" }
      ]
    };
  }
  render() {
    return (
      <>
        <Header />
        <table>
          <tbody>
            {this.state.data.map((country, i) => (
              <Row key={i} data={country} />
            ))}
          </tbody>
        </table>
      </>
    );
  }
}
```

```jsx
const Header = () => {
  return (
    <div>
      <h1>Cities</h1>
    </div>
  );
};

const Row = props => {
  return (
    <tr>
      <td>{props.data.id}</td>
      <td>{props.data.city}</td>
      <td>{props.data.country}</td>
    </tr>
  );
};

ReactDOM.render(<App />, document.getElementById("root"));
```

Code sample: https://codesandbox.io/s/react-keys2-vn5ki

3.8 Higher-Order Components (HOC)

Higher-order components are an essential concept in React. HOCs are equivalent to higher-order functions in native JavaScript. A HOC is a function that accepts a Component as an argument and returns a new Component. The returned Component is an enhanced version of the input Component and can be used in the JSX.

We have already learned this concept in native JavaScript. A higher-order function accepts another function as an argument. The array map method falls under this category. A typical example of a higher-order function is as follows:

```
const multiply = (x) => (y) => x * y
multiply(2)(3)      //6
```

If the higher-order function is not a clear concept to you, we would suggest reviewing the Closure section and Hight Order Function section in this book.

A HOC in React is a design pattern used to share common functionality between components without repeating code. The composed component does not need to know anything about the implementation of a HOC other than the names of the properties and methods that it makes available. HOC provides a consistent way to extend the functionality of a pre-existing component by simply wrapping it and injecting its own additional functionality into them.

In the following example, OuterComponent wraps innnerComponent that passes the name to the OuterComponent.

```
import React from "react";
import ReactDOM from "react-dom";

const innerComponent = (props) => (
  <div>
    <h2>Inner component</h2>
    <h3>{props.name}</h3>
  </div>
);

//For OuterComponent, innerComponent is like blackbox.
const myConnect = (OuterComponent) => {
  return (props) => (
    <div>
      <h1>Outer Wrapper</h1>
      <OuterComponent {...props} />
    </div>
  );
};
//connect innerComponent to HigerComponent
const HigherComponent = myConnect(innerComponent);

ReactDOM.render(
  <HigherComponent name="Haskell Curry" />, document.getElementById("root")
);
```

Code sample: https://codesandbox.io/s/react-hoc-scit1

You can add several props in, just as you need.

3.9 Context API

Context API provides a way to pass data through the component tree without passing props down manually at every level.

In a typical React application, data is passed top-down (parent to child) via props, but this can be a nuisance for certain types of props required by many components within an application. What's more, it can also decrease performance if not managed properly. When you pass state many levels down and change state somewhere on the top component, all of its children get rerendered (inside virtual DOM).

Context API provides a way to share values like these between components without explicitly passing props through every level of the tree. However, Context API is not a replacement for Redux or other state management libraries. Context API is not optimized for global state management. Context API can only store a single value, not a multiple set of values, each with its own consumers.

Provider is used to passing the data down to the components. The Provider component is used in a higher hierarchy of the tree. In the below example, the Provider uses a prop called as value. It acts as a root component in the hierarchical tree such that any child in the tree can access the values provided by the context provider.

```
render() {
  return (
    <Provider value={this.state.contextValue}>
      {this.props.children}
    </Provider>
  )
}
```

Consumer is used for receiving the data, which is passed by the Provider component. As the name implies, the consumer consumes the data being passed, regardless of how deeply nested it is located in the component tree. The consumer does not have to be necessarily being the child of the Provider. Instead, it can access data from anywhere deep down the component tree. A consumer renders the data by using a render prop API.

```
render() {
  return (
   <Consumer>
     {contextValue => <Child anyProp={contextValue} />}
   </Consumer>
  )
}
```

You need a predefined function to create a Context:

```
const Context = React.createContext();
```

The following code is a simple Context API example with a **Provider** and a **Consumer**.

React.createContext is used to initialize the Context, and it passes the initial value. It returns an object with a **Provider** and a **Consumer**. Providers and consumers come in pairs. For each provider, there is a corresponding consumer:

```
//sample from "React/Hooks/Redux in 48 hours"
import React from "react";
import ReactDOM from "react-dom";

// HelloContext is created with default value "null"
// returns two components Provider and Consumer
const HelloContext = React.createContext(null);
//Provider
function App() {
  return (
    <div>
      <HelloContext.Provider value="Context ! ">
        <Post />
      </HelloContext.Provider>
    </div>
  );
}
// consuming the ThemeContext data inside Post component
function Post() {
  return (
    <HelloContext.Consumer>
      {(data) => (
        <div>
          <h1>Hello {data}</h1>
        </div>
      )}
    </HelloContext.Consumer>
  );
}
ReactDOM.render(<App />, document.getElementById("root"));
```

Code sample: https://codesandbox.io/s/contextapi-lh0yg

Context API is not a state manager itself. In fact, you have to do all the management yourself. Besides, it can easily lead to unnecessary re-renders. However, you can avoid re-renders caused by Context API if you destructure the context value.

3.10 Props Validation

JavaScript is a dynamically typed language. Types are determined at runtime. React is a JavaScript library, and JavaScript does not provide any type-checking. Passing the wrong type of props to components can cause a lot of bugs in your application.

React encourages developers to build by breaking a UI into components. There will always be a need to pass data from one component to another since we are combing them together, and they rely on one another.

PropTypes ensure that the right type of props is passed to a component — and conversely, receiving the correct type of props. **PropTypes** are runtime type checkers for components that get compiled away in production. Runtime type checks have some clear advantages over compile-time type checking. It is easy to observe what happens in the running app's context when the user's API detects unexpected types at your APIs.

Properties validation is a valuable way to force the correct usage of the components. This will help during development to avoid future bugs and problems when the app becomes larger. It also makes the code more readable since we can see how each component should be used.

To perform type checking on the props for a component, you can assign the special **propTypes** property:

PropsType	Description
PropTypes.any	The props can be of any data type
PropTypes.array	The props should be an array
PropTypes.bool	The props should be a Boolean
PropTypes.func	The props should be a function
PropTypes.number	The props should be a number
PropTypes.object	The props should be an object
PropTypes.string	The props should be a string
PropTypes.symbol	The props should be a symbol
PropTypes.instanceOf	The props should be an instance of a particular JavaScript class
PropTypes.isRequired	The props must be provided
PropTypes.element	The props must be an element
PropTypes.node	The props can render anything: numbers, strings, elements or an array (or fragment) containing these types
PropTypes.oneOf()	The props should be one of several types of specific values
PropTypes.oneOfType ([PropTypes.string,PropTypes.number])	The props should be an object that could be one of many types

Appending *isRequired* to any PropTypes option will cause React to return an error if that property is missing.

In the following example, we import PropTypes from 'prop-types'. If some of the props do not use the correct type assigned, we will get an error. For example, If we delete *propArray: [1, 2, 3, 4, 5, 6, 7]* from the *App.defaultProps* object, it will give an error. If we set the value of *propArray* to 1, React will warn us that the *propType* validation has failed since we expect an array.

```
import React from "react";
import ReactDOM from "react-dom";
import PropTypes from "prop-types";

const App = (props) => {
  return (
    <>
      <h1>Props Validation Example</h1>
      <h2>Array: {props.propArray}</h2>
      <h2>Boolean: {props.propBool ? "true" : "False"}</h2>
      <h2>String: {props.propString}</h2>
      <h2>Number: {props.propNumber}</h2>
      <h2>Object: {props.propsObject.object1}</h2>
      <h2>Object: {props.propsObject.object2}</h2>
      <h2>Function: {props.propFunc(100)}</h2>
    </>
  );
};

App.propTypes = {
  propArray: PropTypes.array.isRequired,
  propBool: PropTypes.bool.isRequired,
  propString: PropTypes.string,
  propNumber: PropTypes.number,
  propsObject: PropTypes.object,
  propFunc: PropTypes.func
};
App.defaultProps = {
  propArray: [1, 2, 3, 4, 5, 6, 7],
  propBool: true,
  propFunc: function (x) {
   return x + 1;
  },
  propNumber: 2020,
  propString: "Hello World",
  propsObject: {
    object1: "object 1",
    object2: "object 2"
  }
};

ReactDOM.render(<App />, document.getElementById("root"));
```

Code sample: https://codesandbox.io/s/react-props-validation-4ih9i

3.11 Server-Side Rendering

When rendering our React component using the ReactDOMServer API, we will send static HTML to the client. In order to deal with the dynamic events you have programmed in your React component, you will have to attach this HTML markup to its original React component. React achieves this by sending identification to the generated markup. This way, it is possible to resolve later which event should be attached to which element in the DOM.

ReactDOMServer API

With ReactDOMServer object, you can render components to static markup. Typically, it is used on a Node.js server.

renderToString() and **renderToStaticMarkup()** can be used in both server and browser environments. **renderToNodeStream()** and **renderToStaticNodeStream()** work on the server only.

ReactDOM.hydrate( )

When building a SPA, all you need to use is ReactDOM at the entry point of your app and then subsequently load all components. However, if you build an SSR or static-site-generator, your web application is being built before deployment. If you attempt to render those pre-created components with ReactDOM, an error will occur. Because ReactDOM does not support the server-side rendering.

ReactDOM.hydrate() is similar to ReactDOM.render(), but it is used when we want to render our React Application on the server-side and hydrate the JavaScript on the client-side. This makes our apps fast and also allows search engines to crawl our pages. As a result, the SEO (Search Engine Optimization) will be improved. ReactDOM.hydrate() expects the container-element in our HTML to be already rendered by ReactDOMServer and only takes care of attaching event listeners.

The syntax of ReactDOM.hydrate() is identical to ReactDOM.render ():

ReactDOM.hydrate(<App />, document.getElementById('root'))

You should only use ReactDOM.hydrate( ) on a container whose HTML contents were rendered by ReactDOMServer.

4. REACT HOOKS

(10 hours reading and exercise)

History is a record of these class struggles and displacement.

(Karl Marx 1818-1883)

If you are used to functional programming, you will likely enjoy using hooks.
If you come from class-based programming such as Java, ES6 Class components may be more natural. Although hooks are trendy nowadays, there is nothing wrong with using Class components. The choice is mostly a matter of personal preference.

React Hooks allows us to use only functional components for all our needs to avoid complicated patterns. Hooks are a simpler way to encapsulate stateful behavior and side effects in a user interface while using less code and increasing readability.

React Hooks let us use state and other React features without using ES6 Classes and allow us to access state and Lifecycle methods in a functional component. Hooks relies on closures to store data.

Before Hooks had been released, the most common way to use state was with ES6 Classes. We had to use *this.state* and *this.setState( )* to refer and update state respectively. With **Hooks** API, setState and ES6 Classes are not needed anymore. No more confusing *this*, but now we have to understand the JavaScript closures.

React hooks present a new set of functionality that allows React to be written in a completely functional manner, opening the door to all sorts of possibilities for performance, lower memory usage, and responsive (non-blocking / concurrent) web applications.

There are only several rules to follow to use Hooks.
- Declare Hooks at the top level in your function components before the return declaration.
- Do not call within a conditional statement, loop statement.
- Do not call within nested functions.
- Do not call from Class components. You can call Hooks from React Functions only. i.e., Functional Components and Custom Hooks.

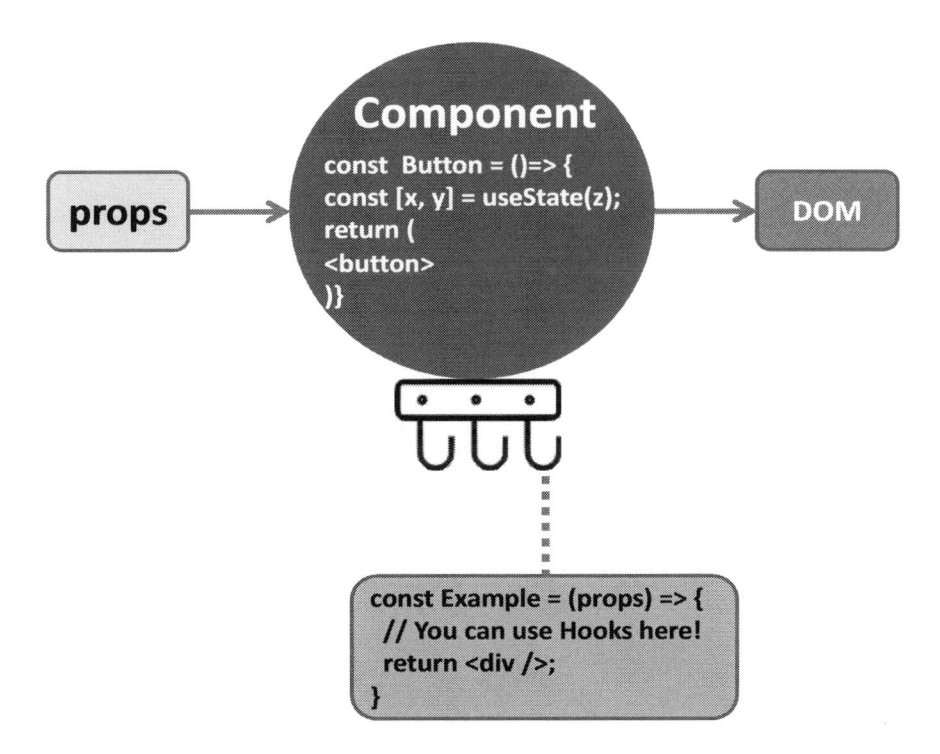

Component
```
const Button = ()=> {
const [x, y] = useState(z);
return (
<button>
)}
```

props → Component → DOM

```
const Example = (props) => {
  // You can use Hooks here!
  return <div />;
}
```

Since React is a component-oriented UI library, creating and managing a global state requires a third-party dependency like Redux. With the introduction of React Hooks, it can be done easily with React without installing any third-party dependency. However, its use case and performance are limited when using in large-scale projects. This means that state managers (such as Redux, Recoil, MobX) are still required for many cases. Hooks and state managers are not mutually exclusive.

The concept of Hooks is easy and clean, but in practice, Hooks APIs are not simple. As a result, you may need considerable time practicing to use it properly.

4.1 useState

As the name implies, **useState** is a hook that allows you to use state in your function. **useState** accepts the initial value of the state item and returns an array containing the state variable and the function you call to update the state. Since it returns an array, we use ES6 array destructuring to access each item, for example, like this:
const [state, setState] = useState(0)

The first variable is the value that is similar to *this.state* in the class components. The second variable is a function to update that value, which is identical to *this.setState*. The final part is the argument that we pass to it. (initial state value).

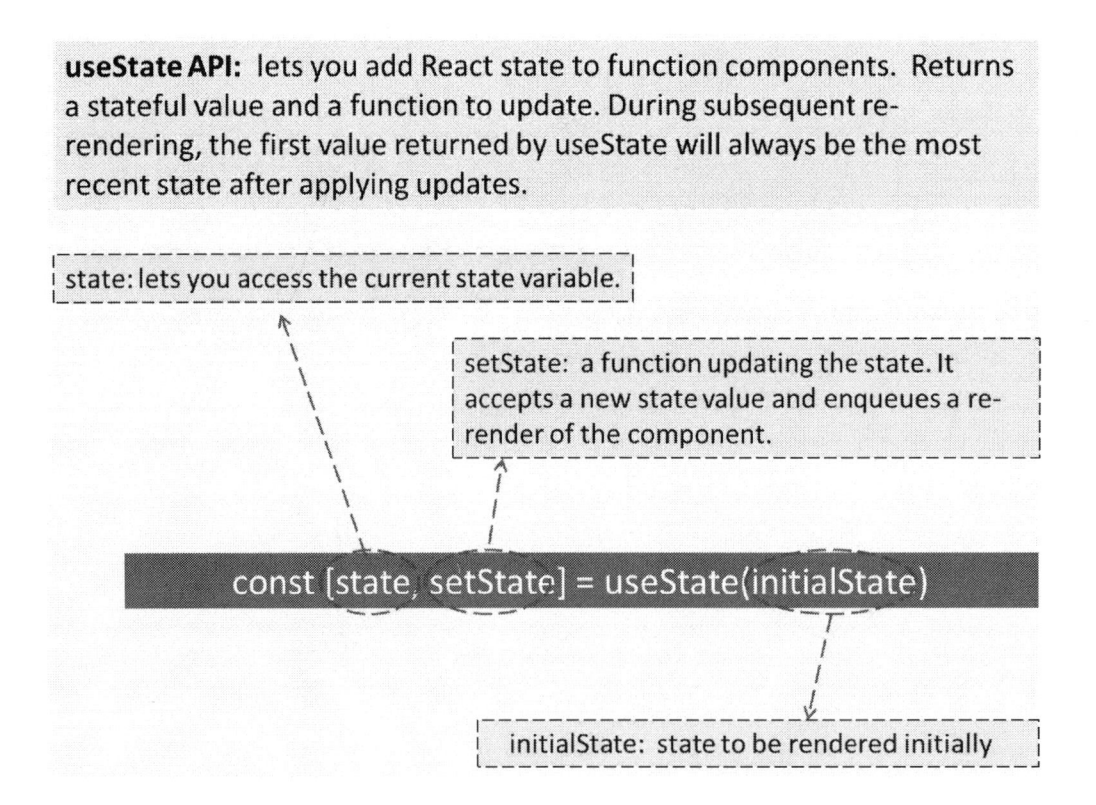

> **useState API:** lets you add React state to function components. Returns a stateful value and a function to update. During subsequent re-rendering, the first value returned by useState will always be the most recent state after applying updates.

state: lets you access the current state variable.

setState: a function updating the state. It accepts a new state value and enqueues a re-render of the component.

`const [state, setState] = useState(initialState)`

initialState: state to be rendered initially

Besides the different syntax, useState( ) works differently than setState( ) in class-based components. **Unlike class-based components, the state is not getting merged. When you set a new state with React Hooks, the old state will always be replaced by a new state.**

(Basic pattern 1)

The simplest example is like this. It displays the "Hello world" using the initial value:

```
import React, { useState } from "react";
import ReactDOM from "react-dom"

const App = () => {
  const [greeting] = useState( "Hello world" );

  return (
    <div>
      <h1>{greeting}</h1>
    </div>
  );
};

ReactDOM.render(<App />, document.getElementById("root"));
```

(Basic pattern 2)

You can initialize state variable with function:

```
import React, { useState } from "react";
import ReactDOM from "react-dom";

const App = () => {
  const [greeting] = useState( ( ) => "Hello world" );

  return (
    <div>
      <h1>{greeting}</h1>
    </div>
  );
};

ReactDOM.render(<App />, document.getElementById("root"));
```

(Basic pattern 3)
You can use a function to update the state variable.
The initial message "Hello World" will be replaced by "Hello Mars":

```jsx
import React, { useState } from "react";
import ReactDOM from "react-dom";

const App = () => {
  const [greeting, updateGreeting] = useState("Hello world" );

  return (
    <div>
      <h2>{greeting}</h2>
      <button onClick={() => updateGreeting("Hello Mars") }>
        Update greeting
      </button>
    </div>
  );
};
ReactDOM.render(<App />, document.getElementById("root"));
```

(Basic pattern 4)
Instead of object, use a function parameter to access the previous state variable.

```jsx
import React, { useState } from "react";
import ReactDOM from "react-dom";
const App = () => {
  const [greeting, updateGreeting] = useState( "Hello world" );
  return (
    <div>
      <h2>{greeting}</h2>
      <button
        onClick={() => updateGreeting((greeting) => `${greeting} + Hello Mars`) }
      >
        Update greeting
      </button>
    </div>
  );
};
ReactDOM.render(<App />, document.getElementById("root"));
```

Code sample: https://codesandbox.io/s/hook-usestate1-f7wn6

In the following example, *count* holds the current state, *setCount* is a function that increments or decrements the count depending on the button clicked.

```jsx
import React, { useState } from "react"
import ReactDOM from "react-dom"

function App() {
  const [count, setCount] = useState(0);
  return (
    <div>
       <h1>count: {count} </h1>
       <button onClick={() => setCount(count + 1)}>increment</button>
       <button onClick={() => setCount(count - 1)}>decrement</button>
    </div>
  )
}

ReactDOM.render(<App />, document.getElementById("root"))
```

Code sample: https://codesandbox.io/s/hook-usestate0-jddjq

useState() confusing part

Much like setState in the class component, the usage of useState is a bit tricky.

1. Objects being used as a function updater parameter

In the class component, initialization is in the constructor and runs only one. On the other hand, in the useState hook, every time the component re-renders, initialization takes place. In the below code, no matter how many times setCount(count+1) runs, the result is always 1 because functions overwrite the values.

```
function App() {const [count, setCount] = useState(0);

const incrementCount1 = () => {
        setCount(count + 1);           //1
        setCount(count + 1);           //1  (we expect 2)
        setCount(count + 1);           //1  (we expect 3)
};
```

2. Functions being used as a function updater parameter

If you intend to use the previous value to update the state, you must pass a function that receives the previous value and returns an updated value. In the code below, every time setCount((prevCount) => prevCount + 1) are executed, values are incremented from the previous value.

```
function App() {const [count, setCount] = useState(0);

const incrementCount3 = () => {
        setCount((prevCount) => prevCount + 1);   //1
        setCount((prevCount) => prevCount + 1);   //2
        setCount((prevCount) => prevCount + 1);   //3  (as you expect)
};
```

You can play around with the following code to get used to the subtlety of the useState parameters:

```javascript
//sample code from "learns React/Hooks/Redux in 48 hours"
import React, { useState } from "react";
import ReactDOM from "react-dom";

function App() {
  const [count, setCount] = useState(0);

  //plus 1. values based on the Redered values.
  //functions overwite the rendered values each other

  const incrementCount1 = () => {
    setCount(count + 1);
    setCount(count + 1);
    setCount(count + 1);
  };
  //plus 3. values based on the previous valus passed into
  const incrementCount3 = () => {
    setCount((prevCount) => prevCount + 1);
    setCount((prevCount) => prevCount + 1);
    setCount((prevCount) => prevCount + 1);
  };
  return (
    <>
      <h1>count: {count} </h1>
      <button onClick={incrementCount1}>increment by 1</button>
      <button onClick={incrementCount3}>increment by 3</button>
    </>
  );
}
ReactDOM.render(<App />, document.getElementById("root"));
```

Code sample : https://codesandbox.io/s/hook-usestate-yvjk2

4.2 useEffect

The **useEffect** hook takes the side-effect function (asynchronous function) as an argument and runs this function whenever the component is mounted to the DOM. **useEffect** is run after the render. The useEffect hook is like handling **componentDidMount**, **componentDidUpdate**, and **componentWillUnmount** all in one call. It should be used for any side-effects that you are executing in your render cycle. By default, effects run after every completed render, but you can also choose to trigger only when specific values have changed. If you don't want it to be executed after each re-render, then you will add a second parameter with an empty array [ ].

> **useEffect API:** The callback function passed to useEffect will run after the render is committed to the screen. Mutations, subscriptions, timers, logging, and other side effects can be used.

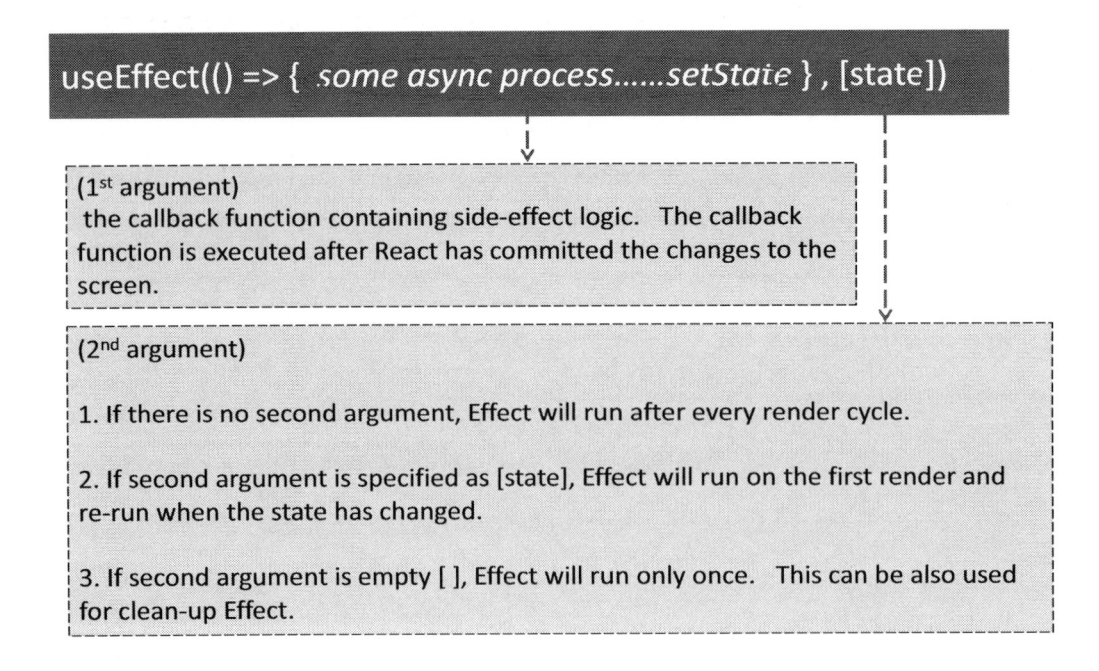

```
useEffect(() => { some async process......setState } , [state])
```

(1st argument)
the callback function containing side-effect logic. The callback function is executed after React has committed the changes to the screen.

(2nd argument)

1. If there is no second argument, Effect will run after every render cycle.

2. If second argument is specified as [state], Effect will run on the first render and re-run when the state has changed.

3. If second argument is empty [ ], Effect will run only once. This can be also used for clean-up Effect.

useEffect() can be called multiple times, which is nice feature to separate unrelated logic.

Cleanup after the effect execution

React performs the cleanup when the component unmounts. As **useEffect** can run for every render and not just once, React also needs to clean up effects from the previous render before running the effects next time. Otherwise, it may affect your application performance.

The **useEffect** Hook provides the ability to run a cleanup after the effect. This can be achieved by specifying a return function at the end of the effect. It is like both **componentDidMount** and **componentDidUnmount** combined into a single effect.

The clean-up function runs before the component is removed from the UI to prevent memory overflows. Additionally, if a component renders multiple times, the previous effect can be cleaned up before executing the next effect.

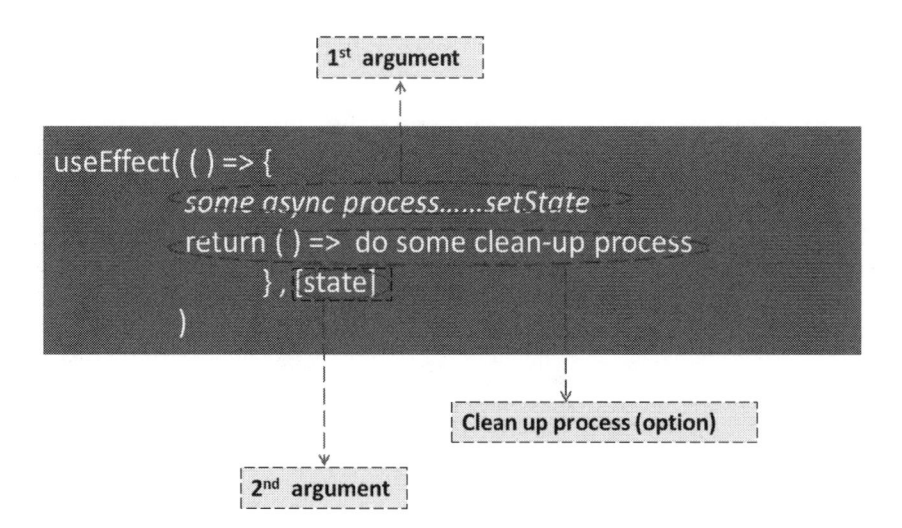

```
useEffect( ( ) => {
        some async process......setState
        return ( ) => do some clean-up process
             }, [state]
    )
```

1st argument → (function body)

2nd argument → [state]

Clean up process (option) → return ( )

Run the effect on every render

React uses the 2nd argument to determine whether it needs to execute the function passed to **useEffect**. If there is no 2nd argument, **useEffect** is run upon every render. This may cause performance issues or just be overkill.

```jsx
import React, { useState, useEffect } from "react";
import ReactDOM from "react-dom";

// useEffect will be called whenever count state changes
function App() {
  const [count, setCount] = useState(0);

  useEffect(() => {
    console.log("effect runs upon render!");
    return () => {
      //clearn-up
      console.log("clean-up done!");
    };
  });
  const handleClick = () => {
    setCount(count + 1);
  };
  return (
    <>
      <h2>count: {count}</h2>
      <button onClick={handleClick}>Click me</button>
    </>
  );
}

const rootElement = document.getElementById("root");
ReactDOM.render(<App />, rootElement);
```

Code sample: https://codesandbox.io/s/hooks-useeffect-ozxnt

Run the effect only once

If we only like to run the effect for a single time, pass an empty [ ] as the 2nd argument to **useEffect**. It is a replacement for **componentDidMount**. The below code accesses the external resource using the Fetch API.

```
import React from "react";
import { useState, useEffect } from "react";
import ReactDOM from "react-dom";

function App() {
  const [url, setUrl] = useState([]);
  //effect will run only once
  useEffect(() => {
    fetch("https://dog.ceo/api/breeds/image/random")
      .then((res) => res.json())
      .then((url) => setUrl(url.message));
  }, []);

  return (
    <>
      <h2>useEffect random dogs - click the reload button</h2>
      <img src={url} alt="loading images...." />
    </>
  );
}

ReactDOM.render(<App />, document.getElementById("root"));
```

Code sample: https://codesandbox.io/s/hooks-dogs-x7zx0rrqqo

Note: In order to focus on understanding the useEffect API concept, error handling procedures are intentionally omitted in this example.

Run the effect when data changes

If you want to run the effect only when a specific value changes (for example, updating some local storage or triggering an HTTP request), you can pass values that you are monitoring.

In the following code, setTimeout is called inside of the useEffect Hook. JavaScript setTimeout( ) function invokes a setCount function after 1 second. As the 2nd argument is specified as [count], the Effect will run on the first render and re-run when the count is changed.

To clear the setTimeout, we need to call the clearTimeout method by setting our timeout variable as an argument.   *return () => clearTimeout(timeout)*

```
import React, { useState, useEffect } from "react"
import ReactDOM from "react-dom"

function App() {
 const [count, setCount] = useState(0)

 useEffect(() => {
   const timeout = setTimeout(() => {
     setCount(count + 1)
   }, 1000)
   return () => clearTimeout(timeout)
 }, [count])

 return <div>count: {count}</div>
}

ReactDOM.render(<App />, document.getElementById("root"))
```

Code sample: https://codesandbox.io/s/039p9zwomv

Using setInterval( ) in useEffect. (a bit tricky)

setInterval( ) and setTimeout( ) are JavaScript methods of Windows object. setInterval( ) allows us to repeatedly run a function, starting after the interval of time, then repeating continuously at that interval. In contrast, setTimeout( ) runs a function once after the interval of time. If you use setInterval() within react hooks, the component may not work as you expect.

Counter example 1 (may not work as you expect)

By giving [ ] as the second argument, useEffect will call the function once after mounting. Even though setInterval() is called only once, this code run incorrectly.
The count will increase from 0 to 1 and stay that way.

In the first rendering, the closure captures the count variable. However, the useEffect() is not invoked the second time. Even if the count increases later, it still uses a stale closure. It always has a value of 0 within the setInterval callback. The count is always the same.

The reason is that the callback passed into setInterval's closure that only accesses the variable in the first rendering. It doesn't have access to the new count value in the subsequent render because the useEffect() is not invoked the second time.

```
import React, { useState, useEffect } from "react";
import ReactDOM from "react-dom";

function App() {
  console.log("render");
  const [count, setCount] = useState(0);

  useEffect(() => {
    const interval = setInterval(() => {
      setCount(count + 1);
    }, 1000);
    return () => clearInterval(interval);
  }, [ ]);

  return <div> count: {count}</div>;
}

ReactDOM.render(<App />, document.getElementById("root"));
```

Counter Example 2 (works correctly, but clumsy)

One of the solutions is to add [count] as a dependency. This way, **useEffect( ) has the closure of [count] and correctly handles the reset of interval.** With the dependencies properly set, useEffect( ) updates the closure as soon as the count changes. Proper management of hooks dependencies is an efficient way to solve the stale closure problem.

However, this is not an ideal solution, as a new setInterval( ) will be created and executed on every change of count. You would need to clean it up on every render. Each setInterval( ) is always executed once. Then why not using a setTimeout( ) instead?

```
import React, { useState, useEffect } from "react";
import ReactDOM from "react-dom";

function App() {
  const [count, setCount] = useState(0);

  useEffect(() => {
    const interval = setInterval(() => {
      setCount(count + 1);
    }, 1000);
    return () => clearInterval(interval);
  }, [count]);

  return <div> count: {count}</div>;
}

ReactDOM.render(<App />, document.getElementById("root"));
```

Code sample: https://codesandbox.io/s/hooks-useeffect2x-3xep6

Counter Example 3 (Recommended solution)

Like the setState, useEffect hooks have two forms of parameters:
(1) object: takes in the updated state.
(2) function: callback form in which the current state is passed.

You should use the second form and read the latest state value within the callback to ensure that you have the newest state value before incrementing it.

In the following sample, useState updates the previous state without capturing the current value. To do that, we need to provide a callback. This code works correctly and more efficiently. We are using a single setInterval during the lifecycle of a component. The clearInterval will only be called once after the component is unmounted.

```
import React, { useState, useEffect } from "react";
import ReactDOM from "react-dom";

function App() {
  const [count, setCount] = useState(0);

  useEffect(() => {
    const interval = setInterval(() => {
      setCount(count => count + 1);  //uses callback function
    }, 1000);
    return () => clearInterval(interval);
  }, [ ]);

  return <div> count: {count}</div>;
}

ReactDOM.render(<App />, document.getElementById("root"));
```

Code sample: https://codesandbox.io/s/hooks-useeffect3x-ve8zl

4.3 useContext

The React Context API is a simple alternative to prop-drilling up and down your component tree. Instead of passing local data around and through several layers of components, it helps data that needs to be shared across components. The downside is that using React Context will cause unnecessary re-renders for any components (within the Consumer) update.

The useContext hook provides all the same functionality you would expect from the Context API. The useContext lets you use context without using a Consumer keyword, which is a bit simpler than Context API.

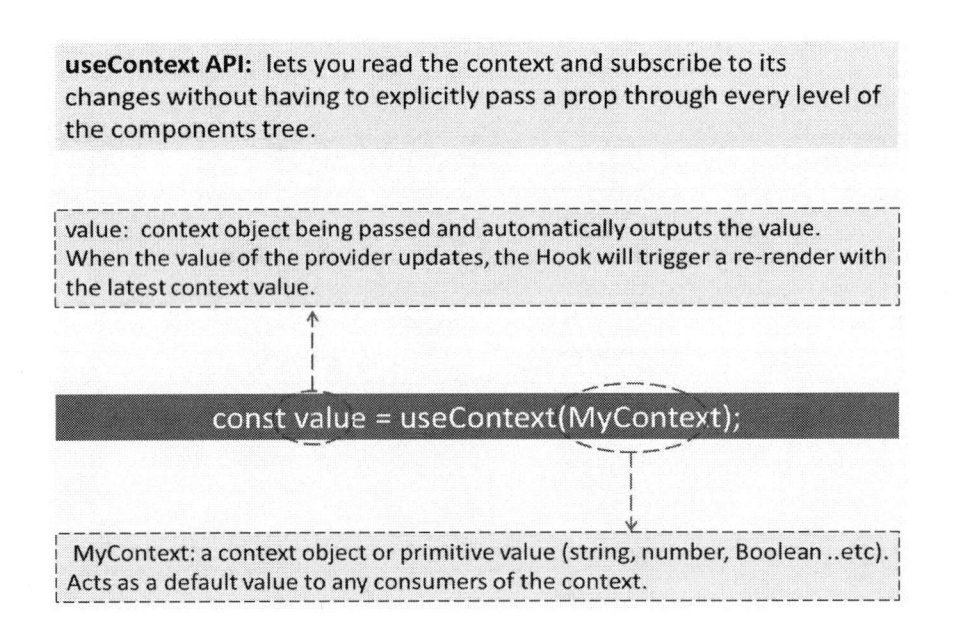

useContext API: lets you read the context and subscribe to its changes without having to explicitly pass a prop through every level of the components tree.

value: context object being passed and automatically outputs the value. When the value of the provider updates, the Hook will trigger a re-render with the latest context value.

```
const value = useContext(MyContext);
```

MyContext: a context object or primitive value (string, number, Boolean ..etc). Acts as a default value to any consumers of the context.

```jsx
import React, { useContext } from "react";
import ReactDOM from "react-dom";

// *GreetingContext is created with default value
// *it returns two components Provider and Consumer
const GreetingContext = React.createContext(null);

//* context provider
function App() {
  return (
    <div>
      <GreetingContext.Provider value="World">
        <Post />
      </GreetingContext.Provider>
    </div>
  );
}

// *consuming the GreetingContext data inside Post component
function Post() {
  const theme = useContext(GreetingContext);
  return (
    <div>
      <h1>Hello {theme}</h1>
    </div>
  );}

ReactDOM.render(<App />, document.getElementById("root"));
```

Code sample: https://codesandbox.io/s/usecontext-vo95t

4.4 useRef

useRef hook is a solution to use React *refs* within functional components. *useRef* can be used when you want to avoid re-render or when you want to access the DOM element imperatively. Much like *refs*, *useRef* should not be overused.

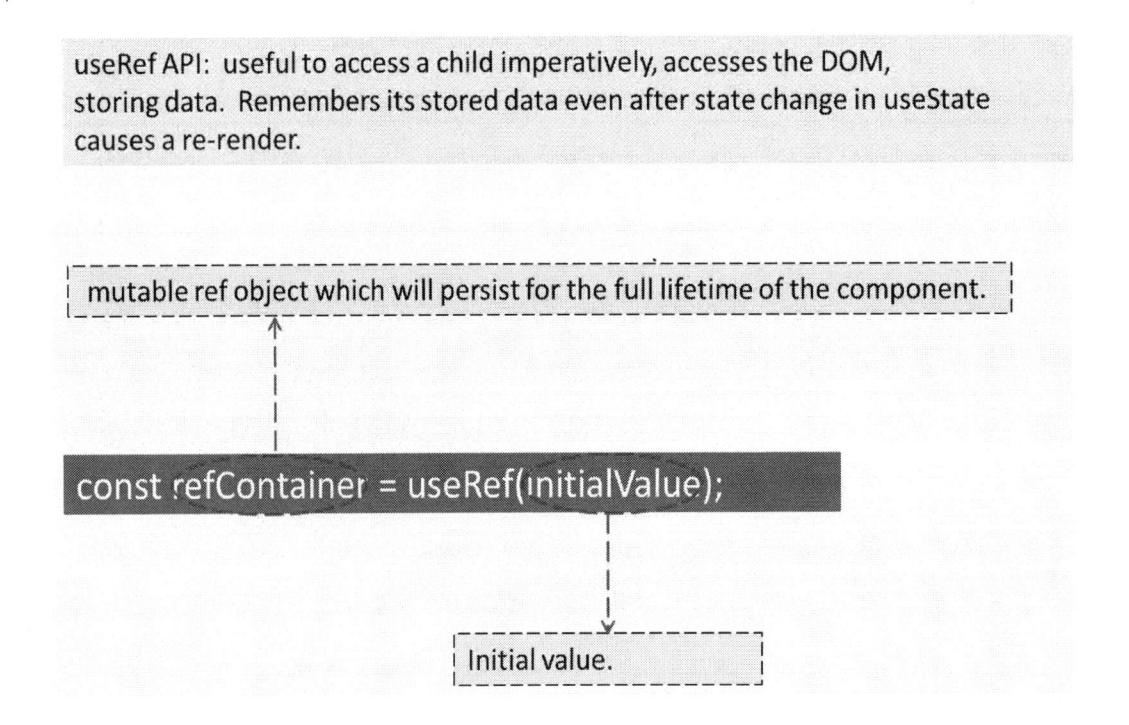

useRef API: useful to access a child imperatively, accesses the DOM, storing data. Remembers its stored data even after state change in useState causes a re-render.

mutable ref object which will persist for the full lifetime of the component.

```
const refContainer = useRef(initialValue);
```

Initial value.

```jsx
import React, { useState, useRef } from "react";
import ReactDOM from "react-dom";

function App() {
  const [name, setData] = useState("Enter Your Name");

  const dataRef = useRef(null);

  const submitData = () => {
    setData(dataRef.current.value);
  };
      //React will set its current property (dataRef.current.value)
      //to the corresponding DOM node whenever that node changes.
  return (
    <div className="App">
      <p>{name}</p>

      <div>
        <input ref={dataRef} type="text" />
        <button type="button" onClick={submitData}>
          Submit
        </button>
      </div>
    </div>
  );
}

ReactDOM.render(<App />, document.getElementById("root"));
```

Code sample: https://codesandbox.io/s/useref-7q7zs

4.5 useReducer

useReducer is an alternative to useState. The recommended way to manage component state when your application is more complex, containing objects with multiple sub-values, or when the next state depends on the previous one.

***useReducer* allows you to update parts of your component's state when specific actions are dispatched.** In a way, it is similar to Redux. However, *useReducer* cannot be used as a global state container because the dispatch function operates only on one reducer function.

While Redux creates one global state container located somewhere above your whole application, ***useReducer* creates an independent state container within your component.**

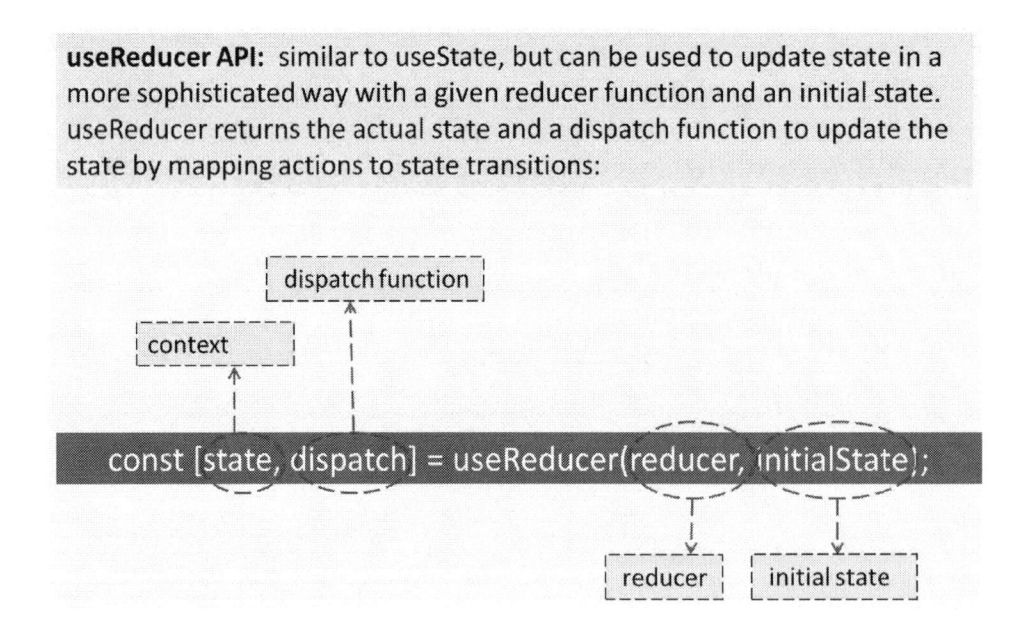

> **useReducer API:** similar to useState, but can be used to update state in a more sophisticated way with a given reducer function and an initial state. useReducer returns the actual state and a dispatch function to update the state by mapping actions to state transitions:
>
> ```
> const [state, dispatch] = useReducer(reducer, initialState);
> ```
>
> - state → context
> - dispatch → dispatch function
> - reducer → reducer
> - initialState → initial state

Counter example 1

The following example is a counter that increments by 10. When you click the button, value 10 is dispatched. The reducer returns current state + 10.

```
import React, { useReducer } from "react";
import ReactDOM from "react-dom";

function App() {
  const [value, dispatch] = useReducer((state, action) => {
    return state + action;
  }, 0);

  return (
    <div>
       <h2>count: {value}</h2>
       <button onClick={() => dispatch(10)}>increment by 10</button>
    </div>
  );
}

ReactDOM.render(<App />, document.getElementById("root"));
```

Code sample: https://codesandbox.io/s/usereducer-px8ld

Counter example 2

In the following example, a counter will be incremented, decremented, or reset depending on the dispatched action.type. With useRedux, you can easily create a Finite State Machine (FSM):

```js
const ACTIONS = {
  INCREMENT: "increment",
  DECREMENT: "decrement",
  RESET: "reset"
};

const reducer = (state, action) => {
  console.log(state, action);
  switch (action.type) {
    case ACTIONS.INCREMENT:
      return { count: state.count + 1 };
    case ACTIONS.DECREMENT:
      return { count: state.count - 1 };
    case ACTIONS.RESET:
      return { count: (state.count = 0) };
    default:
      return state;
  }
};

function App() {
  const [state, dispatch] = useReducer(reducer, { count: 0 });

  const increment = () => {dispatch({ type: "increment" })
  };
  const decrement = () => {dispatch({ type: "decrement" })
  };
  const reset = () => {dispatch({ type: "reset" })
  };
  return (
    <div>
      <h2>count: {state.count}</h2>
      <button onClick={increment}>+</button>
      <button onClick={decrement}>-</button>
      <button onClick={reset}>Reset</button>
    </div>
  );
}
ReactDOM.render(<App />, document.getElementById("root"));
```

Reducer to update the state based on the action.type

Dispatch action.type selected by user

Code sample: https://codesandbox.io/s/usereducer1-qrx0f

Todo list example

With useReducer, the Todo list is simpler than using useState.

```jsx
function App() {
  const [todoValue, setTodoValue] = useState();
  let dataRef = useRef(null);

//***reducer***
  const reducer = (state, action) => {
    switch (action.type) {
      case "add":                    //*add todo item and ID
        setTodoValue("");
        return [...state, { id: state.length + 1, text: todoValue }];

      case "remove":                 //*remove the selected todo item
        const newList = state.filter((item) => item.id !== action.id);
        return newList;
      default:
        return state;
    }
  };
//***end reducer***
  const [state, dispatch] = useReducer(reducer, []);

  return (
    <div className="App">
      <form onSubmit={(e) => e.preventDefault()}>
        <input type="text"  ref={dataRef} onChange={(e) => setTodoValue(e.target.value)}/>
        <button onClick={ () => dispatch({ type: "add", text: todoValue }) }>
          Add Todo
        </button>
      </form>
      <div>
        {state.map((todo) => (
          <div className="Row" key={todo.id}>
            <p>{todo.text}</p>
            <button onClick={ () => dispatch({ type: "remove", id: todo.id }) }>
              Remove
            </button>
          </div>
        ))}
      </div>
    </div>
  );
}
ReactDOM.render(<App />, document.getElementById("root"));
```

Code sample: https://codesandbox.io/s/usereducer-todo-nid5i

If the action.type is "add", then add a todo item and generate its id.

If the action.type is "remove", since we already have a value of id property, we simply filter the source array against this id. The filter method removes items that have a value of id equal to the target id.

```
const reducer = (state, action) => {
  switch (action.type) {
    case "add":                      //*add todo item and ID
      setTodoValue("");
      return [...state, { id: state.length + 1, text: todoValue }];

    case "remove":                   //*remove the selected todo item
      const newList = state.filter((item) => item.id !== action.id);
      return newList;

    default:
      return state;
  }
};
```

4.6 useMemo

In a nutshell, memoization is the programming pattern to make long recursive/iterative functions run much faster. When React checks for changes in a component, it may cause unnecessarily re-rendering to the component tree. This is where a software technique called memoization comes in.

useMemo prevents unnecessary re-renders, making your code way more efficient by returning a **memoized value** resulting from the callback function.

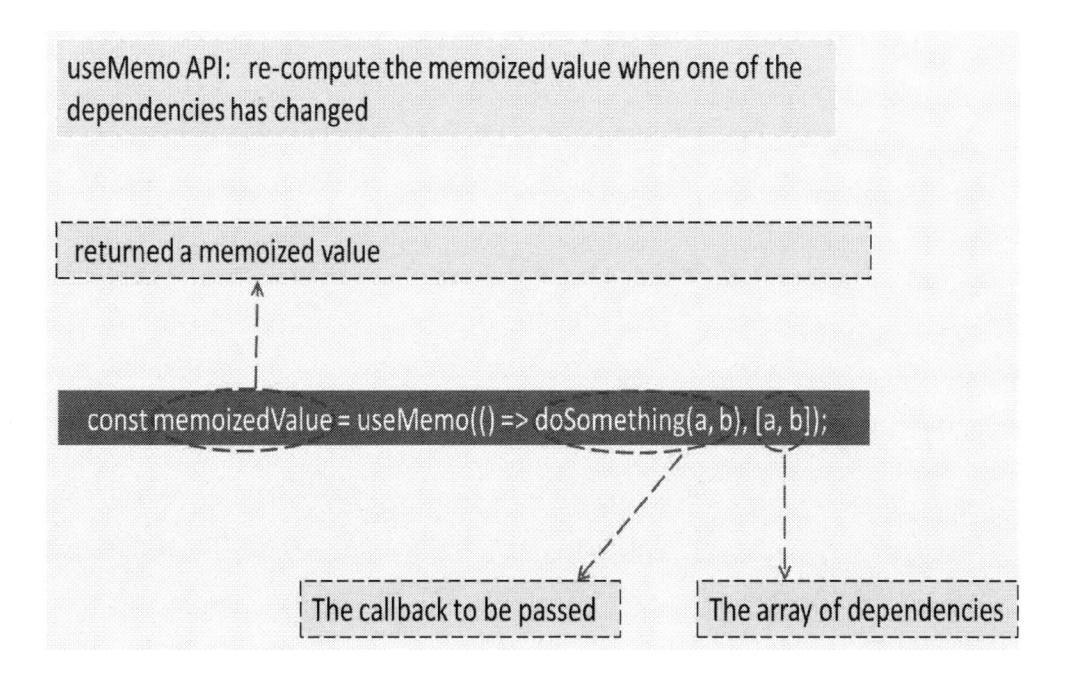

useMemo API: re-compute the memoized value when one of the dependencies has changed

returned a memoized value

```
const memoizedValue = useMemo(() => doSomething(a, b), [a, b]);
```

The callback to be passed

The array of dependencies

In the following example, useMemo allows you to cache the value of a variable along with a dependency list (*memoCount*). If any variables in this dependency list change, React will re-run the processing for this data and re-cache it.

If the variable value in the dependency list was previously cached, React gets the value from the cache. In this way, you can improve the performance of repetitive processing.

```
import React, { useState, useMemo } from "react";
import ReactDOM from "react-dom";

const App = () => {
  const [memoCount, setMemoCount] = useState(0);
  const memoFunction = () => {
    console.log("memoized value", memoCount);
    /* You can add code that requires heavy processing */
  };

  /* create the memo hook, when memoCount changes, memoFunction will be executed again */
  useMemo(memoFunction, [memoCount]);

  /* After creating useMemo, each change of memoCount triggers the function passed to the hook,
     otherwise the memoized value will be returned */

  return (
    <div>
      <button onClick={() => setMemoCount(memoCount + 1)}>
        Increment memo count
      </button>
      <p>click the Console below</p>
    </div>
  );
};

ReactDOM.render(<App />, document.getElementById("root"));
```

Code sample: https://codesandbox.io/s/usememo-b29ug

4.7 useCallback

useCallback prevents unnecessary re-renders, making your code more efficient by returning a memoized callback function. *useCallback* helps memoize the callback function, which requires heavy computation. **useCallback returns its function when the dependencies change.** (On the other hand, *useMemo* calls its function and returns the memoized value.)

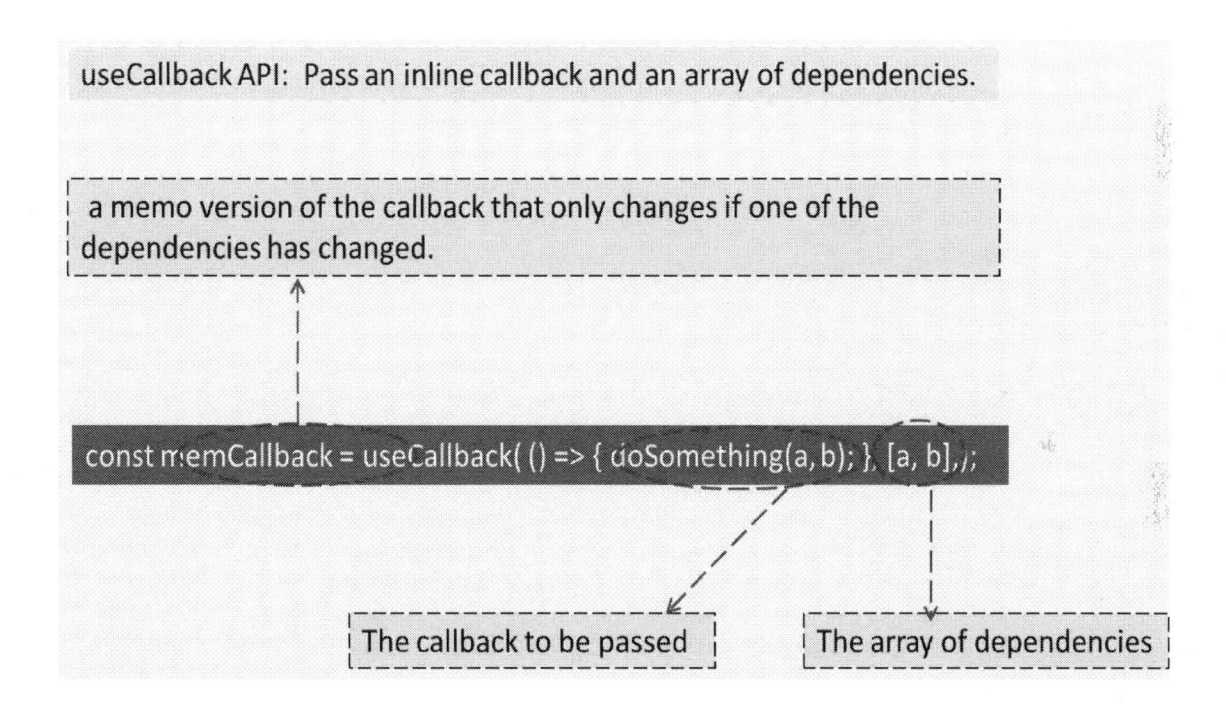

useCallback API: Pass an inline callback and an array of dependencies.

a memo version of the callback that only changes if one of the dependencies has changed.

```
const memCallback = useCallback( () => { doSomething(a, b); }, [a, b],);
```

The callback to be passed

The array of dependencies

```jsx
import React, { useEffect, useState, useCallback } from "react";
import ReactDOM from "react-dom";

const App = () => {
  const [callbackCount, setCallbackCount] = useState(0);

  /* if we give an empty array of dependencies,
     the callback function will return the old value of callbackCount
     because useCallback will return its memoized version */

  const callbackFunction = useCallback(() => {
    console.log("callback", callbackCount);
    return callbackCount;
  }, [callbackCount]);

  return (
    <>
      {/* It will receive a function that will change when the dependency value changes */}
      <Child action={callbackFunction} />

      {/* Change the callback hook dependency to trigger a change in the child */}
      <button onClick={() => setCallbackCount(callbackCount + 1)}>
        Increment callback count
      </button>
      <p>click the Console below</p>
    </>
  );
};

const Child = ({ action }) => {
  const [value, setValue] = useState(0);

  useEffect(() => {
    const number = action();
    setValue(number);
  }, [action]);

  return <p>callback count: {value}</p>;
};

ReactDOM.render(<App />, document.getElementById("root"));
```

Code sample: https://codesandbox.io/s/usecallbak-rnhci

4.8 Custom Hooks

You can create your own custom hooks to avoid code repetition and make the code cleaner. Custom hooks are normal JavaScript functions that can use other hooks with the *use* prefix. Custom hooks are just functional components, and so it is easy to understand. The general rules of hooks also apply to custom hooks:

- Only call hooks at the top level. Do not call hooks inside loops, conditions, or nested functions. React relies on the order in which hooks are called to associate the hooks with a specific local state. Placing a hook inside conditions may change this order resulting in subsequent hooks failing to get called.
- Only call hooks from React function components. You cannot call hooks from regular JavaScript functions.
- You can call custom hooks from your own custom hooks.

In the following example, we create a custom hook *useCounter* that processes increment, decrement or reset, depending on the input parameters.

```
import React, { useState } from "react";
import ReactDOM from "react-dom";

// custom hook to count up/down/reset
const useCounter = (initialValue) => {
  const [count, setCount] = useState(initialValue);
  return {
    value: count,
    increase: () => setCount((prevCount) => prevCount + 1),
    decrease: () => setCount((prevCount) => prevCount - 1),
    reset: () => setCount(initialValue)
  };
};

// counter calling useCounter hook.
const Counter = ({ initialValue }) => {
  const counter = useCounter(initialValue);
  return (
    <>
      <h2>count: {counter.value}</h2>
      <button onClick={counter.increase}>increment</button>
      <button onClick={counter.decrease}>decrement</button>
      <button onClick={counter.reset}>Reset</button>
    </>
  );
};

function App() {
  return (
    <div className="App">
      <Counter initialValue={0} />
    </div>
  );
}

ReactDOM.render(<App />, document.getElementById("root"));
```

Code sample: https://codesandbox.io/s/custom-hooks-v02fj

In the following example, we create a custom hook *useClock* that displays a local time by calling a JavaScript Date method.

```
import React from "react";
import ReactDOM from "react-dom";
import { useState, useEffect } from "react";

import "./index.css";
//using custom hook
const App = () => {
  return (
    <div>
      <h1>Current local time</h1>
      <br />
      <h2> {useClock()} </h2>
      <h3> {useClock()} </h3>
      <h4> {useClock()} </h4>
    </div>
  );
};
//customer hook
const useClock = () => {
  const [clock, setClock] = useState(new Date().toLocaleTimeString());

  useEffect(() => {
    const myInterval = setInterval(() => {
      setClock(new Date().toLocaleTimeString());
    }, 1000);

    return () => clearInterval(myInterval);
  }, []);

  return clock;
};

ReactDOM.render(<App />, document.getElementById("app"));
```

Code sample: https://codesandbox.io/s/react-custom-hooks1-c6obt

4.9 React Hook Form library

React Hook Form is the third-party custom hooks library, having a clean structure with a single hook call abstracting away many underlying setups, and it is flexible for many different situations. It includes local validation, the ability to pass in a validation schema, ability to change output shape within its form. PropTypes becomes much easier for defining your form components because React Hook Form manages it. React Hook Form must be used within a functional component.

Try this CodeSandbox sample from the official docs.
https://codesandbox.io/s/kw7z2q2n15

We encourage you to take a closer look if you think it might be for you.

official docs: https://react-hook-form.com/

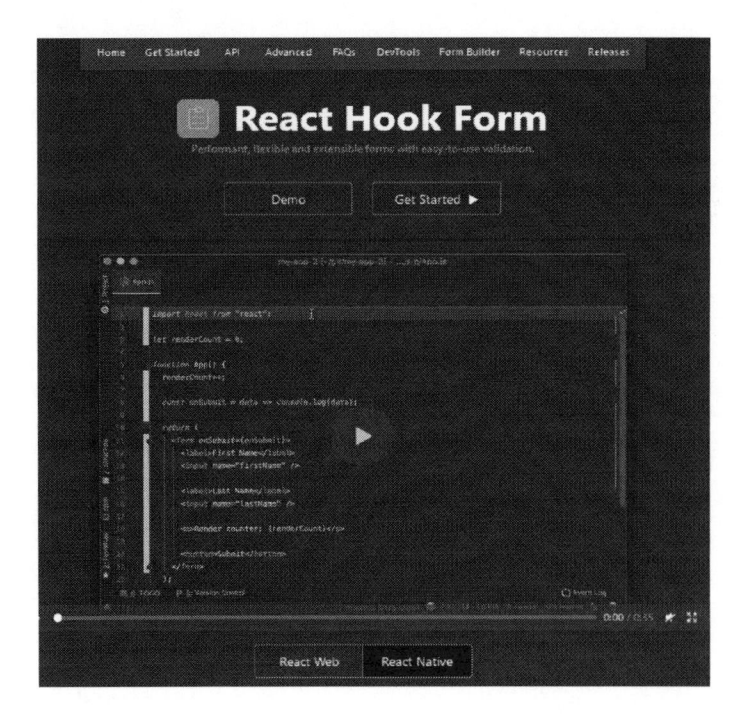

4.10 SWR

SWR (Stale-While-Revalidate) is a data fetching library made by the team at ZEIT, the same team that created Next.js. This new library is made for React applications as a custom hook with a straightforward interface.

SWR first returns the data from cache (stale), then sends the fetch request (revalidate), and finally comes with the up-to-date data. With SWR, components will get a stream of data updates constantly and automatically.

The following example demonstrates the fundamental API of SWR. The useSWR hook accepts a key string and a fetcher function. A key is a unique identifier of the data (the URL API) and passed to the fetcher. The fetcher is an asynchronous function that returns the data. The hook returns two values: data and error, based on the status of the request. In this example, we use fetch API, but you can use any library you like (such as Axois).

```
import useSWR from "swr";

const fetcher = (url) => fetch(url).then((res) => res.json());

export default function App() {
  const { data, error } = useSWR(
    "https://dog.ceo/api/breeds/image/random",
    fetcher
  );

  if (error) return "An error has occurred.";
  if (!data) return "Loading...";
  return (
    <div>
      <h2>SWR random dogs</h2>
      <h4>click the reload button to change</h4>
      <img src={data.message} alt="loading images...." />
    </div>
  );
}
```

Sample code: https://codesandbox.io/s/react-swr1-f7nom

SWR official docs: https://swr.vercel.app/

5. REACT ROUTER

(2 hours reading and exercise)

React router official docs: https://reacttraining.com/react-router/

Many modern websites are made up of a single page. They look like conventional multiple pages applications because they contain components that render like separate pages. These are referred to as SPAs (Single Page Applications). SPA is an app that works inside a browser and does not require page reloading during use. These types of applications are, for instance: Netflix, WhatsApp, Gmail, Google Maps, Twitter, Facebook, Instagram, Wix, Uber, etc.

SPA can serve an outstanding UX because of no page reloads, no extra wait time. It is just one web page that you visit, then loads all other content using JavaScript, which they heavily depend on. SPA requests the markup and data independently and renders pages in the browser. Single-page sites help keep the user in one comfortable web space where content is presented to the user in a simple, easy, and workable fashion.

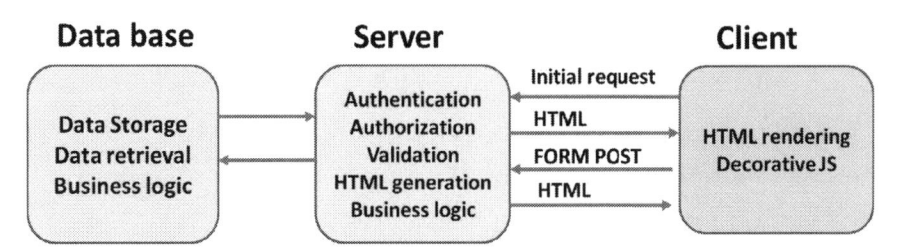

Traditional Multi Page Application

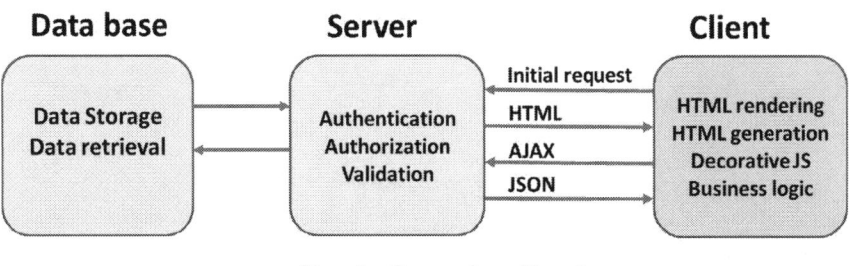

Single Page Application

Why do SPAs need routing in the first place?

In SPA, when the rendered component changes and the screen updated, the URL doesn't change. Therefore, the user cannot return to the previous screen by pressing the "back button". SPA's advantage is that the screen changes smoothly without page transitions, but it can be frustrating if you cannot use the "back button" of the browser.

What React Router does is conditionally render certain components to display depending on the route being used in the URL. While a combination of the protocol and the hostname direct us to a certain website, the pathname references a specific resource on that site. In other words, the pathname references a specific location in our application. React Router is a collection of navigational components that compose declaratively with your application.

There are three primary categories of components in React Router:

- **Routers**

    <Router> The common low-level interface for all router components. Typically apps will use one of the high-level routers like <BrowserRouter> <HashRouter> <MemoryRouter> <NativeRouter> <StaticRouter> instead. The most common use-case for the low-level <Router> is to synchronize a custom history with a state management library like Redux.

    <BrowserRouter> Using the HTML5 history API (pushState, replaceState, and the popState event) to keep the UI in sync with the URL. It can be used when using service calls request.

    <HashRouter> Using the hash portion of the URL (i.e., window.location.hash) to keep the UI in sync with the URL. It can be used when using a static file server.

- **Route matchers**

    <Route> The Route component is the most important component in React Router. Its primary responsibility is to render some UI when its path matches the current URL.

    <Switch> Renders the first child **<Route>** or **<Redirect>** that matches the location. It's useful for grouping routes. It will iterate through child route elements and render the route element which is matching to the current path/location.

- **Navigation**

    <Link> component to create links in the application and be rendered as <a> anchor on the page.

    <NavLink> A special version of the **<Link>** that will add styling attributes to the rendered element when it matches the current URL.

    <Redirect> component for page transition. Rendering a **<Redirect>** will navigate to a new location. The new location will override the current location in the history stack.

React Router Example

The App component is used as the main menu. The other three components - Home, Products, and Contact will be rendered by the Router when the route changes. <Switch> is used for grouping routes. <Route> renders the route element which is matching to the current path/location.

(Index.js)

```
import React from "react";
import ReactDOM from "react-dom";
import App from "./App";

ReactDOM.render(<App />, document.getElementById("root"));
```

(App.js)

```jsx
import React from "react";
import { BrowserRouter as Router, Switch, Route, Link } from "react-router-dom";
import Home from "./Home";
import Products from "./Products";
import Contact from "./Contact";

const App = () => {
  return (
    <Router>
      <div>
        <h2>React Router Example</h2>
        <nav className="navbar navbar-expand-lg navbar-light bg-light">
          <ul className="navbar-nav mr-auto">
            <li>
              <Link to={"/"} className="nav-link">
                {" "}
                Home{" "}
              </Link>
            </li>
            <li>
              <Link to={"/products"} className="nav-link">
                Products
              </Link>
            </li>
            <li>
              <Link to={"/contact"} className="nav-link">
                Contact
              </Link>
            </li>
          </ul>
        </nav>
        <hr />
        <Switch>
          <Route exact path="/" component={Home} />
          <Route path="/products" component={Products} />
          <Route path="/contact" component={Contact} />
        </Switch>
      </div>
    </Router>
  );
};

export default App;
```

(Home.js)

```javascript
import React from "react";

const Home = () => {
  return (
    <div>
      <h2>Home</h2>
    </div>
  );
};
export default Home;
```

(Products.js)

```javascript
import React from "react";

const About = () => {
  return (
    <div>
      <h2>Products</h2>
    </div>
  );
};

export default Products;
```

(Contacts.js)

```javascript
import React from "react";

const Contact = () => {
  return (
    <div>
      <h2>Contact</h2>
    </div>
  );
};

export default Contact;
```

Code sample: https://codesandbox.io/s/react-router-j9oev

6. TEST DRIVEN DEVELOPMENT

(2 hours reading and exercise)

The unexamined life is not worth living.

(Socrates 470-399BC)

There are several ways to test React applications.

- **Unit test**

A unit test examines each small piece of your code. This is the simplest and least expensive testing option. We could add unit tests after we create the production code. However, if components are straightforward and simple, writing unit tests can be overkill.

- **Integration test**

If you have lots of components, you may want to test how they interact with each other. You can do this by mocking your endpoints as part of an integration test.

- **End-to-end test**

Running a complete app in a browser environment.

Jest

Official site: https://jestjs.io/docs/en/tutorial-react

Jest is a testing framework created and maintained by Facebook. Jest lets you access the DOM via jsdom. It includes a command-line tool for test execution. It also allows us to create mock functions with simple configuration and provides a useful set of matchers that makes assertions easier to read.

Furthermore, it offers snapshot testing, which helps us check and verify the component rendering result. We can use snapshot testing to capture a component's tree and save it into a file so that we can compare it against a rendering tree (or whatever we pass to the expected function as the first argument.)

If you would like to assert and manipulate your rendered components, you could use React Testing Library, Enzyme, or React TestUtils. So far React Testing library is the easiest to use.

React Testing library

Official site: https://testing-library.com/docs/react-testing-library/intro

React Testing Library is a lightweight solution for testing React components. It provides light utility functions on top of react-dom and react-dom/test-utils. It is a set of helper utilities that let you test React components without relying on their implementation details. Your tests resemble the way your software is actually used. The utilities in this library facilitate querying the DOM in the same way the user would access the DOM, searching for elements by their label text, finding links, and buttons from their text.

Example 1
The following example shows the test utility searching for the string "hello world" in the hello.js.

(index.js)

```
import React from "react";
import ReactDOM from "react-dom";
const App = () => <div>React Testing Library introduction</div>;
ReactDOM.render(<App />, document.getElementById("root"));
```

(hello.js)

```
import React from "react";
export default ({ name }) => <h1>Hello {name}!</h1>;
```

(__tests__/hello.js)

```js
import "@testing-library/jest-dom/extend-expect";
import React from "react";
import { render } from "@testing-library/react";
import Hello from "../hello";

test("React Testing Library example", () => {
  const { getByText } = render(<Hello name="World" />);
  expect(getByText(/hello world/i)).toBeInTheDocument();
});
```

Code sample: https://codesandbox.io/s/react-testing-library-1qnpi

Test results will be displayed by clicking the Tests button on the right top. The Browser button lets you display the normal mode.

Examples 2

The following example is counters using Hooks. App.test.js is a test script for App.js. Button.test.js is a test script for Button.js.

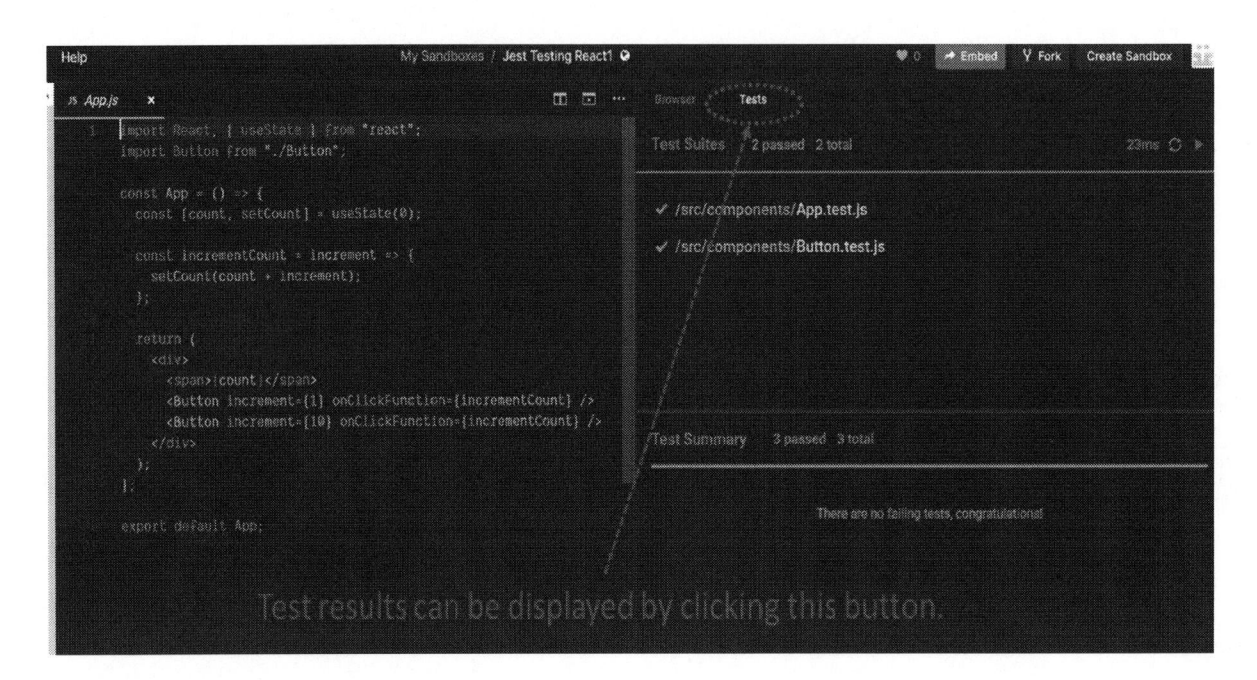

```
import React, { useState } from "react";
import Button from "./Button";

const App = () => {
  const [count, setCount] = useState(0);

  const incrementCount = increment => {
    setCount(count + increment);
  };

  return (
    <div>
      <span>{count}</span>
      <Button increment={1} onClickFunction={incrementCount} />
      <Button increment={10} onClickFunction={incrementCount} />
    </div>
  );
};

export default App;
```

Test results can be displayed by clicking this button.

Test Suites: 2 passed, 2 total
✓ /src/components/App.test.js
✓ /src/components/Button.test.js

Test Summary: 3 passed, 3 total

There are no failing tests, congratulations!

(index.js)

```
import React from "react";
import ReactDOM from "react-dom";
import App from "./components/App";

ReactDOM.render(<App />, document.getElementById("root"));
```

(App.js)

```javascript
import React, { useState } from "react";
import Button from "./Button";

const App = () => {
  const [count, setCount] = useState(0);

  const incrementCount = increment => {
    setCount(count + increment);
  };

  return (
    <div>
      <span>{count}</span>
      <Button increment={1} onClickFunction={incrementCount} />
      <Button increment={10} onClickFunction={incrementCount} />
    </div>
  );
};

export default App;
```

(App.test.js)

```javascript
import React from "react";
import { render, fireEvent } from "react-testing-library";
import App from "./App";

test("App test", () => {
  const { container } = render(<App />);
  console.log(container);
  const buttons = container.querySelectorAll("button");

  expect(buttons[0].textContent).toBe("+1");
  expect(buttons[1].textContent).toBe("+10");

  const result = container.querySelector("span");
  expect(result.textContent).toBe("0");
  fireEvent.click(buttons[0]);
  expect(result.textContent).toBe("1");
  fireEvent.click(buttons[1]);
  expect(result.textContent).toBe("11");
});
```

(Button.js)

```js
import React from 'react'

const Button = ({ increment, onClickFunction }) => {
  const handleClick = () => {
    onClickFunction(increment)
  }
  return <button onClick={handleClick}>+{increment}</button>
}
```

(Button.test.js)

```js
import React from "react";
import { render, fireEvent } from "react-testing-library";
import Button from "./Button";

let count;

const incrementCount = increment => {
  count += increment;
};

test("+1 Button test", () => {
  count = 0;
  const { container } = render(
    <Button increment={1} onClickFunction={incrementCount} />
  );
  const button = container.firstChild;
  expect(button.textContent).toBe("+1");
  expect(count).toBe(0);
  fireEvent.click(button);
  expect(count).toBe(1);
});

test("+10 Button test", () => {
  count = 0;
  const { container } = render(
    <Button increment={10} onClickFunction={incrementCount} />
  );
  const button = container.firstChild;
  expect(button.textContent).toBe("+10");
  expect(count).toBe(0);
  fireEvent.click(button);
  expect(count).toBe(10);
});
```

Code sample: https://codesandbox.io/s/jest-testing-react1-fr717

7. REDUX

(12 hours reading and exercise)

When the analysis is finite, we can reach the final truth.

(Gottfried Leibniz 1646-1716)

Redux official site: https://redux.js.org/

There is a considerable learning curve involved. Learning Redux can become further difficult as knowledge of functional programming is mandatory. Redux is not only for React but also can be used with libraries such as View or Angular. Therefore, the Redux official site does not cover how to bind Redux with React. You have to refer to the following site as well.

React-Redux official site: https://react-redux.js.org/

7.1 Redux Concept

Using Redux is an option. You can use React without Redux. Probably most of the simple apps do not require the Redux. If what you want is only to avoid transferring props, Context API/useContext are sufficient. However, Redux improves testability, extensibility using middleware (Thunks, Reselect, Saga, etc.). Besides, Redux decouples state from components lifecycle and I/O. If you have a complex state/business logic that you want to decouple from your UI components, Redux can be helpful.

With Redux, we can store data in a central location in our JavaScript apps. It can work standalone, and it's also a state management solution for React apps when combined with React-Redux.

As Redux uses a single central store that holds the entire state of the application, all components can access this store and, as such, removes the need to pass parameters and properties between components. Redux consists of three main building blocks - actions, reducers, and a single store.

Rule 1 — Single source of truth (single Store)

The state of your whole application is stored in an object tree in a **store**, which is a single unit that holds **state trees.** The store supports the following methods so that your component can interact with a state tree. There is no other way to interact with a state inside the store except through those methods:

- Getting the state ---- getState()
- Updating the state ---- dispatch()
- Listening to the changes in the state ---- subscribe()

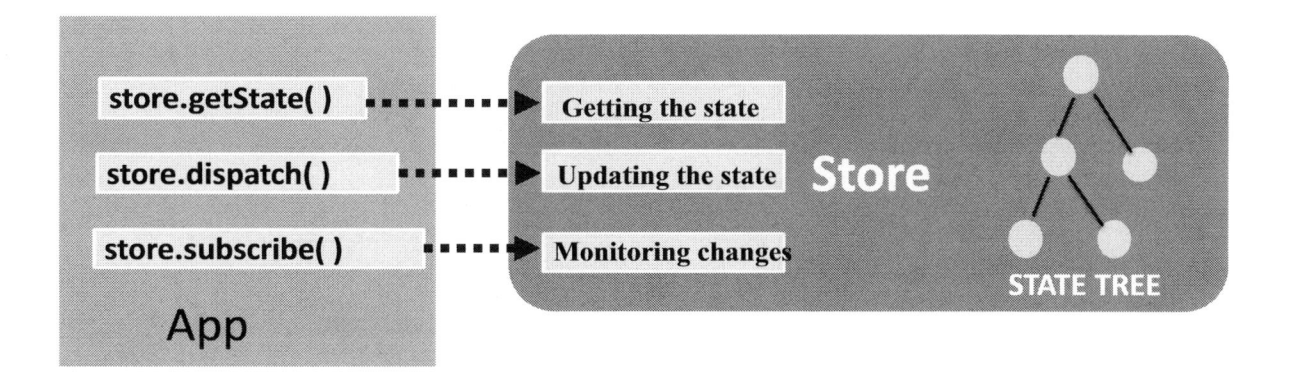

Rule 2 — State is read-only (Actions)

Actions are plain objects describing what happened in the app and serve **as the only way to describe the specific event taking place in the application.**

The **type** property is mandatory and should be descriptive about the action. The main purpose of the **type** property is to let Redux know about the event taking place:

{**type**: "ADD_ORDER_TO_THE_CART"}

Action objects are dispatched to the store to let Redux know which events happened. Normally, the dispatch method is used to trigger the action from your component:

store.dispatch({ **type**: "ADD_ORDER_TO_THE_CART"})

Along with the **type** property, it can have other information about the event. Actions can have as much information as you want. However, it is a good practice to provide less and necessary information — preferably an **id** or any unique identifier wherever possible:

{**type**: "ADD_ORDER_TO_THE_CART', **payload**: {**id**: "123", **item**: "--------"} }

Whenever you need to change/update the state of your Redux application, you need to dispatch an action, which is the only legitimate way to trigger to change the state.

Normally, an action creator function is used instead of plain objects. We are learning more details in the next section.

Rule 3 — Changes are made with pure functions (Reducers)

Reducers are pure, predictable functions in Redux. **Reducers are the only way to update the state in the store.** The Reducer function will accept the current state of the apps and action being dispatched, determine the next state, and returns the new object.

Since Reducer is a pure function, it does not mutate the original state. Instead, it returns the updated state in the new object. One application can have multiple Reducers. Each Reducer can have a relevant state to perform specific tasks.

State changes are based on a user's interaction or event like a network request. If the application's state is managed by Redux, the changes happen inside a Reducer function.

The naming can be a bit confusing. Reducer does not reduce multiple states to one. It simply updates the current state.

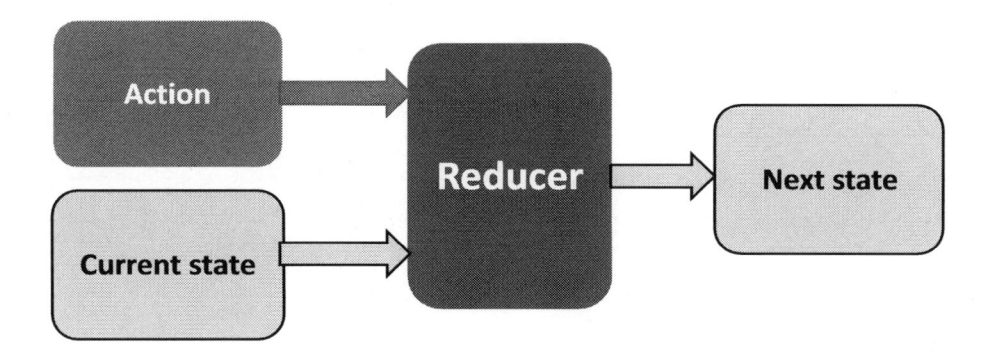

The following JS methods are recommended to avoid mutations in Redux.

- For arrays, slice( ), concat( ), or spread operator (…).
- For objects, Object.assign() or spread operator (…).

Redux data flow

Redux architecture revolves around a strict unidirectional data flow. React application data will follow in the one-way binding data flow. Therefore, managing updated states is straightforward, even if your apps become complicated. In addition to holding the application state and controlling access, the store also allows the state to be updated and handle registering and unregistering listeners via subscribing.

Using Redux with React is not that difficult, thanks to the React-Redux library, which provides the connect function to create higher-order components with access to the Redux store to set their props. If the higher-order component does not fit in with your mental model, you could use useSelecter() and useDispatch() hooks instead.

The following diagram will help you understand the Redux data flow visually. Action from React components is sent to the Reducers, which return the new state based on the older state of the object. The new state is saved in the store, which is the central entity in Redux applications.

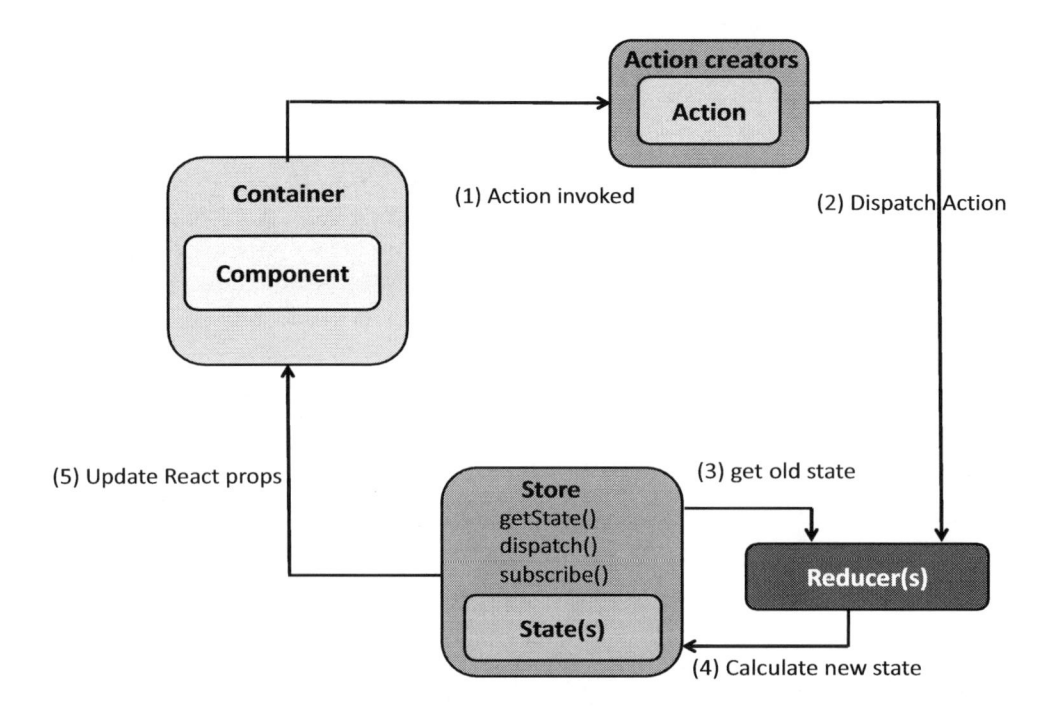

View/UI Layer - Presentational and Container Components

React/Redux separates presentational components from container components. This approach can make your app easier to understand and allow you to reuse components easily.

In React, a presentational component renders HTML. The presentational component's only function is markup. The presentational component accepts props from a container component.

The container component specifies the data that a presentational component should render. The container component also determines behavior. If the presentational component has any user activity –such as a button, the container component will dispatch an action to the Redux store.

Presentational Components and Container Components

	Presentation Components	**Container Components**
Purpose	How things look (markup, styles, appearance……)	How things work (data fetching, triggering state updates…….)
Aware of Redux	No	Yes
To read data	Read data from props	Subscribe to Redux state – subscribe(listener)
To change data	Invoke callbacks from props	Dispatch Redux actions - dispatch({type: xyz……..})
How written ?	By hand	By hand and generated by React-Redux

Note: Whether a component is presentational or a container component is an implementation detail. You don´t always have to follow this design pattern strictly.

7.2 Learn Redux implementation

We are learning simple Redux implementation, which uses minimum parameters.

Store

A **store** is a single unit that holds the **state tree** and the **methods to interact with the state tree**. There is no other way to interact with a state inside the store except through these given methods. The store provides the following three important methods.

- **getState( )** — Returns the current state of the application.
- **dispatch(action)** — The only way to update a state is by dispatching an action.
- **subscribe(listener)** — The purpose of this method is to listen for the state changes. Every time a state is changed, it will be called and will return the updated state. Unregistering of listeners can be handled via the function returned by subscribe(listener). Since it is a low-level API, you will most likely use React-Redux standard bindings instead of using the subscribe method directly.

You don't need to use getState( ) and subscribe( ) explicitly in this example because there are handled by the React-Redux library.

You can create a store by using **createStore()**. There should only be a single store in your apps.

(store.js)

```js
import { createStore } from "redux";
import addReducer from "./reducer";

const store = createStore(addReducer);

export default store;
```

Actions

An **action** is plain JavaScript objects signaling the specific event taking place in the application. In other words, an **action** describes a change that we want to make. "dispatching an action" means sending out an event signal to the store. (through Reducer)

The *type* property is mandatory.

{*type*: "INCREMENT"}

The main purpose of the *type* property is to let Redux know about the event taking place. The *type* should be descriptive about the action. Along with the *type* property, it can have other information about the event taking place. This is how an action looks like, for example:

{type: 'ADD_ARTICLE', payload: { title: 'learn React while sleeping', id: 1} }

Actions can have as much information as you want. Redux actions are nothing more than JavaScript objects. It is a good practice to provide less and necessary information — preferably an *id* or any unique identifier wherever possible. Deeply nested action objects should be avoided.

Action creators

An action creator is a function that returns an action object. You can dispatch an action with plain objects described above, but normally an action creator function is used to dispatch. Using action creators, a component doesn't have to know any of the details of creating and dispatching the action. It is easy to write tests for the component that passes in a mock version of the function. It also helps to reuse the component in other situations.

In the following example,
function incrementAction returns an object {type: INCREMENT}.
function decrementAction returns an object {type: DECREMENT}.

(actions.js)

```javascript
export const INCREMENT = "INCREMENT";
export const DECREMENT = "DECREMENT";

//******defining Actions********
export function incrementAction() {
  return {
    type: INCREMENT
  };
}
export function decrementAction() {
  return {
    type: DECREMENT
  };
}
```

Reducers

Reducer is the only place where state changes happen. The reducer function uses a *current state* (or an initial state) and *action* to determine a *new state*. Although the store is only one in your apps, you can have multiple reducers if necessary.

Reducers are not allowed to modify the existing state. Instead, they must make immutable updates by copying the existing state and making changes to the copied values. By default Redux setting, Reducers must not do any asynchronous logic or other "side effects".

In the following code, the Reducer takes the current state and an action to figure out the new state. When the current state is {state.value} and if the Reducer received an action {type: "INCREMENT"}, then {state.value+1} will replace {state.value}. Since Reducers have to be pure functions, in this example, ES6 spread operator (...state) is used.

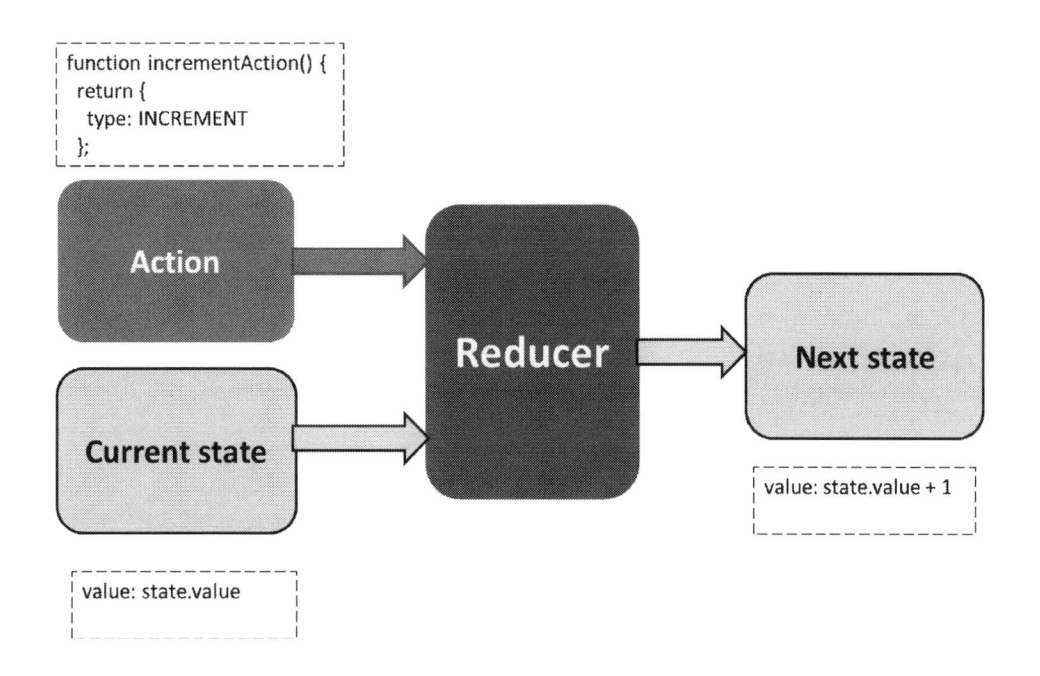

```
function incrementAction() {
  return {
    type: INCREMENT
  };
};
```

Action → **Reducer** → **Next state**

Current state →

value: state.value + 1

value: state.value

(reducer.js)

```
import { INCREMENT, DECREMENT } from "./actions";

const initialState = {
  value: 0
};
//*****Depending on Actions type, calculate the next state
function addReducer(state = initialState, action) {
  switch (action.type) {
   case INCREMENT:
    return { ...state, value: state.value + 1 };
   case DECREMENT:
    return { ...state, value: state.value - 1 };
   default:
    return state;
  }
}

export default addReducer;
```

You can use an if/else statement instead of a switch statement if you like.

Connecting React with Redux

React-Redux is a library that connects a React component with the Redux store. **Provider** is a React component given by the React-Redux library, which provides the store with its child components. The <Provider> makes the Redux store available to any nested components that have been wrapped in the connect() function. Since any React components in a React-Redux app can be connected, most applications will render the <Provider> at the top level, with the entire app's component tree inside of it.

connect( ) HOC with **mapStateToProps( )** and **mapDispatchToProps( )** functions abstract relevant logic from the main logic and magically append the resulting output to the props.

mapStateToProps( ) subscribes to redux store changes and append the required store data to the React props.

mapDispatchToProps( ) dispatches redux actions by appending the dispatch function to the React props. It allows you to dispatch multiple actions from a single action creator.

In the following example, we are wrapping the App component within the Provider to connect the required functions.

(Index.js)

```js
import React from "react";
import ReactDOM from "react-dom";
import { Provider } from "react-redux";

import store from "./store";
import App from "./main";

ReactDOM.render(
  <Provider store={store}>
    <App />
  </Provider>,
  document.getElementById("root")
);
```

If Provider's concept is not clear to you, please quickly review JavaScript Higher-Order functions, closure, currying, and React HOC.

The **connect()** function connects a React component to a Redux store. It provides its connected component with the pieces of the data it needs from the store. It returns a new, connected component that wraps the component you passed in. Using **connect( )** leads to some performance improvements and a clean structure.

Alternatively, you could use useSelector( ) hook and useDispatch( ) hook, if you don't like using connect(). We will cover this later.

The **connect()** function has the following parameters to set. For the time being, you can ignore the 3rd and 4th parameters, which are not used in this counter example.

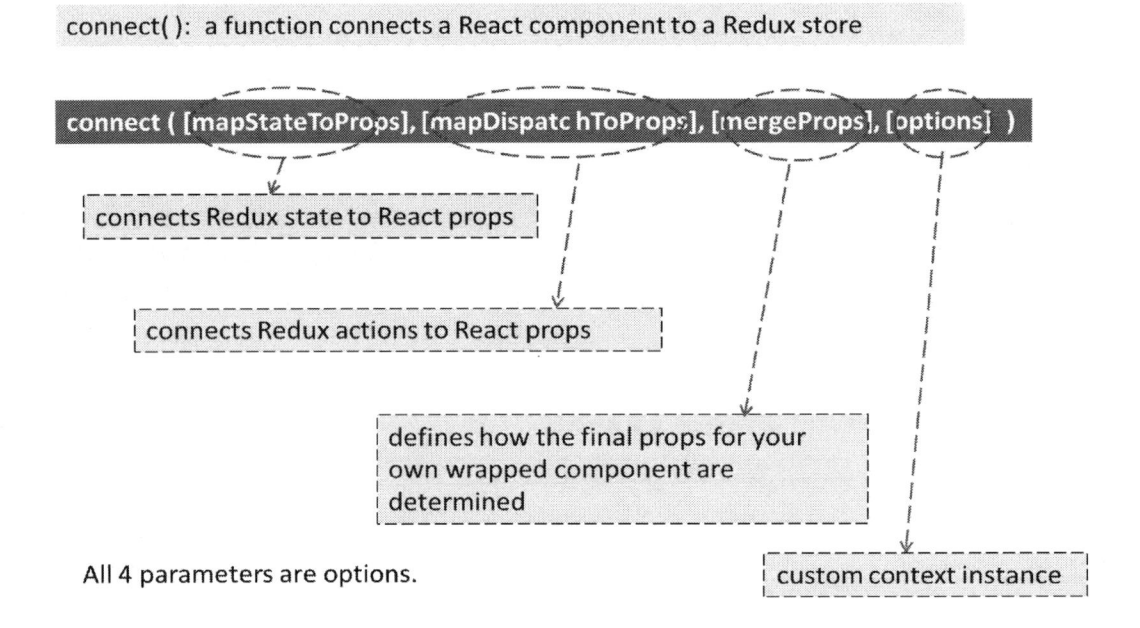

connect( ): a function connects a React component to a Redux store

connect ([mapStateToProps], [mapDispatchToProps], [mergeProps], [options])

- connects Redux state to React props
- connects Redux actions to React props
- defines how the final props for your own wrapped component are determined
- custom context instance

All 4 parameters are options.

The concept of **mapStateToProps** and **mapDispatchToProps** may be a bit difficult to grasp. Many new react developers struggle with it. However, once you understand and use them properly, your React components are supposed to be concerned only with user interface. The only place that a React component is supposed to get information from is their props.

The 1st and 2nd parameters are named as **mapStateToProps** and **mapDispatchToProps** by convention. You can use any name as long as meeting the connect( ) syntax requirements.

mapStateToProps connects a part of the Redux state to the props of a React component. mapStateToProps receives the Redux store state, and any props passed into the connected component. They are used to return any additional data from the Redux store that is needed to render the component. This way, a connected React component will have access to the **exact part of the store it needs**. Optionally the second parameter, *ownProps,* will also be passed directly to the component.

mapStateToProps( ): function to get the required state and assign them to the props of the component. The return value will be an object derived from state (as it lives in the store), whose keys will be passed to your target component as props.

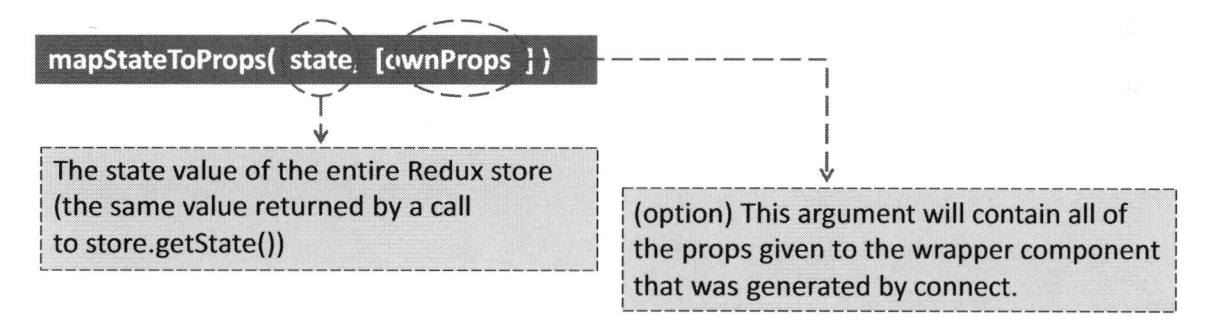

mapStateToProps(state, [ownProps])

The state value of the entire Redux store (the same value returned by a call to store.getState())

(option) This argument will contain all of the props given to the wrapper component that was generated by connect.

Return plain object containing the required data
- Each field in the object will become a prop for the actual component
- The values in the fields will be used to determine if your component needs to re-render.

	(state) => stateProps	(state, ownProps) => stateProps
mapStateToProps runs when:	store state changes	store state changes or any field of ownProps is different
component re-renders when:	any field of stateProps is different	any field of stateProps is different or any field of ownProps is different

In our counter example, the 2nd parameter (ownProps) is not used, you can focus on the 1st parameter for the time being.

mapDispatchToProps is a utility that will help your component to signal an action event (dispatching action, which may cause a change of the application state). **mapDispatchToProps connects Redux actions to React props so that a connected React component will be able to send messages to the store**.

mapDispatchToProps wraps your action creator in the redux's dispatch method and passes it as props to your container. Therefore, the global store's state and action creators wrapped with dispatch are combined and passed as props to your component.

mapDispatchToProps takes two arguments: the dispatch function (coming from Redux) and, as an option, the props being passed down into this container called ownProps.

The main benefit of using **mapDispatchToProps** is that the components do not have to be aware of dispatch. Components only see the resulting props and only need to bother with what they do and when using them. This significantly increases the reusability and testability of the component.

---

mapDispatchToProps( ): allows you to specify which actions your component might need to dispatch. It lets you provide action dispatching functions as props.

---

mapDistpatchToProps(dispatch, [ownProps])

a function of the Redux store. You can call store.dispatch to dispatch an action.

There are two cases.
-pass in a plain action object directly.
 You cannot use ownProps.
-pass in the result of an action creator
 You can use ownProps optionally.

(option) This argument will contain all of the props given to the wrapper component that was generated by connect.

Return plain object:
   -Each field in the object will become a separate prop for your own component, and the value should normally be a function that dispatches an action when called.
   -If you use action creators (as oppose to plain object actions) inside dispatch, it is a convention to simply name the field key the same name as the action creator:

In the counter example, the 2nd parameter is not used, so you can focus on the 1st parameter for the time being.

For beginners, mapStateToProps and mapDispatchToProps are the most difficult part of the Redux. The below diagram would help you understand the concept.

The **Connect HOC** takes care of access to any actions and dispatch calls needed to work with the Redux store without having any special code to access it. It's important to note that only components within the Provider can be connected.

mapStateToProps and **mapDispatchToProps** are both pure functions that return an object, whose keys will then be passed on as the props of the component they are connected to.

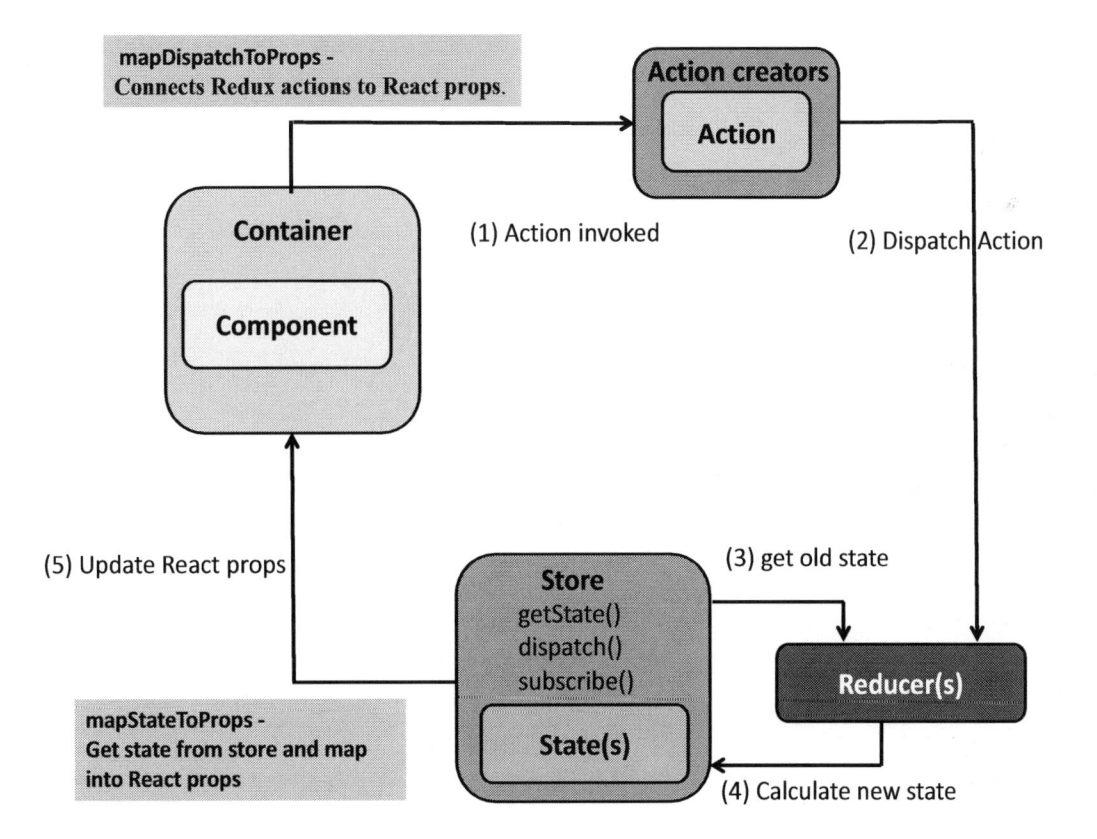

In the following code:
- *mapStateToProps* returns an object *state.value*. It connects *state.value* from the store to the React props. In this way, a connected React component will have access to the exact part of the store it needs.
- *mapDispatchToProps* returns an object with the *"INCREMENT"* or *"DECREMENT"* keys. It connects *incrementAction( )* or *decrementAction( )* to the selected React props. In this way, a connected React component will be able to send messages to the store.
- You can't use *mapStateToProps* for the same purpose as *mapDispatchToProps* because you don't have access to dispatch inside *mapStateToProp*.

(main.js)

```js
import React from "react";
import { connect } from "react-redux";
import { incrementAction, decrementAction } from "./actions";

//**********issues actions*********
function App({ value, incrementAction, decrementAction }) {
  return (
    <div>
      <h1>count: {value}</h1>
      <button onClick={incrementAction}>increment</button>
      <button onClick={decrementAction}>decrement</button>
    </div>
  );
}

//****** Map Redux state to component props********
const mapStateToProps = state => ({
  value: state.value
});

//****** Map Redux actions to component props*******
const mapDispatchToProps = dispatch => ({
  incrementAction: () => dispatch(incrementAction()),
  decrementAction: () => dispatch(decrementAction())
});

//********Hight Order Component*********
export default connect(
  mapStateToProps,
  mapDispatchToProps
)(App);
```

Code sample: https://codesandbox.io/s/reactredux-basic-3dx81

7.3 Learn Redux with ToDoList

This ToDoList example (originally written by Dan Abramov) is forked from the Redux official docs. It is an excellent example but a bit challenging for React beginners. As there are many small files, you might be much more productive with several display monitors. Even if you don't understand the details, don't worry. This example can be simplified by using Redux Toolkit (RTK) anyway. If you don't have time, skip this section for now and go to the Middleware section. After going through the rest of this book, you can come back to this section.

User interface and usages example

This example app supports the following user operations, for instance.

A. Add Todo item

B. Click Add Todo button

C. Add other Todo items

D. Complete one item

E. Display active item

F. Display completed item

Data and Control Flow

There are many small files, which might confuse beginners. Visualizing structure would help you understand the code later.

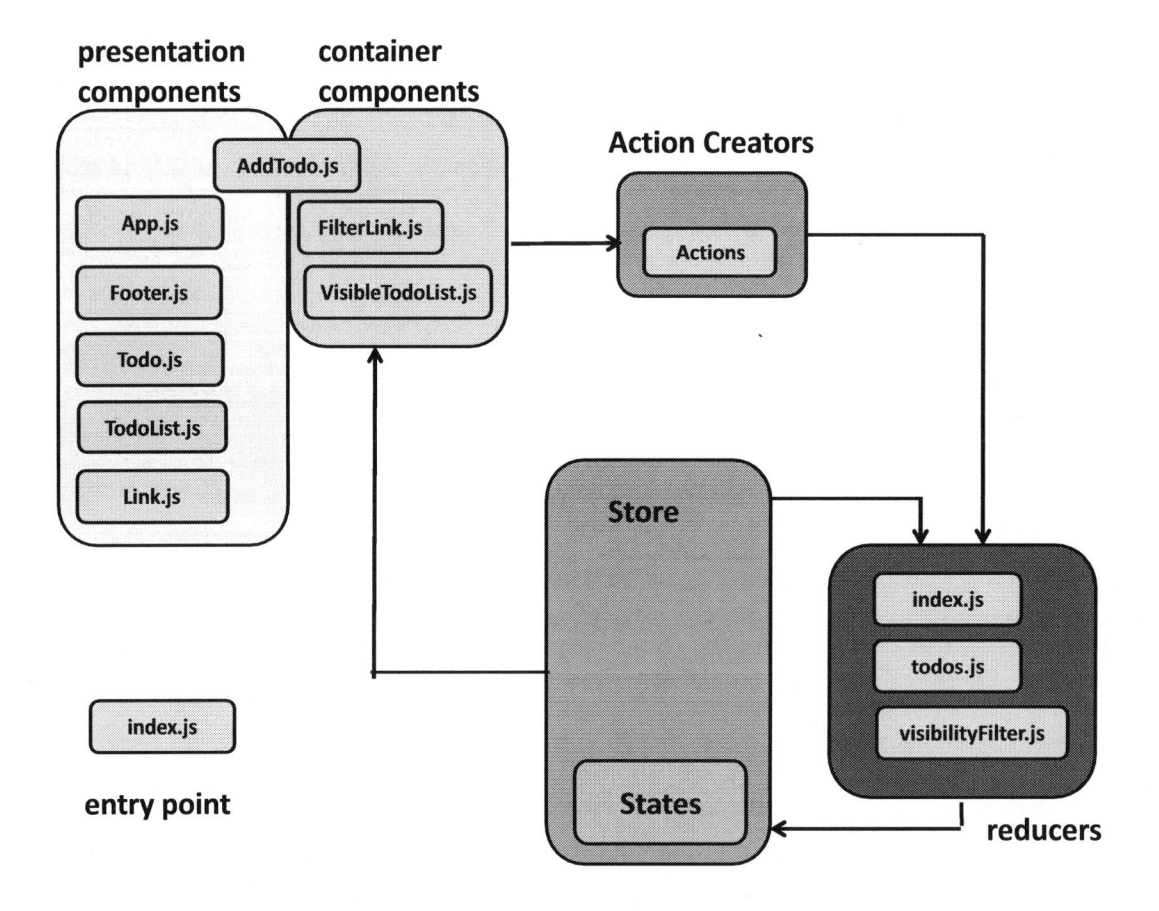

277

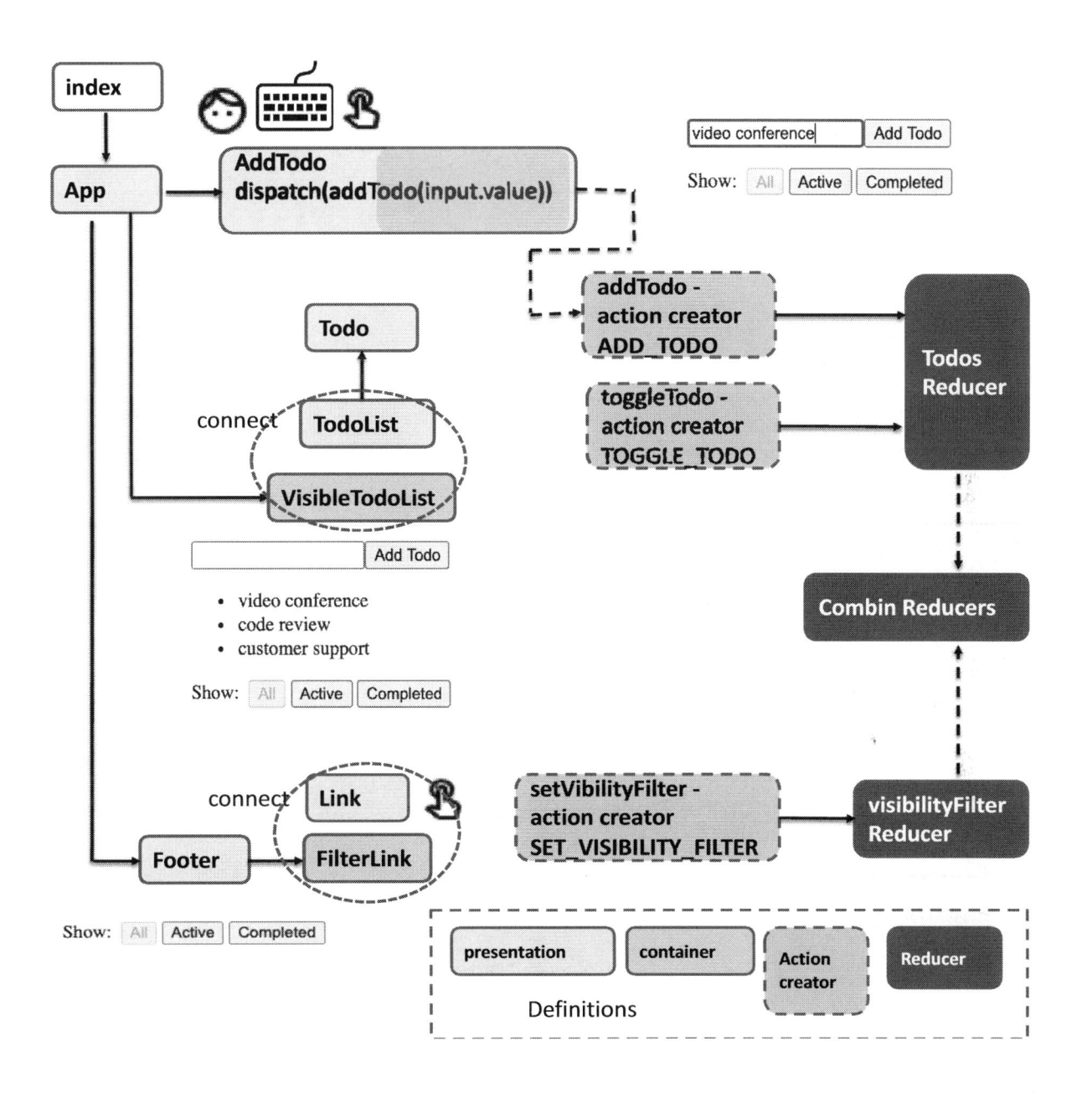

Entry point and Store Creation

The store holds the following two objects:
- *todos*: A normalized reducer of *todos*. It contains a *byIds* map of all *todos* and *allIds* that contains the list of all *ids*.
- *visibilityFilters*: A simple string all, completed, or incomplete.

Index.js renders our app to the DOM. We need to make the store available to our app. To do this, we wrap our app with the <Provider /> API provided by React-Redux.

(index.js)
```
import React from 'react'
import { render } from 'react-dom'
import { createStore } from 'redux'
import { Provider } from 'react-redux'
import App from './components/App'
import rootReducer from './reducers'

const store = createStore(rootReducer)

render(
  <Provider store={store}>
    <App />
  </Provider>,
  document.getElementById('root')
)
```

Action Creators

Action creators are functions that create actions. Action creators return an action object. *addToDo* function returns an action object to add a new item. *setVisibilityFilter* function returns an action object to set a visibility filter, which indicates either "SHOW_ALL", "SHOW_COMPLETE" or "SHOW_ACTIVE". *toggleTodo* function returns a flag that disables or enables the *todo* item.

(actions/index.js)

```
let nextTodoId = 0
export const addTodo = text => ({
  type: 'ADD_TODO',
  id: nextTodoId++,
  text
})
```
→ action creator to add a new item to todos. It takes a single string variable content and returns an ADD_TODO action with payload containing a self-incremented id

```
export const setVisibilityFilter = filter => ({
  type: 'SET_VISIBILITY_FILTER',
  filter
})
```
→ action creator to set a visibility filter. It creates the action to set the app's active filter. It takes a single string variable filter

```
export const toggleTodo = id => ({
  type: 'TOGGLE_TODO',
  id
})
```
→ action creator to toggle todos item. It takes a single number variable id and returns a TOGGLE_TODO action with payload containing id only

```
export const VisibilityFilters = {
  SHOW_ALL: 'SHOW_ALL',
  SHOW_COMPLETED: 'SHOW_COMPLETED',
  SHOW_ACTIVE: 'SHOW_ACTIVE'
}
```
→ Common const data for the whole app

Reducers

combineReducers() is a helper function included with the Redux library. It is used for "splitting" the root reducer into separate functions that each manage one branch of the state tree.

It takes an object where
- each *key* is a name
- each *value* is a reducer function

It returns a single reducer that combined them all into a single reducer. The resulting reducer calls every child reducer and combines their results into a single state object.

The important point is that a single store can be pseudo-divided. There is no difference in having only one single store in the application, but with a key, various store trees spread underneath.

In the following example, we want to store two different things:
- The currently selected visibility filter.
- The actual list of *todos*.

We can have multiple reducers and combine them into one root reducer, using combineReducers(). We can easily organize our code while still having everything in one root state tree.

(reducers/index.js)

```js
import { combineReducers } from 'redux'
import todos from './todos'
import visibilityFilter from './visibilityFilter'

export default combineReducers({
  todos,
  visibilityFilter
})
```

The following reducer handles two types of actions. ADD_TODO is used for text input. TOGGLE_TODO is used for enabling/disabling the todo items.

(reducers/todos.js)

```
const todos = (state = [], action) => {
  switch (action.type) {
    case 'ADD_TODO':
      return [
        ...state,
        {
          id: action.id,
          text: action.text,
          completed: false
        }
      ]                                             // text input
    case 'TOGGLE_TODO':
      return state.map(todo =>
        (todo.id === action.id) ? {...todo, completed: !todo.completed} : todo
      )                                             // toggle todo item
    default:
      return state
  }
}

export default todos
```

VisibilityFilters is a reducer that selects one of the visibility filter - VisibilityFilters.SHOW_ALL, VisibilityFilters.SHOW_ACTIVE or VisibilityFilters.SHOW_COMPLETED.

- It accepts an activeFilter prop from the parent that indicates which filter is currently selected by the user. An active filter is rendered with an underscore.
- It dispatches the setFilter action to update the selected filter.

(reducers/visibilityFilter.js)

```
import { VisibilityFilters } from '../actions'

const visibilityFilter = (state = VisibilityFilters.SHOW_ALL, action) => {
  switch (action.type) {
    case 'SET_VISIBILITY_FILTER':
      return action.filter
    default:
      return state
  }
}

export default visibilityFilter
```

Container Components

The container components connect the presentational components to the Redux store. For example, the presentation component TodoList needs a container like VisibleTodoList that subscribes to the Redux store and knows how to apply the current visibility filter. To change the visibility filter, we will provide a container component FilterLink that renders a Link dispatching an appropriate action on click.

The *mapStateToProps* and *mapDispatchToProps* have a second parameter, *ownProps*, as an option. If the *ownProps* parameter is present, react-redux will pass the props (that were already passed to the component) into your connect functions. The *ownProps* refer to the props that were passed down by the parent.

In the following code, the component Link is wrapped by the FilterLink container, and the *ownProps* gives access to the properties which are being passed into the FilerLink.

(containers/FilterLink.js)

```
import { connect } from 'react-redux'
import { setVisibilityFilter } from '../actions'
import Link from '../components/Link'

const mapStateToProps = (state, ownProps) => ({
  active: ownProps.filter === state.visibilityFilter
})

const mapDispatchToProps = (dispatch, ownProps) => ({
  onClick: () => dispatch(setVisibilityFilter(ownProps.filter))
})

export default connect(
  mapStateToProps,
  mapDispatchToProps
)(Link)
```

→ FilterLink component wraps the Link component.

VisibleTodoList calculates todos to pass to the TodoList, so we define a function that filters the state.todos according to the state.visibilityFilter, and use it in its mapStateToProps.

(containers/VisibleTodoList.js)

```
import { connect } from 'react-redux'
import { toggleTodo } from '../actions'
import TodoList from '../components/TodoList'
import { VisibilityFilters } from '../actions'

const getVisibleTodos = (todos, filter) => {
  switch (filter) {
    case VisibilityFilters.SHOW_ALL:
      return todos
    case VisibilityFilters.SHOW_COMPLETED:
      return todos.filter(t => t.completed)
    case VisibilityFilters.SHOW_ACTIVE:
      return todos.filter(t => !t.completed)
    default:
      throw new Error('Unknown filter: ' + filter)
  }
}

const mapStateToProps = state => ({
  todos: getVisibleTodos(state.todos, state.visibilityFilter)
})

const mapDispatchToProps = dispatch => ({
  toggleTodo: id => dispatch(toggleTodo(id))
})

export default connect(
  mapStateToProps,
  mapDispatchToProps
)(TodoList)
```

Presentation Components

App is the root component for our app. It renders the header, the AddTodo, TodoList, and VisibilityFilters components.

(components/App.js)

```
import React from 'react'
import Footer from './Footer'
import AddTodo from '../containers/AddTodo'
import VisibleTodoList from '../containers/VisibleTodoList'

const App = () => (
 <div>
   <AddTodo />
   <VisibleTodoList />
   <Footer />
 </div>
)

export default App
```

Footer is where we let the user change currently visible todos.

(components/Footer.js)

```
import React from 'react'
import FilterLink from '../containers/FilterLink'
import { VisibilityFilters } from '../actions'

const Footer = () => (
 <div>
   <span>Show: </span>
   <FilterLink filter={VisibilityFilters.SHOW_ALL}>
     All
   </FilterLink>
   <FilterLink filter={VisibilityFilters.SHOW_ACTIVE}>
     Active
   </FilterLink>
   <FilterLink filter={VisibilityFilters.SHOW_COMPLETED}>
     Completed
   </FilterLink>
 </div>
)

export default Footer
```

Link component binds active and children with a callback.
onClick() is a callback function to invoke when the link is clicked.

(components/Link.js)

```
import React from 'react'
import PropTypes from 'prop-types'

const Link = ({ active, children, onClick }) => (
  <button
    onClick={onClick}
    disabled={active}
    style={{
      marginLeft: '4px',
    }}
  >
    {children}
  </button>
)

Link.propTypes = {
  active: PropTypes.bool.isRequired,
  children: PropTypes.node.isRequired,
  onClick: PropTypes.func.isRequired
}

export default Link
```

Todo is the component that renders a single todo item:
It renders the todo content and shows if a todo is completed, crossing out the strings. It dispatches the action to toggle the todo's complete status upon onClick.

- text: string is the text to show.
- completed: boolean is whether the todo should appear crossed out.
- onClick() is a callback to invoke when the todo is clicked.

(components/Todo.js)

```js
import React from 'react'
import PropTypes from 'prop-types'

const Todo = ({ onClick, completed, text }) => (
  <li
    onClick={onClick}
    style={{
      textDecoration: completed ? 'line-through' : 'none'
    }}
  >
    {text}
  </li>
)

Todo.propTypes = {
  onClick: PropTypes.func.isRequired,
  completed: PropTypes.bool.isRequired,
  text: PropTypes.string.isRequired
}

export default Todo
```

TodoList is the component that renders the list of todos. It renders the filtered list of todos when one of the VisibilityFilters is selected.

- todos is an array of todo items with { id, text, completed } object shape.
- onToggleTodo(id: number) is a callback function to invoke when a todo is clicked.

(components/TodoList.js)

```js
import React from 'react'
import PropTypes from 'prop-types'
import Todo from './Todo'

const TodoList = ({ todos, toggleTodo }) => (
  <ul>
    {todos.map(todo =>
      <Todo
        key={todo.id}
        {...todo}
        onClick={() => toggleTodo(todo.id)}
      />
    )}
  </ul>
)

TodoList.propTypes = {
  todos: PropTypes.arrayOf(PropTypes.shape({
    id: PropTypes.number.isRequired,
    completed: PropTypes.bool.isRequired,
    text: PropTypes.string.isRequired
  }).isRequired).isRequired,
  toggleTodo: PropTypes.func.isRequired
}

export default TodoList
```

Other Components (mixture of Presentation and Container)

AddToDo is a mixture of presentation and Container components. It allows a user to input a todo item and add it to the list upon clicking its "Add Todo" button.

- It uses a controlled input that sets the state upon onChange.
- When the user clicks on the "Add Todo" button, it dispatches the action to add the todo to the store.

(containers/AddTodo.js)

```javascript
import React from 'react'
import { connect } from 'react-redux'
import { addTodo } from '../actions'

const AddTodo = ({ dispatch }) => {
  let input

  return (
    <div>
      <form onSubmit={e => {
        e.preventDefault()
        if (!input.value.trim()) {
          return
        }
        dispatch(addTodo(input.value))
        input.value = ''
      }}>
        <input ref={node => input = node} />
        <button type="submit">
          Add Todo
        </button>
      </form>
    </div>
  )
}
export default connect()(AddTodo)
```

Code sample: https://codesandbox.io/s/redux-todo-yqv6z

Highly recommended to read this blog by Patrick Bacon
https://spin.atomicobject.com/2018/04/02/redux-rerendering/

7.4 Middleware

Middleware generally refers to software that combines separate features in existing software. In a non-web environment, Middleware locates between an operating system and the applications. Data communication, Data management, application services, messaging, authentication, and API management are all commonly handled by middleware.

In Redux, Middleware locates between Action Creators and Reducer. Middleware allows you to inject custom functions into the middle of the action/update cycle and centralize your logic. It intercepts the action object before Reducer receives it and gives the functionality to perform additional actions or enhancements. Middleware in Redux can hold your application logic, which is decoupled from the React components.

Middleware provides a third-party extension point between dispatching an action and handing the action off to the Reducer. The Middleware includes logging, crash reporting, routing, handling asynchronous requests, etc.

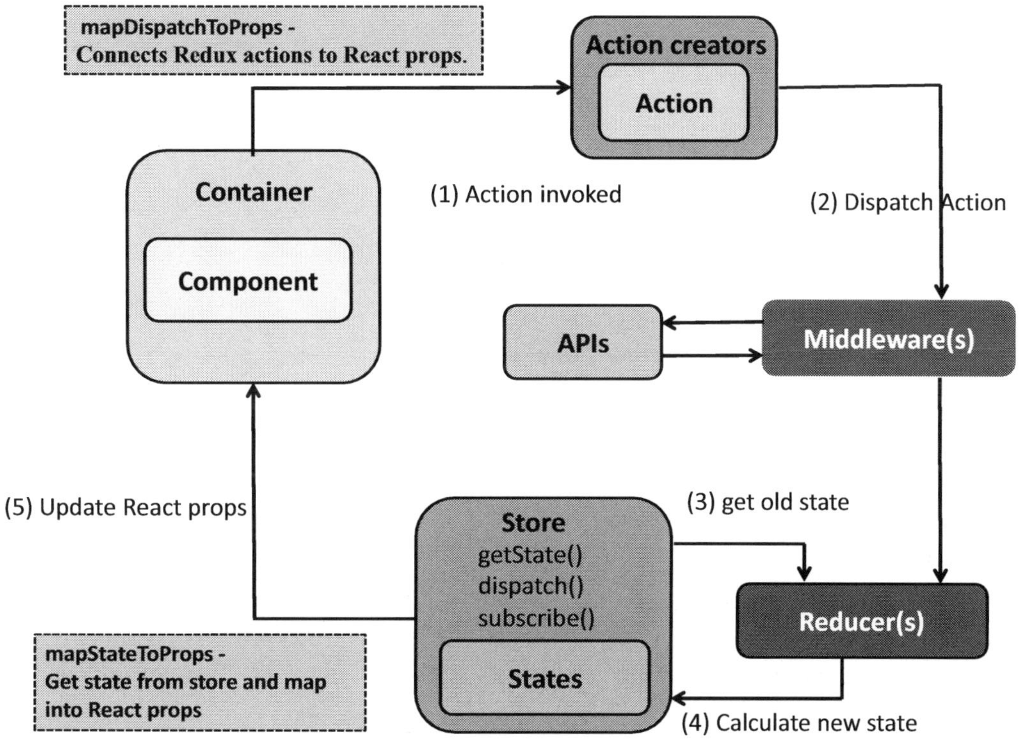
mapDispatchToProps -
Connects Redux actions to React props.
Action creators
Action
Container
Component
(1) Action invoked
(2) Dispatch Action
APIs
Middleware(s)
(5) Update React props
Store
getState()
dispatch()
subscribe()
States
(3) get old state
Reducer(s)
(4) Calculate new state
mapStateToProps -
Get state from store and map
into React props

Creating a custom Redux middleware (store => next => action)

Redux middleware is a function that can intercept and perform the actions accordingly before they reach the reducer. Redux middleware returns a function, which takes the next function as a parameter. Then the inner function returns another function that takes action as a parameter and finally returns next(action). It is a triple curried function that brings below into its scope.

- store's state
- next function
- dispatched action

Currying minimizes the number of changes to a program's state known as side effects using immutable data and pure (no side effects) functions. Currying helps you write little code modules that can be reused and configured with ease to avoid frequently calling a function with the same argument and in partial applications.

A conventional un-curry function is like this:

```
const myMiddleware = (store, next, action) => {..................}
```

Instead, triple currying function can be used like this:

```
const myMiddleware = store => next => action => {
            // we can use values from the store
            // we have access to action that's currently being dispatched
    next(action);    // call next if necessary
}
```

By using a conventional function, it is like this:

```
const myMiddleware = function(store) {
  return function(next) {
    return function(action) {
                    // we can use values from the store
                    // we have access to action that's currently being dispatched
      next(action);           // call next if necessary
    }
  }
}
```

Below three arguments are used:

- **store** - The Redux store. You can use the store object directly in middleware when making decisions based on an existing state, which can be obtained using **store.getState( )** method.
- **next** - A function that will be called when you are ready to pass the action to the next middleware in the chain.
- **action** - The action being dispatched. Generally, your middleware will be executed with every action.

In order to configure Middleware, applyMiddleware() has to be specified as a store enhancer parameter in the createStore().

For example, you can add more than one middleware like applyMiddleware(….myMiddleware) or applyMiddleware(myMiddleware1,myMiddleware2).

createStore API

createStore( ): Creates a Redux store that holds the complete state tree of your app. There should only be a single store in your app.

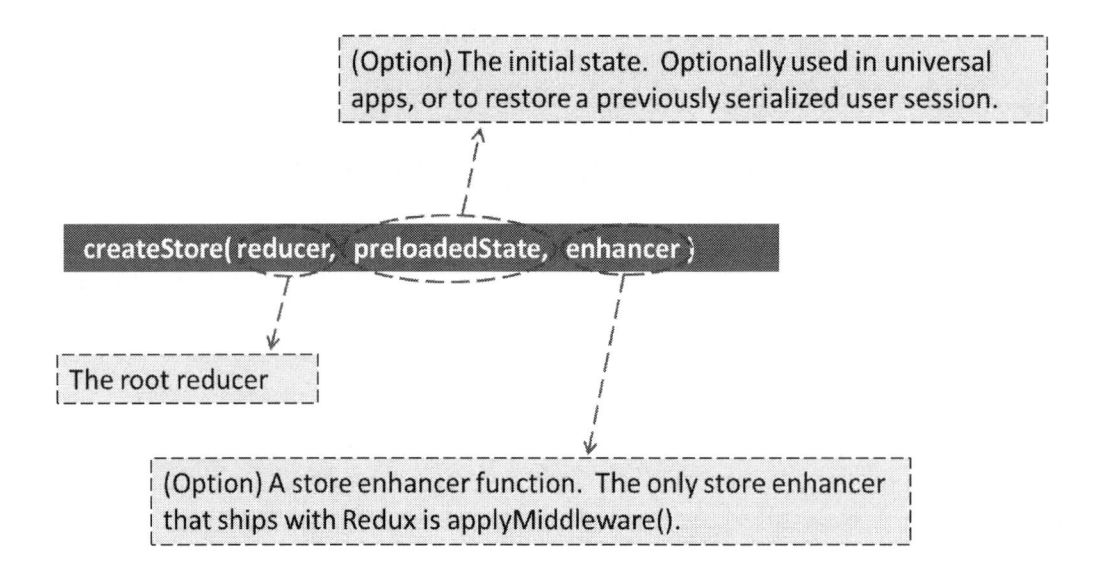

createStore(reducer, preloadedState, enhancer)

- The root reducer
- (Option) The initial state. Optionally used in universal apps, or to restore a previously serialized user session.
- (Option) A store enhancer function. The only store enhancer that ships with Redux is applyMiddleware().

Middleware example

We are adding a custom-made logger middleware to the code we had built in the React-Redux.

(store.js)

```
import addReducer from "./reducer";

import { createStore, applyMiddleware } from "redux";
//import addReducer from "./reducer";
import logger from "./logger";
//***** add array to use multiple middleWares in the future
const middleWares = [logger];

//****** apply middleware by using applyMiddleware()
const store = createStore(addReducer, applyMiddleware(...middleWares));

export default store;
```

Logger intercepts the action object before Reducer receives it. It logs action type, current state, dispatching actions, and the next state.

(logger.js)

```
const logger = store => next => action => {
  console.log("action type:", action.type);
  console.log("current state:", store.getState());
  console.log("dispatching:", action);
  const result = next(action);
  console.log("next state:", store.getState());
  return result;
};

export default logger;
```

Code sample: https://codesandbox.io/s/reactredux-middleware1-y67f8

7.5 Redux-Thunk

Redux expects action creators to return an action object. It works perfectly for synchronous action creators. Unfortunately, with out-of-the-box Redux, there is no clear way to handle asynchronous calls to the API (backend) or any other side effects.

Redux-Thunk is the most popular middleware for handling asynchronous events. Thunk is a programming concept where a function is used to delay the evaluation/calculation. **The Redux-Thunk middleware allows us to write action creators that return a callback function instead of an action object.** The Redux-Thunk middleware intercepts every action before reaching a reducer, ensuring that the asynchronously-retrieved data will be added to the Redux store. In this way, the Redux-Thunk can delay the dispatch of action or dispatch only if a specific condition is met.

A callback function returned from action creators has access to specific parameters, including dispatch and getState. The action creators can dispatch multiple actions, and action can be dispatched after an asynchronous call is resolved. Redux-Thunk gives us the ability to trigger actions in a specific order and provides us with a way of handling asynchronous actions.

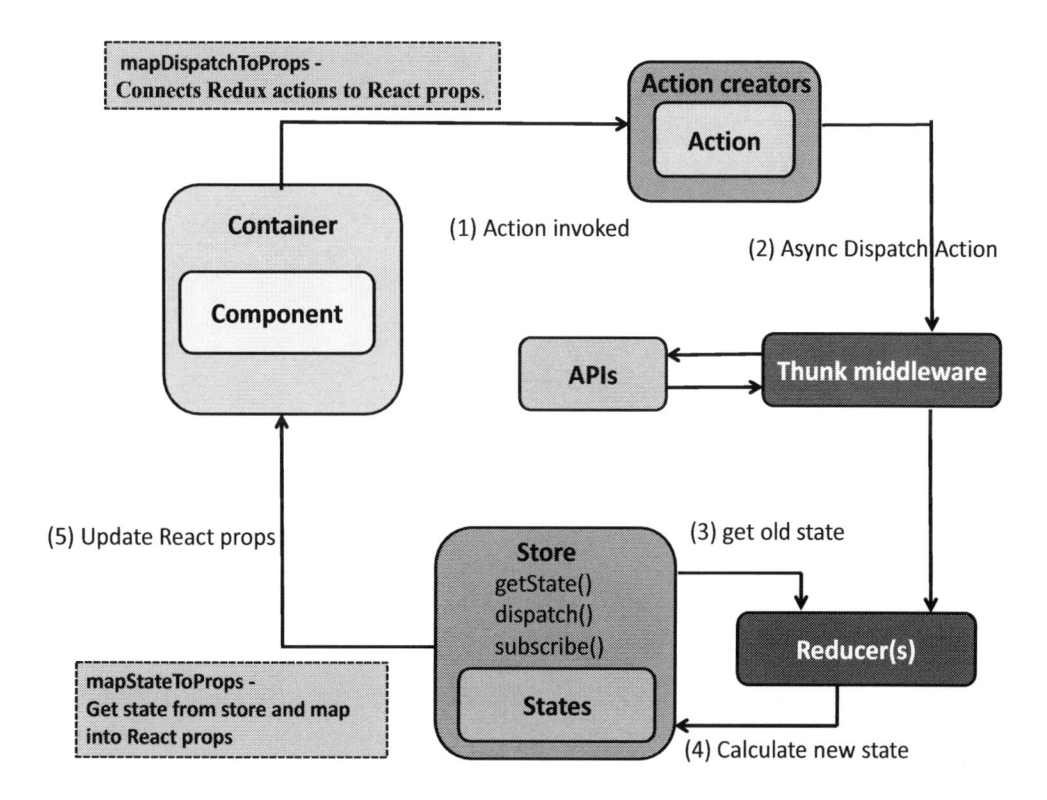

Redux-Thunk example

The following code imports Thunk from the library and create a store with Thunk middleware. The App component is placed within the Provider.

There are four counters in this example. "plus" and "minus" are synchronous counters. "asyncPlus" counter and "asyncMinus" counter are emulating asynchronous operations by adding a 2-second delay.

Entry point, Store creation and UI

(index.js)

```javascript
import React from "react";
import ReactDOM from "react-dom";
//****** middleware is used in the store
import { createStore, applyMiddleware } from "redux";
import rootReducer from "./reducers";

import { Provider } from "react-redux";

import App from "./containers";

//***** redux-thunk
import thunk from "redux-thunk";

//****** create store using thunk middleware
const store = createStore(rootReducer, applyMiddleware(thunk));

ReactDOM.render(
  <Provider store={store}>
    <App />
  </Provider>,
  document.getElementById("root")
);
```

(components.js)

```
import React from "react";

const App = ({ number, plus, minus, asyncPlus, asyncMinus }) => (
  <div>
    <h2>counter: {number}</h2>
    <button onClick={plus}>increment</button>
    <button onClick={minus}>decrement</button>
    <button onClick={asyncPlus}>increment Async</button>
    <button onClick={asyncMinus}>decrement Async</button>
  </div>
);

export default App;
```

Container Component

In the code below, mapStateToProps connects a part of the Redux state to the props of a React component. A connected React component will have access to the exact part of the store it needs. mapDispatchToProps connects Redux actions to React props. In this way, a connected React component will be able to send messages to the store.

(containers.js)

```js
import App from "./components";
import { connect } from "react-redux";
import { minus, plus, asyncPlus, asyncMinus } from "./actions";

const mapStateToProps = (state) => {
  return {
    number: state.number
  };
};

const mapDispatchToProps = (dispatch) => {
  return {
    plus: () => {
      dispatch(plus());
    },
    minus: () => {
      dispatch(minus());
    },
    asyncPlus: () => {
      dispatch(asyncPlus());
    },
    asyncMinus: () => {
      dispatch(asyncMinus());
    }
  };
};

export default connect(mapStateToProps, mapDispatchToProps)(App);
```

Action Creators

In the following code, **synchronous actions "plus" and "minus" return objects, Asynchronous actions "asyncPlus" and "asyncMinus" return callback functions.** Asynchronous actions use Thunk library automatically. This is a key concept of Redux-Thunk.

(Actions.js)

```javascript
//***** synchronous action creators, returning objects.
export const plus = () => {
  return { type: "INCREASE_COUNT" };
};
export const minus = () => {
  return { type: "DECREASE_COUNT" };
};

//***** asynchronous action creators, returning function
export const asyncPlus = () => {
  return (dispatch) => {
    setTimeout(() => {
      dispatch({ type: "INCREASE_COUNT" });
    }, 2000);
  };
};
export const asyncMinus = () => {
  return (dispatch) => {
    setTimeout(() => {
      dispatch({ type: "DECREASE_COUNT" });
    }, 2000);
  };
};
```

Reducer

The reducer updates the state based on the **action.type**. combineReducers() is not necessary for this code sample, but we keep it for the future expansion.

(reducers.js)

```js
import { combineReducers } from "redux";

const number = (state = 0, action) => {
  switch (action.type) {
    case "INCREASE_COUNT":
      return state + 1;

    case "DECREASE_COUNT":
      return state - 1;

    default:
      return state;
  }
};

        // combine reducers not necessary in this case, but only for future expansion
export default combineReducers({
  number
        // ----- you can add other reducers here
});
```

Code sample: https://codesandbox.io/s/redux-thunk1-pme3i

Redux-Thunk library

The Redux-Thunk library is simple. You could create a similar library to practice functional programming. However, we recommend using the Redux-Thunk library as it is for commercial projects - no need to reinvent the wheel unless you come up with a better idea.

GitHub link: https://github.com/reduxjs/redux-thunk

Redux-Thunk library -- index.js

```js
function createThunkMiddleware(extraArgument) {
  return ({ dispatch, getState }) => (next) => (action) => {
    if (typeof action === 'function') {
      return action(dispatch, getState, extraArgument);
    }
    return next(action);
  };
}
const thunk = createThunkMiddleware();
thunk.withExtraArgument = createThunkMiddleware;
export default thunk;
```

7.6 Redux with Hooks

React-Redux offers a set of Hooks as an alternative to the existing connect() higher-order components. These Hooks allow you to connect to the Redux store and dispatch actions without wrapping your components using connect().

useSelector

useSelector is similar to connect's **mapStateToProps**. It creates subscription to the store. You pass a function that takes the Redux store state and directly returns the pieces of the state you intend to use.

useSelector API: extract data from the Redux store state, using a selector function.

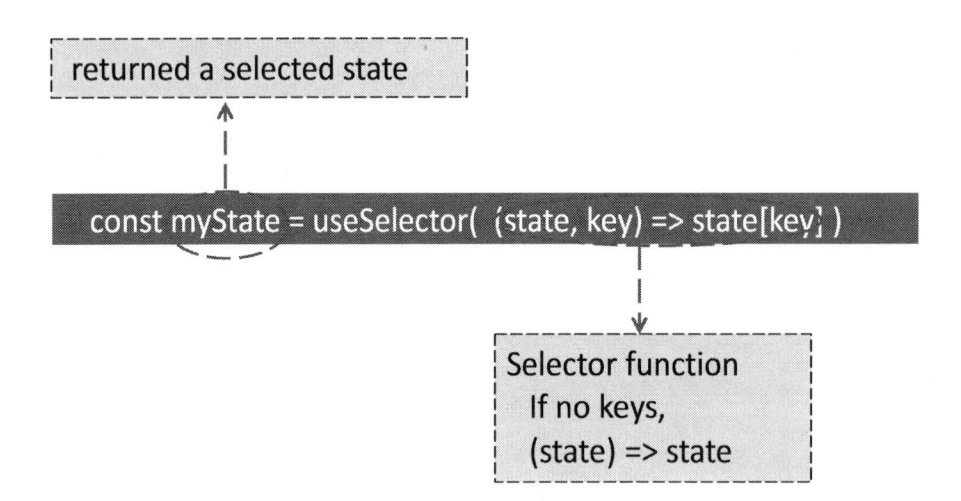

returned a selected state

```
const myState = useSelector( (state, key) => state[key] )
```

Selector function
If no keys,
(state) => state

useDispatch

useDispatch replaces connect's **mapDispatchToProps**. However, **useDispatch** is not fully an alternative to mapDispatchToProps since it does not map anything. **useDispatch** returns your store's dispatch method so that you can dispatch actions manually.

useDispatch API: returns a reference to the dispatch function from the Redux store.

returned a reference to the distpach function

const dispatch = useDispatch( )

When passing a callback using dispatch to a child component, you can memoize it with useCallback, just like memoizing any passed callback. This avoids unnecessary rendering of child components due to the changed callback reference.

Data flow

The main benefit of using the Redux Hooks is that they are conceptually simpler than connect( ). With connect( ), you are wrapping your component and injecting props into it. This can make it difficult to determine in the component which props come from Redux and which are passed in.

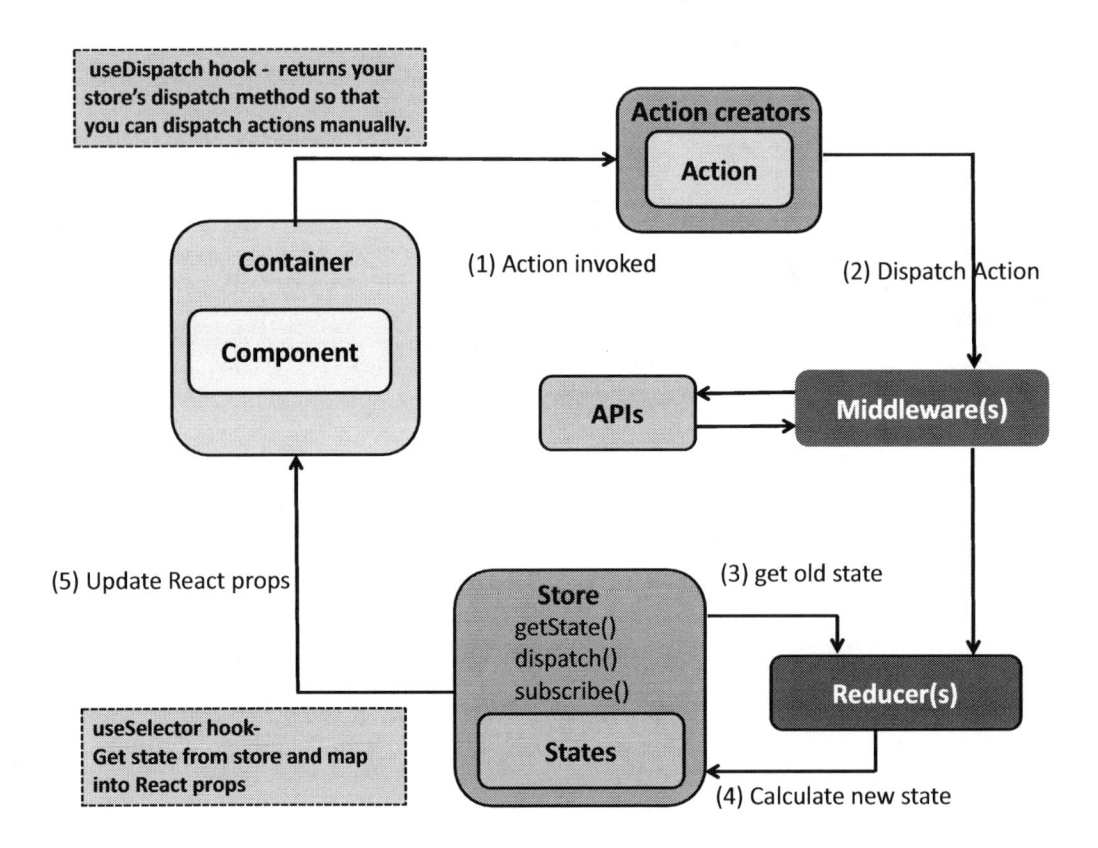

Redux-Thunk Hooks example

We are creating counters example using useSelector, useDispatch and useCallback instead of connect( ).

Entry Point

As with connect(), we start by wrapping your entire application in a Provider component to make the store available throughout the component tree.

(index.js)

```js
import React from "react";
import ReactDOM from "react-dom";
import { Provider } from "react-redux";

import configureStore from "./store";
import Counter from "./main";

const store = configureStore();

const App = () => {
  return (
    <div>
      <div>
        <Counter />
      </div>
    </div>
  );
};

ReactDOM.render(
  <Provider store={store}>
    <App />
  </Provider>,
  document.getElementById("root")
);
```

Store

Redux-Thunk and applyMiddleware are not required for this simple example but are included as platform template.

(store.js)
```js
import { createStore, applyMiddleware } from "redux";

import thunk from "redux-thunk";
import rootReducer from "./reducers";

export default function configureStore(initialState = {}) {
  return createStore(rootReducer, initialState, applyMiddleware(thunk));
}
```

Presentation and Container

useSelector and **useDispatch** are hooks functions imported from the React-Redux library. We can use these hooks for every functional component that needs to either read data from the state or dispatch an action without writing the extra amount of code.

useSelector takes the current state as an argument and returns whatever data you want from it. It allows you to store the return values inside a variable within the scope of our functional components instead of being passing down as props.

With **useDispatch**, we can dispatch any action to the store by simply adding action as an argument to the new variable like the code below

Besides, we can use **useDispatch** in conjunction with React's **useCallback** hook, wrapping the dispatch method and treating it as the only dependency. When the dependency [dispatch] changed, increaseCount() or decreaseCount() will be dispatched.

(main.js)

```js
import React, { useCallback } from "react";
import { useSelector, useDispatch } from "react-redux";
import { increaseCount, decreaseCount } from "./actions";

const Counter = () => {
  const { count } = useSelector((state) => ({
    ...state.reducer
  }));
  const dispatch = useDispatch();
  const increase = useCallback(() => dispatch(increaseCount()), [dispatch]);
  const decrease = useCallback(() => dispatch(decreaseCount()), [dispatch]);
  return (
    <div>
      <h2>counter: {count} </h2>
      <div>
        <button onClick={increase}>increment</button>
        <button onClick={decrease}>decrement</button>
      </div>
    </div>
  );
};
export default Counter;
```

Actions

(actions.js)

```
export const increaseCount = () => {
 return {
  type: "INCREASE_COUNT"
 };
};

export const decreaseCount = () => {
 return {
  type: "DECREASE_COUNT"
 };
};
```

Reducers

(reducers.js)

```
import { combineReducers } from "redux";
// Set up reducer and switch
const reducer = (state = { count: 0 }, action) => {
 switch (action.type) {
  case "INCREASE_COUNT":
   return {
    ...state,
    count: state.count + 1
   };
  case "DECREASE_COUNT":
   return {
    ...state,
    count: state.count - 1
   };
  default:
   return state;
 }
};
// added combineReducers for future reducers addtions
export default combineReducers({
 reducer
});
```

Code sample: https://codesandbox.io/s/redux-hooks-counter1-fvcif

Redux-Thunk Hooks Asynchronous example

We are modifying the previous example to support asynchronous counters using Redux-Thunk. All we need to do is to add action creators that return functions to handle the side effect. There are no modifications in the reducer.

(actions.js)

```js
//***** synchronous actions creator, returing object
export const increaseCount = () => {
  return {
   type: "INCREASE_COUNT"
  };
};
export const decreaseCount = () => {
  return {
   type: "DECREASE_COUNT"
  };
};

//***** asynchronous actions, after 2sec delay,  returning function
export const increaseCountAsync = () => {
  return (dispatch) => {
    setTimeout(() => {
     dispatch({ type: "INCREASE_COUNT" });
    }, 2000);
  };
};
export const decreaseCountAsync = () => {
  return (dispatch) => {
    setTimeout(() => {
     dispatch({ type: "DECREASE_COUNT" });
    }, 2000);
  };
};
```

We are adding two asynchronous counters buttons and useCallback hooks.

(main.js)

```js
import React, { useCallback } from "react";
import { useSelector, useDispatch } from "react-redux";
import { increaseCount, decreaseCount } from "./actions";
import { increaseCountAsync, decreaseCountAsync } from "./actions";

const Counter = () => {
  const { count } = useSelector((state) => ({
    ...state.reducer
  }));
  const dispatch = useDispatch();
  const increase = useCallback(() => dispatch(increaseCount()), [dispatch]);
  const decrease = useCallback(() => dispatch(decreaseCount()), [dispatch]);
  const increaseAsync = useCallback(() => dispatch(increaseCountAsync()), [dispatch]);
  const decreaseAsync = useCallback(() => dispatch(decreaseCountAsync()), [dispatch]);
  return (
    <div>
      <h2>counter: {count} </h2>
      <div>
        <button onClick={increase}>increment</button>
        <button onClick={decrease}>decrement</button>
        <button onClick={increaseAsync}>increment Async</button>
        <button onClick={decreaseAsync}>decrement Async</button>
      </div>
    </div>
  );
};

export default Counter;
```

Code sample: https://codesandbox.io/s/redux-hooks-counter2-27onu

Pros and Cons of using useSelector and useDispatch

There are tradeoffs in using useSelector and useDispatch.

Pros
- More readable code.
- No more connect() HOCs, fewer nodes in our component hierarchy.
- no conflicts between props coming from connect, props coming from a parent, and props injected by wrappers from 3rd party libraries

Cons
- Performance is not optimized by default, compared to connect().
- Must follow the Hooks rules.
- To get the ownProps object, we need to write our own logic/hook.

7.7 Redux-Saga

Redux Saga official docs: https://redux-saga.js.org/

Redux-Saga is a library bringing the concept of "task" to Redux. A task here is an independent unit of execution, like a process that runs independently and concurrently. Each task runs separately and in parallel. Redux-Saga provides an execution environment for this task. In a nutshell, it is like a separate thread in our application that is solely responsible for side effects. Redux-Saga also provides **Effects**, a tool for describing asynchronous processing as tasks, and a method.

Redux-Saga listens for dispatched actions, performs side effects, and returns its own actions to the standard reducer. It intercepts actions with side effects and handles them so that Redux reducers remain pure.

Redux-Saga subscribes to the store and can trigger a saga to run or continue when a specific action is dispatched. Redux-Saga library is implemented using ES6 generator functions that yield objects to the redux-saga middleware. Unlike normal functions, generator functions can be paused and resumed on demand and can return (more accurately yield) multiple values. If you forget the generator functions, please refer to the 2.8 Asynchronous systems.

In Redux-Saga, generators typically yield effects. They are JavaScript objects containing instructions to be performed by the middleware. We don't have to call next() in our code because Redux-Saga handles it under the hood. Besides, it also provides tools for describing asynchronous processing as tasks. We can define our **async flow** using a simple synchronous style and familiar control flows **(if/else, loops, try/catch...)**.

Redux-Sagas has some architectural benefits. In Redux-Saga applications, since all side effects are moved into sagas, UI components do not typically perform any business logic. Only dispatch actions as pure JavaScript objects to notify what happened. It allows for much simpler and more readable code by centralizing asynchronous logic for more manageable and sophisticated async flows.

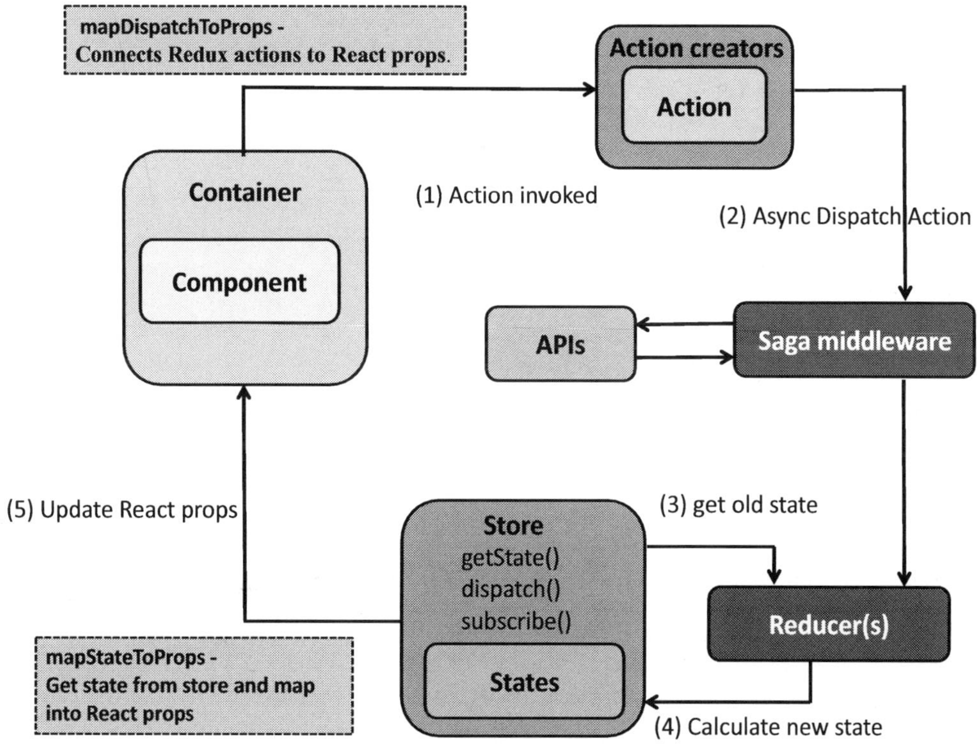

Saga architecture

Sagas are broken down into the root, watchers, and workers. All other Sagas you write are consolidated into the root.

- **Root** - All Sagas will be registered with a root Saga. Combined with an **all()** function, they are allowed to start all at the same time each time.

- **Watcher** - watches for specific actions and call Worker Saga to execute.

- **Worker** – handles the actions, termination, and specific business logic.

Effects Library

The Effects Library provides primitives and operators to manage concurrency between tasks (e.g., coordinate concurrent AJAX requests). We can fork multiple background tasks in parallel. We can also cancel a running task. An Effect is simply an object that contains some information to be interpreted by the middleware. Actions are like commands (instructions, primitives) for describing tasks, such as the following.

- **call** (blocking) —Runs a function passing the specified arguments. If the function returns a Promise, it pauses the saga until the promise is either resolved or rejected.
- **put** (non-blocking) —Dispatches a Redux action.
- **fork** (non-blocking) —Runs the function passed in a non-blocking way.
- **take** (blocking)—Pauses the saga until the specified Redux action is received.
- **takeEvery** (non-blocking)—Returns result for every call triggered for the specified Redux action.
- **takeLatest** (non-blocking) —Returns the result of only the last call triggered for the specified. Redux action, ignoring the rest. This effect can be used to implement some form of action cancellation.
- **race (blocking)** —Runs multiple effects simultaneously and terminates them when one task is completed.

The Saga library provides the following Objects Effects.

Name	Blocking
takeEvery	No
takeLatest	No
takeLeading	No
Throttle	No
Debounce	No
Retry	Yes
Take	Yes
take(channel)	Sometimes (see API reference)
takeMaybe	Yes
Put	No
putResolve	Yes
put(channel, action)	No
Call	Yes
Apply	Yes
Cps	Yes
Fork	No
Spawn	No
Join	Yes
Cancel	No
Select	No
actionChannel	No
Flush	Yes
Cancelled	Yes
Race	Yes
Delay	Yes
All	Blocks if there is a blocking effect in the array or object

7.8 React Saga counters example

Entry point and create store

The counter component is wrapped within the Provider.

(Index.js)

```
import React from "react";
import ReactDOM from "react-dom";
import { Counter } from "./Counter";
import { store } from "./store";
import { Provider } from "react-redux";

const App = () => (
 <Provider store={store}>
   <Counter />
 </Provider>
);

ReactDOM.render(<App />, document.getElementById("root"));
```

Import rootSaga from saga.js. Calling sagaMiddleware.run(rootSagas) is to run the app.

(store.js)

```js
import { createStore, applyMiddleware } from "redux";
import createSagaMiddleware from "redux-saga";

import { rootSagas } from "./sagas";
import { reducer } from "./reducers";

const sagaMiddleware = createSagaMiddleware();

export const store = createStore(reducer, applyMiddleware(sagaMiddleware));

sagaMiddleware.run(rootSagas);
```

(constants.js)

```js
export const INCREMENT = "INCREMENT";
export const DECREMENT = "DECREMENT";
export const INCREMENT_ASYNC = "INCREMENT_ASYNC";
export const DECREMENT_ASYNC = "DECREMENT_ASYNC";
```

Presentation and container

We implement two synchronous counters and two asynchronous counters with a 2-second delay.

(Counter.js)

```javascript
import React from "react";
import { connect } from "react-redux";

import {DECREMENT, INCREMENT, INCREMENT_ASYNC, DECREMENT_ASYNC
} from "./constants";

const myCounter = ({
  value,
  onIncrementAsync,
  onDecrementAsync,
  onIncrement,
  onDecrement
}) => (
  <div>
    <div> SAGA counter: {value}</div>
    <button onClick={onIncrement}>Sync +</button>
    <button onClick={onDecrement}>Sync -</button>
    <button onClick={onIncrementAsync}>Async +</button>
    <button onClick={onDecrementAsync}>Async -</button>
  </div>
);

export const mapStateToProps = (state) => ({ value: state });

export const mapDispatchToProps = (distpatch) => ({
  onIncrement: () => distpatch({ type: INCREMENT }),
  onDecrement: () => distpatch({ type: DECREMENT }),
  onIncrementAsync: () => distpatch({ type: INCREMENT_ASYNC }),
  onDecrementAsync: () => distpatch({ type: DECREMENT_ASYNC })
});
export const Counter = connect(mapStateToProps, mapDispatchToProps)(myCounter);
```

Reducers

If async operation, action.type is passed from the Saga middleware.
If sync operation, action.type is directly from the actions creator.

(reducers.js)

```js
import { INCREMENT, DECREMENT } from "./constants";

export function reducer(state = 0, action) {
  switch (action.type) {
    case INCREMENT:
      return state + 1;
    case DECREMENT:
      return state - 1;
    default:
      return state;
  }
}
```

Sagas watcher and worker

- The Root Saga combines all other Sagas (generators) and coordinates all Sagas in this app.
- Saga Watcher checks for specific actions (DECREMENT_ASYNC, INCREMENT_ASNC) and calls Worker Saga to execute.
- Saga Worker calls a function for a 2-second delay and dispatches an action.

(sagas.js)

```javascript
import { delay } from "redux-saga";
import { put, takeEvery, all, call } from "redux-saga/effects";
import {INCREMENT,DECREMENT,INCREMENT_ASYNC, DECREMENT_ASYNC
} from "./constants";

function* hello() {
  console.log("Hello SAGA!");
  yield 1;
}
const delay = (ms) => new Promise(res => setTimeout(res, ms))

//****** Saga Worker *********************
function* incrementAync() {
  yield call(delay, 2000);           //2 sec delay
  yield put({ type: INCREMENT }); //dispatch an action
}

function* decrementAync() {
  yield call(delay, 2000);           //2 sec delay
  yield put({ type: DECREMENT }); //dispatch an action
}

//******Saga Watcher. *********************
function* watchIncrementAsync() {
  yield takeEvery(INCREMENT_ASYNC, incrementAync);
}

function* watchDecrementAsync() {
  yield takeEvery(DECREMENT_ASYNC, decrementAync);
}

//****rootSaga coordinates all sagas used in this application******
export function* rootSagas() {
  yield all([hello(), watchIncrementAsync(), watchDecrementAsync()]);
}
```

Code sample: https://codesandbox.io/s/redux-saga-24ily

7.9 React Saga external resources access example

Entry point and creating store

App component is wrapped within Provider. Import rootSaga from sagas.js. sagaMiddleware.run(watcherSagas) runs the saga.

(index.js)

```javascript
import React from "react";
import ReactDOM from "react-dom";
import "./styles.css";
import App from "./App";
import { createStore, applyMiddleware, compose } from "redux";
import createSagaMiddleware from "redux-saga";
import { Provider } from "react-redux";
import { dogReducer } from "./redux";
import { watcherSaga } from "./sagas";

// create the saga middleware
const sagaMiddleware = createSagaMiddleware();

// create a redux store with our reducer above and middleware
let store = createStore(dogReducer, compose(applyMiddleware(sagaMiddleware)));

// run the saga
sagaMiddleware.run(watcherSaga);

ReactDOM.render(
  <Provider store={store}>
    <App />
  </Provider>,
  document.getElementById("root")
);
```

(constants.js)

```javascript
// action types
export const API_CALL_REQUEST = "API_CALL_REQUEST";
export const API_CALL_SUCCESS = "API_CALL_SUCCESS";
export const API_CALL_FAILURE = "API_CALL_FAILURE";
```

Presentation and Container

UI providing a button to update random dog pictures. mapStateToProps connects required states to props.

(App.js)

```javascript
import React from "react";
import { connect } from "react-redux";

function App(props) {
  const { fetching, dog, onRequestDog, error } = props;
  return (
    <div className="App">
      <header className="App-header">
        {dog && <img src={dog} className="App-logo" alt="logo" />}
      </header>
      {fetching ? ( <button disabled>Fetching...</button> ) :
      (<button onClick={onRequestDog}>Request a Dog</button>)}

      {error && (<p style={{ color: "red" }}>Probably network problem. Try again!</p>)}
    </div>
  );
}

const mapStateToProps = (state) => {
  const { fetching, dog, error } = state;
  return {
    fetching,
    dog,
    error
  };
};

const mapDispatchToProps = (dispatch) => {
  return {
    onRequestDog: () => dispatch({ type: "API_CALL_REQUEST" })
  };
};
export default connect(mapStateToProps, mapDispatchToProps)(App);
```

Reducers

Reducer checks action.type (API_CALL_REQUEST, API_CALL_REQUEST, API_CALL_FAILURE) and updates the state based on the action.type.

(reducers.js) *redux.js*

```js
import {
 API_CALL_REQUEST, API_CALL_SUCCESS, API_CALL_FAILURE} from "./constants";

// reducer with initial state
const initialState = {
  fetching: false,
  dog: null,
  error: null
};

export function dogReducer(state = initialState, action) {
  switch (action.type) {
   case API_CALL_REQUEST:
     return { ...state, fetching: true };
   case API_CALL_SUCCESS:
     return { ...state, fetching: false, dog: action.dog };
   case API_CALL_FAILURE:
     return { ...state, fetching: false, error: action.error };
   default:
     return state;
  }
}
```

Saga watcher and worker

- Saga Watcher checks for specific actions (API_CALL_REQUEST, API_CALL_SUCCESS, API_CALL_FAILURE) and calls Worker Saga to execute, if necessary.
- Saga Worker makes the API calls to fetch a random dog picture site and dispatches a success action to the store. If failed, dispatch a failure action.

(sagas.js)

```js
import { takeLatest, call, put } from "redux-saga/effects";
import axios from "axios";
import {API_CALL_REQUEST, API_CALL_SUCCESS, API_CALL_FAILURE
} from "./constants";

// watcher saga: watches for actions dispatched to the store, starts worker saga
export function* watcherSaga() {
  yield takeLatest(API_CALL_REQUEST, workerSaga);
}

// function that makes the api request and returns a Promise for response
export function fetchDog() {
  return axios({
    method: "get",
    url: "https://dog.ceo/api/breeds/image/random"
  });
}

// worker saga: makes the api call when watcher saga sees the action
export function* workerSaga() {
  try {
    const response = yield call(fetchDog);
    const dog = response.data.message;

    // dispatch a success action to the store with the new dog.
    yield put({ type: API_CALL_SUCCESS, dog });
  } catch (error) {
    yield put({ type: API_CALL_FAILURE, error });
  }
}
```

Code sample: https://codesandbox.io/s/redux-saga2-3q6i3

7.10 Reselect library

Reselect is a popular helper library for Redux. Selectors are functions that select a subset of data from more massive data collection. In Redux, a selector is a piece of logic that gets a specific state from the store. The selector extracts only relevant information from the whole state tree and performs the necessary calculations.

Most importantly, selectors built with Reselect supports memoization as well. A memoized function has a buffer, keeping track of the previous arguments that were passed into it and checking the last result. It will only re-run if the arguments change.

Reselect is a memoized selector function composed of selectors that returns something you want in your component's props. Reselect selectors can be composed and chained together. They can even be used as input to other selectors.

Reselect is beneficial in complex apps structured to have a minimal store and rely on selectors to compute derived data.

createSelector API: memoizes an output of every input selector and recalculates the resulting value only if any of the input selectors changes its output.

Input Functions: one or more pure javaScript functions or selectors created with Reselect

```
const mySelector = createSelector (

inputSelector1,
inputSelector2,
inputSelector3,

(result1, result2, result3) = { do something...............}
)
```

Output result function: always one result

Reselect library example

The following example was forked from Reselect official docs. The createSelector( ) function memoizes an output of every input selector and recalculates the resulting value only if any of the input selectors changes its output.

```
import { createSelector } from "reselect";

const shopItemsSelector = state => state.shop.items;
const taxPercentSelector = state => state.shop.taxPercent;

const subtotalSelector = createSelector(
  shopItemsSelector,
  items => items.reduce((acc, item) => acc + item.value, 0)
);

const taxSelector = createSelector(
  subtotalSelector,
  taxPercentSelector,
  (subtotal, taxPercent) => subtotal * (taxPercent / 100)
);

const totalSelector = createSelector(
  subtotalSelector,
  taxSelector,
  (subtotal, tax) => ({ total: subtotal + tax })
);

let exampleState = {
  shop: {
    taxPercent: 8,
    items: [{ name: "apple", value: 1.2 }, { name: "orange", value: 0.95 }]
  }
};

console.log(subtotalSelector(exampleState)); // 2.15
console.log(taxSelector(exampleState)); // 0.172
console.log(totalSelector(exampleState)); // { total: 2.322 }
```

Code sample: https://codesandbox.io/s/redux-reselect-basic-1goyd

Official docs : https://github.com/reduxjs/reselect

7.11 Immer

Immer is a library that helped us improve our JavaScript code's readability, ensuring our state was never modified by accident. Immer allows us to write mutable code but execute it immutably under the hood. It is based on the "copy-on-write" and "Proxies" mechanism and built-in support to use plain JavaScript objects and arrays syntax.

Immer works by writing a producer function, which takes two arguments - the currentState and a producer callback function. The current state determines our starting point, and the producer expresses what needs to be changed. The producer function receives one argument, the draft, which is a proxy to the current state you passed in. Any modification you make to the draft will be recorded and used to produce nextState. The currentState will be untouched during this process. Because immer uses structural sharing, and our example producer above didn't modify anything.

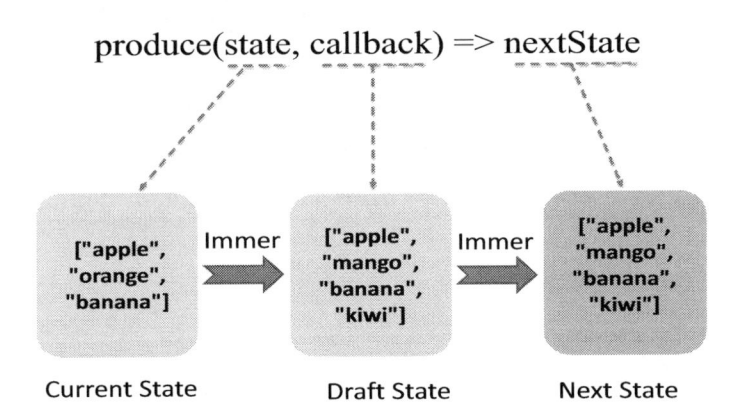

Immer library example

The following code is a simple example of the produce function:

```
import produce from "immer";

const baseState = [
  {
    todo: "Learn React",
    done: true
  },
  {
    todo: "Learn immer",
    done: false
  }
];

const nextState = produce(baseState, (draftState) => {
  draftState.push({ todo: "Learn RTK" });
  draftState[1].done = true;
});

//Any modification to the draft will be recorded
//and used to produce nextState. The currentState will be untouched

console.log(`baseState: ${JSON.stringify(baseState)}`);
console.log(`nextState: ${JSON.stringify(nextState)}`);
```

Code sample: https://codesandbox.io/s/immer-q21m9

The mutable data updating can be frown upon by pure functional programmers. However, the Immer library does not alter the original object. You can specify the value directly in order to update the value of deeply nested objects.

Immer can be used together with Reducer. When updating the value of a deeply nested object, you can specify the value to be updated directly. For example, nested objects like {... store, foo: {... store.foo, bar:'newValue'}} is already painful to read, although it has only two nesting level layers.

By using the Immer library, it is more straightforward:

```
const reducer = (draft: State = initialState, action: Action) => {
  switch (action.type) {
    case 'LEARN_REDUX':
      draft.foo.bar = 'newValue'
      break
    // ...
  }
}
```

There are many good code examples in the CodeSandBox:
https://codesandbox.io/examples/package/immer

Immer library official docs: https://immerjs.github.io/immer/docs/introduction

7.12 Redux Toolkit (RTK)

Redux Toolkit library simplifies common use cases like store setup, creating reducers, immutable update logic, and more. It is an opinionated and batteries-included library that provides useful defaults pattern and includes the most commonly used add-on libraries such as Redux-Thunk, immer, and Reselect.

By default, RTK includes the following three middlewares:

- **Redux-Thunk:** A middleware recommended for handling side effects.

- **redux-immutable-state-invariant:** Used in the development stage only, this library will throw an error if you try to mutate state directly. If you're using regular objects and arrays, this library is useful to avoid mutations.

- **serializable-state-invariant-middleware:** Detects if your state tree and actions have non-serialized data, such as functions, Promises, and non-plain JavaScript data values. Any non-serializable values detection will be logged to the console.

These three middlewares are added by default with the function getDefaultMiddleware() unless you would like to customize by adding additional middlewares or removing them.

Redux Toolkit includes the following APIs:

- **configureStore():** wraps createStore to provide simplified configuration options and default parameters. It can automatically combine your slice reducers, adds whatever Redux middleware you supply, includes Redux-Thunk by default, and enables the use of the Redux DevTools Extension.

- **createReducer():** simplifies immutable update logic by writing "mutative" code in your reducers and supports directly mapping specific action types to case reducer functions that will update the state when that action is dispatched. You can avoid writing switch statements. Under the hood, it uses the Immer library, which allows you to write mutative logic, but it does not alter the original object.

- **createAction():** generates an action creator function for the given action type string. The function itself has toString() defined so that it can be used in place of the type constant. With createAction, you can get rid of action creators and named actions to place all in one place.

- **createSlice():** accepts an object of reducer functions, a slice name, and an initial state value and automatically generates a slice reducer with corresponding action creators and action types. You don't have to use createAction and createReducer separately. You can keep everything in a single place: action creators, reducers, and state.

- **createAsyncThunk:** accepts an action type string and a function that returns a promise, and generates a thunk that dispatches pending/fulfilled/rejected action types based on that promise.

- **createEntityAdapter:** generates a set of reusable reducers and selectors to manage normalized data in the store.

- **createSelector utility** from the Reselect library, re-exported for ease of use.

RTK does not cover every use case. For example, it is not compatible with data fetching libraries such as React Query and SWR. If you would like to use a query library, RTK Query, which is currently in an alpha stage of development, can be a good solution.

RTK Query official docs: https://rtk-query-docs.netlify.app/

Using TypeScript in classic Redux is pretty tough. On the other hand, default RTK works well with TypeScript. If you plan to use TypeScript, RTK makes development more straightforward. However, using TypeScript with Redux-Saga is a bit challenging even if you use RTK. There are fundamental problems with generators in general in Typescript and unconventional use of generator functions in Redux-Saga.

The advantages of the Redux Toolkit come at a price. Because of an additional dependency through the RTK and indirectly some dependencies through the toolkit libraries, for new Redux developers, basic principles working with Redux are hidden, making it more difficult to understand the Redux basic concept. The fundamental building blocks of Redux are still actions => reducers => middleware => store, and you need a good knowledge of these blocks to be proficient with Redux and Redux toolkit. It would be better if you don't use the RTK until you feel comfortable with classic Redux. You could consider using RTK for production projects later.

There are many good examples in the RTK official docs so that you can learn this library quickly.

Basic Tutorial from the official site is an excellent introduction for configureStore, createAction, createReduce, and createSlice:

https://redux-toolkit.js.org/tutorials/basic-tutorial

Intermediate Tutorial from the official site is optional reading material. The ToDoList app we learned in section 7.3 has been RTK converted. Using RTK, readability has improved:

https://redux-toolkit.js.org/tutorials/intermediate-tutorial

RTK official docs: https://redux-toolkit.js.org/

7.13 Connected-React-Router

React-Router is the de-facto standard routing solution for react applications. However, if you try to use React-Router with Redux, you might face fundamental architectural problems in some use cases because both React-Router and Redux expect to have their own state in the app. One of the solutions is to add a library Connected-React-Router (formerly known as React-Router-Redux).

With React-Router, URLs can be modified through <Link>, <Redirect> only. On the other hand, Connected-React-Router enables you to easily achieve screen transition using actions with push, replace, go, goBack, goForward methods. Those methods work for both Redux-Thunk and Redux-Saga as well.

Connected-React-Router synchronizes router state with a redux store through uni-directional flow (i.e. history => store => router => components). Connected-React-Router keeps the state in sync with your Redux store, keeping a copy of the current location hidden in the state.

It is challenging to manage all screens based on the state of the app in large-scale SPAs. Creating a screen for each URL using connected-react-router makes it easier to develop apps. Since Redux manages the routing status, you can easily check "which path you are currently on".

The good thing about this library is that you can still use React-Router API.

Official docs: https://www.npmjs.com/package/react-router-redux

8. Recoil

(2 hours reading and exercise)

*All matter originates and exists only by virtue of a force
which brings the particle of an atom to vibration
and holds this most minute solar system of the atom together.
We must assume behind this force the existence of a conscious
and intelligent mind.*

Max Planck (1858 – 1947)

Recoil is a very powerful and flexible tool to manage complex state and to prevent the confusing passing around of props among components. With Recoil, you can create a data-flow graph that flows from atoms (shared state) through selectors (pure functions) and down into your React components. **Atoms** are units of the state that components can subscribe to. On the other hand, **selectors** are pure functions that transform this state either synchronously or asynchronously.

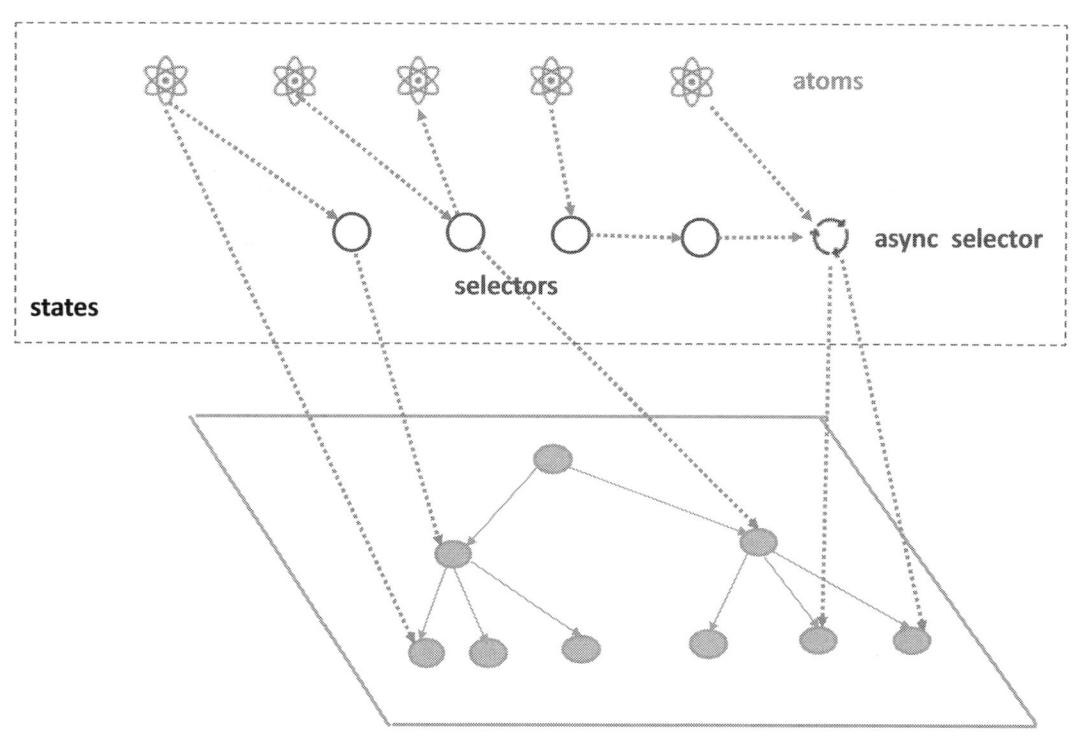

8.1 RecoilRoot

RecoilRoot acts as a global context provider for the entire tree of components in which you want to use shared global states. It can be added somewhere in the parent tree and provides context to all child components. A simple example of using the RecoilRoot is like this:

```
import { RecoilRoot } from "recoil";
function AppRoot() {
 return (
<RecoilRoot>
  <ComponentUsingRecoil />
 </RecoilRoot>
); }
```

Multiple Recoil roots can be used together within an application, with the newest – or innermost root masking any of the outer roots. Atoms can then access the state that has been passed from the Recoil Roots.

8.2 Atoms

Declaring Atoms

In Recoil, the global state (shared by multiple components in the application) is referred to as an atom. An atom is like a chemical element known as atoms that is the smallest unit of ordinary matter. The global state can also be composed of many atoms.

An atom with a value can be created using the atom function provided by the Recoil library. All you need to declare an atom - a unique key and a default value. The *key* is a string that identifies the atom and must be globally unique. The atom declaration itself merely declares the state and does not contain the logic of how the atom is used:

```
const counterState = atom ({{
   key: "uniqueID",
   default: defaultValue
});
```

Using Atoms

Consuming the global state variable is identical to using React useState() hook.

-useRecoilState():

The most basic way to use atoms from a component is to use useRecoilState() provided by Recoil. This hook is used to read and write to an atom. It enables the calling components to subscribe to the atom. For instance, useRecoilState() can be used as follows:

```
const CounterButton = () => {
 const [count, setCount] = useRecoilState(counterState);
 return (
   <p>
     <button onClick={() => setCount(c => c + 1)}>{count}</button>
   </p>
 );
};
```

useRecoilState() is a similar API as useState() API. However, **instead of receiving the default value, it takes an already defined atom as an argument.** The return value is a two-element array like [count, setCount], where the count is a current value of the atom, and setCount is a function that updates the value of the atom.

You can read and write the value of the global state (counterState) in the same manner as the component level local state declared by useState(). The counterState may now be used in different components within the app tree by invoking the useRecoilState() Hook. If you call multiple CounterButton components, all the values will be linked.

In classical Hooks, "declaring a state (belonging to a component)" was done by calling useState(), but in Recoil, atom ({...}) and useRecoilState (atom) work together in a set to declare the state.

React's useState() hook has two roles: "declare a state" and "use the declared state", and states belong to components, so they were inseparable. On the other hand, in Recoil, by making the state (atom) global, it is possible to declare the global state and the component state separately:

// useRecoilState()
const [counter] = useRecoilState(counterValue);

-useRecoilValue(): This hook is used to read an atom. The calling component will be subscribed to the atom:

// useRecoilValue()
const counter = useRecoilValue(counterValue);

-useSetRecoilState(): This is a write-only hook without subscribing to the atom. In other words, a component that only writes to the atom will not be re-rendered when the value of the atom changes. It is a valuable API that updates the atom without unnecessary re-rendering:

// useRecoilState -- subscription to Atom
const [, setCounter] = useRecoilState(counterValue);

// useSetRecoilState -- no subscription to Atom
const setCounter = useSetRecoilState(counterValue);

-useResetRecoilState()

This hook is used to reset an atom to its default value.

-useRecoilCallback()

This hook is used to use a callback that **reads an atom without a subscription**. useRecoilCallback can update asynchronously.

In the following example, alert the current counterState value when clicked. This can also be done using useRecoilValue, but useRecoilCallback can avoid unnecessary re-rendering:

```
const AlertButton = () => {
  const showAlert = useRecoilCallback(async ({ getPromise }) => {
    const counter = await getPromise(counterState);

    alert(counter);
  }, [ ]);

  return (
    <p>
      <button onClick={showAlert}>Show counter value</button>
    </p>
  );
};
```

useRecoilCallback() has a similar interface to useCallback(). It receives a callback function as the first argument, and the second argument is a dependency list. The major difference from useCallback() is that useRecoilCallback() can receive the getPromise function through the object of the first argument of the callback function.

You can use this getPromise function to get the value of the atom. However, the result is a promise. The reason is that Recoil supports asynchronous selectors (will be discussed later).

If you would like to change the value of atoms, you could use set (state, newValue).

Atoms example

(app.js)

```js
import React from "react";
import {atom,useRecoilState, useRecoilValue, useSetRecoilState, useRecoilCallback}
from "recoil";
import "./styles.css";

const counterState = atom({
 key: "counterStateID",
 default: 0
});

//App and useRecoilValue demo
export default function App() {
 const myCount = useRecoilValue(counterState);
 return (
  <div className="App">
   <h1>Recoil Atom APIs example</h1>
   <p>useRecoilValue demo: {myCount}</p>
   <CounterButton />
   <CounterButton />
   <UpdateOnlyButton />
   <AlertButton />
   <h4>click the reload buttom before start</h4>
  </div>
 );
}

//useRecoilState demo
const CounterButton = () => {
 const [myCount1, setCount] = useRecoilState(counterState);
 return (
  <p>
   <button onClick={() => setCount((c) => c + 1)}>
    useRecoilState demo: {myCount1}
   </button>
  </p>
 );
};
//useSetRecoilState demo
const UpdateOnlyButton = () => {
 const setCount2 = useSetRecoilState(counterState);
 return (
  <p>
   <button onClick={() => setCount2((c) => c + 1)}>
    useSetRecoilState demo
   </button>
  </p>
 );
};
```

```
//async demo using useRecoilCallback
const AlertButton = () => {
  const showAlert = useRecoilCallback(async ({ getPromise }) => {
    const counter = await getPromise(counterState);

    alert(counter);
  }, []);

  return (
    <p>
      <button onClick={showAlert}>useRecoilCallback demo</button>
    </p>
  );
};
```

(index.js)

```
import React, { Suspense } from "react";
import ReactDOM from "react-dom";
import { RecoilRoot } from "recoil";

import App from "./App";

ReactDOM.render(
  <React.StrictMode>
    <Suspense fallback={<p>Sus.</p>}>
      <RecoilRoot>
        <App />
      </RecoilRoot>
    </Suspense>
  </React.StrictMode>,
  document.getElementById("root")
);
```

Code sample: https://codesandbox.io/s/recoil-atom-u9oqr

8.3 Selectors

In Redux, the selector calculates values from the state. And when the state is updated, the component will not be re-rendered unless the value calculated by the selector based on that state has changed. Recoil also has a selector, not a one-to-one correspondence with the Redux selector, but achieves a similar result. Recoil doesn't re-render the component unless the selector result changes, even if the state is updated.

A selector serves as an efficient way to get computed values from your application state. **A selector is a pure function that accepts atoms or other selectors as input (chaining selectors).** Much like atoms, selectors need a unique key to identify them. Selectors are used for calculations that rely on the selected state.

Components can subscribe to selectors in the same manner that they can subscribe to atoms and then be re-rendered when they change. When these upstream atoms or selectors are updated, the selector function will be re-evaluated.

In Recoil, **all the hooks such as useRecoilState can be used for Selector as well.** Atom and selector have in common that they provide a value. The only difference is whether they have the value themselves or are calculated from others.

Defining selectors

The selector is created by using the selector function provided by the Recoil library. The selector includes *key* and *get*. The *key* has to be a unique string and shouldn't be the same as any previous atom/selector keys.

The *get* function calculates the value of the selector. It takes a *get* from an argument, and you can use that *get* to use other states (atom or selector) values. The state obtained by calculating the value of the selector is considered to be subscribed from that selector.

For example, we will define a component to increment/decrement the counter, and the selector computes an even or odd number.

```
//define Atom
const myCount = atom({
  key: "myCountID",
  default: 0
});

//define Selector to check if number even or odd ?
const isEvenOdd = selector({
  key: "evenCheckID",
  get: ({ get }) => {
    const myState = get(myCount);
    return myState % 2 === 0 ? "even number" : "odd number";
  }
});
```

In the above example, the myCount value is computed as get(count) % 2 == 0 in the return statement. The JavaScript modulus operator (%) returns the division remainder. If true, it returns an even value. If false, it returns an odd value.

The selector is invoked with an object. A *get* method invoked with an internal *get* function from Recoil. With this *get* function, you may retrieve any state value and do some calculations, as seen above.

Using selector value

Using the computed value within a component is similar to an atom's return value. When obtaining the value within your component, useRecoilValue Hook is used like below:

```
export default function App() {
  const [countState, setCount] = useRecoilState(myCount); //call Atom for counter
  const myValue = useRecoilValue(isEvenOdd);         //call Selector to check even/odd

  return (<div>………………………..</div>);
}
```

The return value from the invoked selector is an object expected to be passed to the Hook useRecoilValue.

Apart from just getting the value, it also creates a subscription to the state. In our example, every time the count changes, a new value for isEvenOdd is recalculated.

Selectors example

(index.js)

```
import React from "react";
import ReactDOM from "react-dom";
import { RecoilRoot } from "recoil";

import App from "./App";

ReactDOM.render(
  <React.StrictMode>
    <RecoilRoot>
      <App />
    </RecoilRoot>
  </React.StrictMode>,
  document.getElementById("root")
);
```

(App.js)

```javascript
import React from "react";
import { atom, selector, useRecoilState, useRecoilValue } from "recoil";
import "./styles.css";

//define Atom
const myCount = atom({
  key: "myCountID",
  default: 0
});

//define Selector to check if number even or odd ?
const isEvenCount = selector({
  key: "evenCheckID",
  get: ({ get }) => {
    const myState = get(myCount);
    return myState % 2 === 0 ? "even number" : "odd number";
  }
});

//App component
export default function App() {
  const [countState, setCount] = useRecoilState(myCount); //call Atom for counter
  const myValue = useRecoilValue(isEvenCount); //call Selector to check even/odd

  return (
    <div className="App">
      <h1>{countState}</h1>
      <button onClick={() => setCount((c) => c + 1)}>Increase</button>
      <button onClick={() => setCount((c) => c - 1)}>Decrease</button>
      <p>{myValue}</p>
    </div>
  );
}
```

Code sample: https://codesandbox.io/s/recoil-selector-counter-dly6d

Writable Selector

Optionally, Recoil's selector can update the object by adding the set property to the object passed to the selector function:

```
const calculateState = selector({
  key: "calculateStateID",
  get: ({get}) => do some calculation),
  set: ({set}, newValue) => set(myState, do another calculation),
});
```

Asynchronous Selector

The calculation of the selector value can be asynchronous. In this case, you need to set the return value as follows:

```
const calculationState = selector ({{
  key: "calculationID",
  get: async ({get}) => {
    await sleep (1000);
    return doComplicatedCalculation;
  }
});
```

The asynchronous selector uses React Concurrent Mode. If the component tries to use the selector value that hasn't been completed processing yet, suspension occurs. There are also hooks related to asynchronous processing called useRecoilStateLoadable and useRecoilValueLoadable, allowing you to get the Loadable object for that state instead of getting the value of the raw state.

As React Concurrent Mode is still in the experimental stage at the time of writing (March 2021), we will not go into the details.

For more information on usage and the other hooks – take a look at https://recoiljs.org/

9. Various State Management Libraries

(one hour reading and exercise)

9.1 MobX

MobX is a scalable library to manage state based on object-oriented concepts and data models of the application. It provides a uniform and unidirectional flow of data throughout the application. MobX uses observables for managing push-based data such as DOM events, interval timers, and sockets and achieves that with a simple description. When observable data is changed, the subscriber is called, and it can be used when running asynchronous processing. Furthermore, by using the filter, the subscriber is called only under specific data conditions.

MobX is easier to learn compared to Redux if you are well versed in functional reactive programming. However, the MobX developer community and the job market are much smaller than Redux.

10 minutes introduction to MobX.
https://mobx.js.org/getting-started

9.2 React Query

React Query is a declarative data-fetching library for fetching, caching, synchronizing, and updating server state in your React applications. You can fetch, cache, and update background data in your React apps without touching any global state. Unlike Redux, there is no global state to manage, reducers, normalization systems, or complicated configurations to understand. Since it is a new library, the React Query community is still small. If Redux or other global state managements are not for you, take a closer look at this library.

React Query Official docs: https://react-query.tanstack.com/

9.3 GraphQL

GraphQL, which was also developed by the Facebook team, is a query language for fetching data from APIs. GraphQL provides a complete and understandable description of the data in your API so that clients can ask for exactly what they need and nothing more. Typically, GraphQL is used together with a GraphQL client. The two most popular client-side solutions are Relay and Apollo-Client.

Apollo-Client is a JavaScript library used for managing local and remote data with GraphQL. It has many benefits like state management, fetching, caching, and modifying application data. It provides an efficient and declarative way to structure code in line with modern development processes. Apollo-Client has native support for React.

Relay is another client library developed by the Facebook team. Similar to Apollo-Client, but Relay enhances the encapsulation already available among React components. It allows components to specify what data they need, and the Relay framework provides the data. Its developer community is smaller than Apollo.

Apollo-client official docs:
https://www.apollographql.com/docs/react/

Relay official docs:
https://relay.dev/docs/en/introduction-to-relay

9.4 XState

XState is a library for creating, interpreting, and executing finite state machines (FSM) and statecharts, as well as managing invocations of those machines as actors.

A finite state machine (FSM) is a mathematical model of computation that describes the behavior of a system that can be in only one state at any given time.

Finite state machines consist of five parts:
- An initial state
- A finite number of states
- A finite number of events
- A transition function that determines the next state given the current state and event
- A set of final states

Any systems where particular inputs cause particular changes in state can be represented using FSMs, which enforce a specific set of "rules" on a logic structure. Each state has state transitions, meaning "Given some event, go to this next state and/or do these actions" :

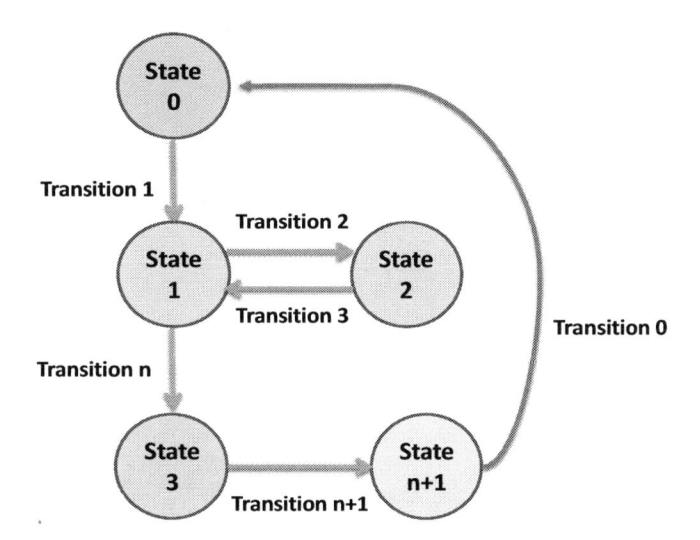

XState allows you to define a state transition in JSON format, instantiate it into an executable state machine and call it from your apps.

As an extension to state machines, statecharts are a formalism for modeling stateful, reactive systems, which is useful for declaratively describing the behavior of your application, from the individual components to the overall application logic.

Statecharts can extend conventional state-transition diagrams with essentially three elements, dealing, respectively, with the notions of hierarchy, concurrency, and communication. These transform the language of state diagrams into a highly structured and economical description language. Therefore, statecharts are compact and expressive. Small diagrams can express complex behavior. Statecharts have been used intensively in many industries (i.e. embedded systems, LSI circuits, telecom protocol, aeronautics, and more).

XState has some similarities with redux, but they are not the same. Instead of having one global store, XState has multiple smaller stores to send events. This architecture is called the Actor model. An actor holds state, can receive a message, decides what to do with the message, sends messages to other actors, and creates more actors.

Although quite a few JavaScript libraries can handle state machines and state transitions, XState has many advantages in features, expressiveness, ease of use in production code, and excellent documentation.

XState supports the following state representations:

Actions - Events and state transitions associated with actions such as onEntry and onExit.
Conditional branching - Branching by conditions such as success/failure and the number of attempts.
Hierarchy - Introduction of the hierarchical structure of states, which contributes to modularization of state.
Orthogonality - a combination of parallel state transitions.
History - Historical history of the state.

The following APIs are available for React:

useMachine(machine, options?) -- A React hook that interprets the given machine and starts a service that runs for the lifetime of the component.
useService(service) -- A React hook that subscribes to state changes from an existing service.
useActor(actor, getSnapshot) -- A React hook that subscribes to emitted changes from an existing actor.
useInterpret(machine, options?, observer?) -- A React hook that returns the service created from the machine with the options if specified. It also sets up a subscription to the service with the observer, if provided.
useSelector(actor, selector, compare?, getSnapshot?) -- A React hook that returns the selected value from the snapshot of an actor, such as a service. This hook will only cause a rerender if the selected value changes, as determined by the optional compare function.
asEffect(action) -- Ensures that the action is executed as an effect in useEffect, rather than being immediately executed.
asLayoutEffect(action) -- Ensures that the action is executed as an effect in useLayoutEffect, rather than being immediately executed.

If you are a digital circuits engineer, telecom engineer, XState may be a straightforward solution. However, not many production projects are using XState at this moment because it is a relatively new library.

If you are interested, there are many code samples in the CodeSandbox: https://codesandbox.io/examples/package/@xstate/react

Official docs: https://xstate.js.org/docs/
Statecharts docs: https://statecharts.github.io/

9.5 Summary

State Management Solutions

- React class components for maintaining legacy projects.
- Hooks (useReducer and useContext) for small size applications that do not require multiple global states.
- Redux-Thunk for medium size applications that require multiple global states. Use RTK to simplify Redux code.
- Redux-Saga for complex/large-size applications. Suited for complex async applications that require complicated unit test cases. Not TypeScript friendly.
- Recoil is simple and can also be used for complicated applications but not matured at the time of writing.
- mobX for programmers prefer not to use functional programming concepts.
- If the finite state machine matches your mental model, XState can be a candidate. For Non-UI engineers, XState is more comfortable grasping the concept compared with Redux.

Data Query/Fetching Libraries

- React Query for efficient data fetching and rendering.
- SWR is a JAMstack-oriented React Hooks library.
- Apollo Client or Relay for GraphQL Schema APIs.
- RTK-Query to use together with RTK, but not matured at the time of writing.

APPENDIX

(2 hours reading and exercise)

Installation

CodeSandbox is a perfect tool for studying React. But in the end, you need to know the real project development environment. We are going to install the simple project using create-react-app to automate the build of your app.

Node.js and npm

Node.js is an open-source, cross-platform, JavaScript runtime environment that executes JavaScript code runs on a server. Node.js lets developers use JavaScript to write command-line tools and for server-side scripting. Node.js includes npm (Node Package Manager), an online repository for publishing open-source Node.js projects, and is a command-line utility for interacting with the repository that aids in package installation, version management, and dependency management.

Although there are many choices for your backend, whether node.js is used as a backend or not, you are likely using it as a JavaScript package manager. Node.js has over one million packages, which you can install with npm. Many front-end tools are distributed through npm, which is part of Node.js.

Node.js official site and download
https://nodejs.org/en/

Yarn

Yarn is another Package-Manager, which is similar to npm, released in 2016. Facebook developed it to fix the performance and security issues in npm, and it was much better than npm. However, npm has now fixed several problems and is catching up.

Yarn and npm download packages from the npm repository. Yarn is still a bit faster than npm as it installs all the packages simultaneously and cashes every download avoiding the need to re-install packages.

For JavaScript beginners, we recommend using npm initially because it is automatically installed via Node.js. Even though Yarn is gaining popularity, npm still has a much larger community. When you launch commercial projects, you could switch to Yarn if necessary.

Official docs: https://yarnpkg.com/

Create React App

Official docs: https://create-react-app.dev/docs/getting-started/

A few years ago, getting your build environment setup was a pain. You had to configure all the required tools manually. Fortunately, Create React App, which the Facebook team had developed, greatly simplified setting up the React SPA environment. You run a few commands on your command line, and your project is created with all of the proper behind-the-scenes configurations automatically hooked up. You don't need to install or configure tools like Webpack, Babel, and others manually.

Step 1: Preparation
Install the latest stable version of Node.js from the official site. Once installed, bring up your favorite command-line tool. In Windows, you can use either PowerShell or BASH Shell. If you are using macOS, launch the Terminal. You can confirm the Node.js installation by simply typing *node*. The following messages will be displayed.

```
Welcome to Node.js v14.17.0.
Type ".help" for more information.
>
```

Step 2: Creating the React Project
Navigate to the folder you wish to create your new project. Once you have navigated to a folder in your command line, enter the following command to create a new project at this location:

```
npx create-react-app my-app
```

Npx is an npm package executor. With npx, you can simply run a node executable anywhere. When you run "npx create-react-app (project name)", npx will always look up the npm registry and run the create-react-app with its latest version.

You will see something like this:

```
Success! Created my-app at /Users/xxxxx/yyyyyy/my-app
Inside that directory, you can run several commands:

  npm start
    Starts the development server.

  npm run build
    Bundles the app into static files for production.

  npm test
    Starts the test runner.

  npm run eject
    Removes this tool and copies build dependencies, configuration files
    and scripts into the app directory. If you do this, you can't go back!

We suggest that you begin by typing:

  cd my-app
  npm start

Happy hacking!
```

Step 3: Building your project

A project folder called 'my-app' was created by the create-react-app. You can navigate to the 'my-app' folder by typing the following:

```
cd my-app
```

From inside this folder, enter the following to start the app:

```
npm start
```

Your project will be built. A local Web server will get started. On the console, the following messages will be displayed:

```
Compiled successfully!
You can now view my-app in the browser.
  Local:            http://localhost:3000
  On Your Network:  http://192.168.0.38:3000

Note that the development build is not optimized.
To create a production build, use npm run build.
```

Open http://localhost:3000 to view it in your default browser.
You will see the following image on your browser:

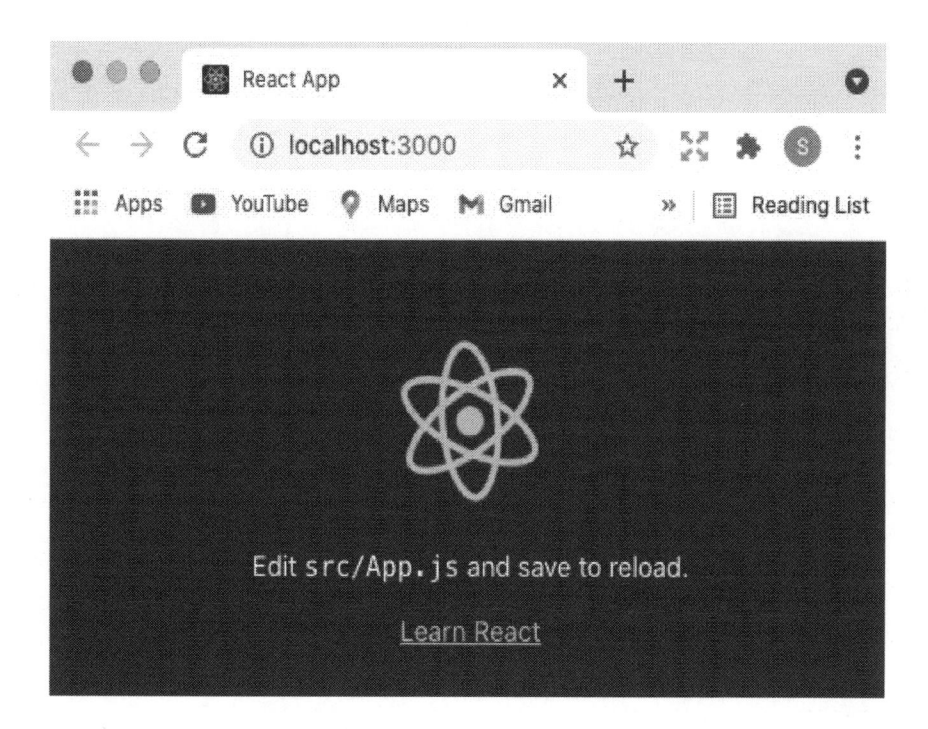

The page will automatically reload if you make changes to the code.
If there are errors, you will see the build errors and warnings in the console.

Step 4: Modifying files for your practice.
The next step is to display "hello world" or any simple messages using this project as a template. Under folder "my-app", you can see the following subfolder and files.

```
README.md          package-lock.json    public
node_modules       package.json         src
```

Under the subfolder "src", the following files were created by default.

```
App.css            index.css            reportWebVitals.js
App.js             index.js             setupTests.js
App.test.js        logo.svg
```

Delete all files under the "src" subfolder and create new JavaScript, css files. If you are busy, you might as well copy all files from the CodeSandbox you had practiced.

Code sample: https://codesandbox.io/s/optimistic-wing-h9y7w

Note: Create-React-App can be used for the SPA only. If you want to do server side rendering with React and Node.js, Next.js is a good solution. If your website is mostly static, consider using Gatsby or Next.js (version 9.3 onwards).

Developer tools

React DevTools, and Redux DevTools are indispensable tools for debugging. For detailed information, please refer to your browser's extension information.

React Developer Tools (React DevTools Extension)

React Developer Tools allow you to inspect a React tree, including the component hierarchy, props, state, and more. It is available as a DevTools extension in Chrome, Firefox, and Edge. It is a powerful tool to debug the React app.

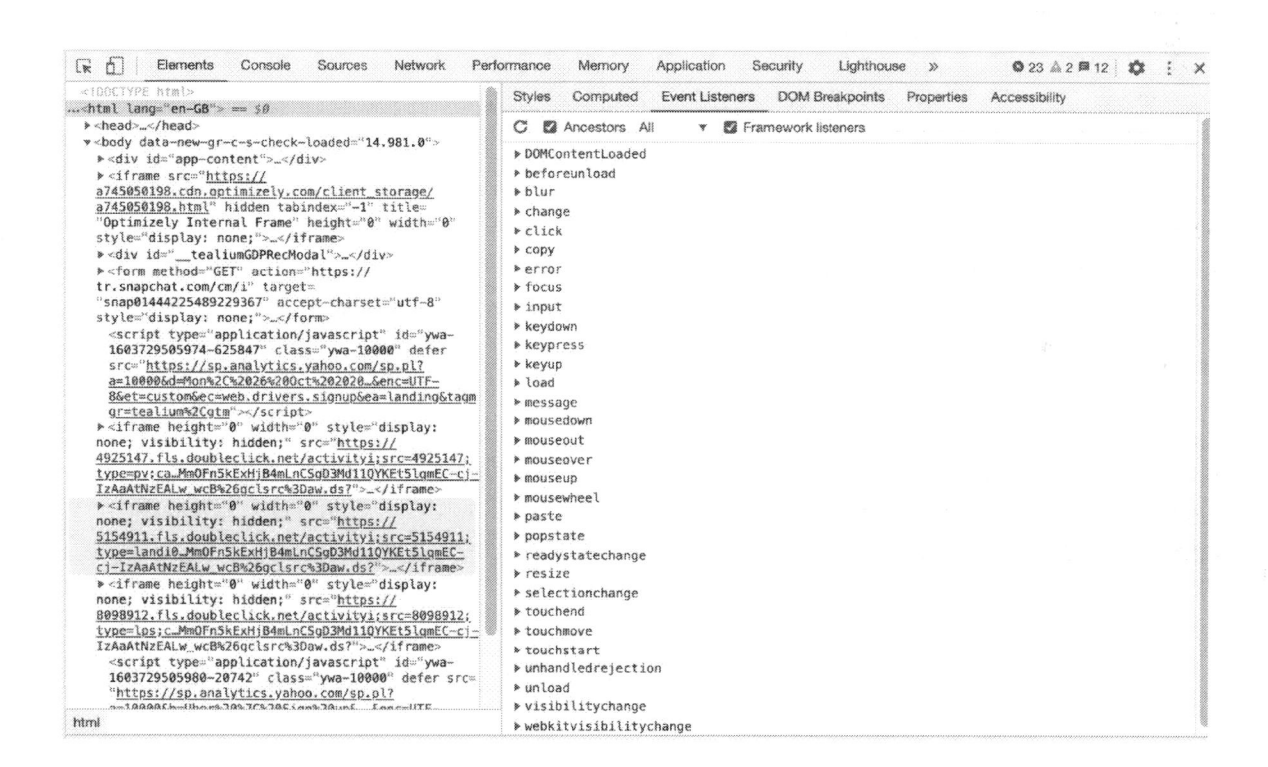

Redux Developer Tools (Redux DevTools Extension)

Redux Developer Tools is a powerful tool to debug your React+Redux app in real-time. Redux DevTools can help you visualize all the complex events in a redux application under the hood. It is available as a DevTools extension in Chrome, Firefox, and Edge. Apart from Redux, it can be used with any other architectures which handle the global state.

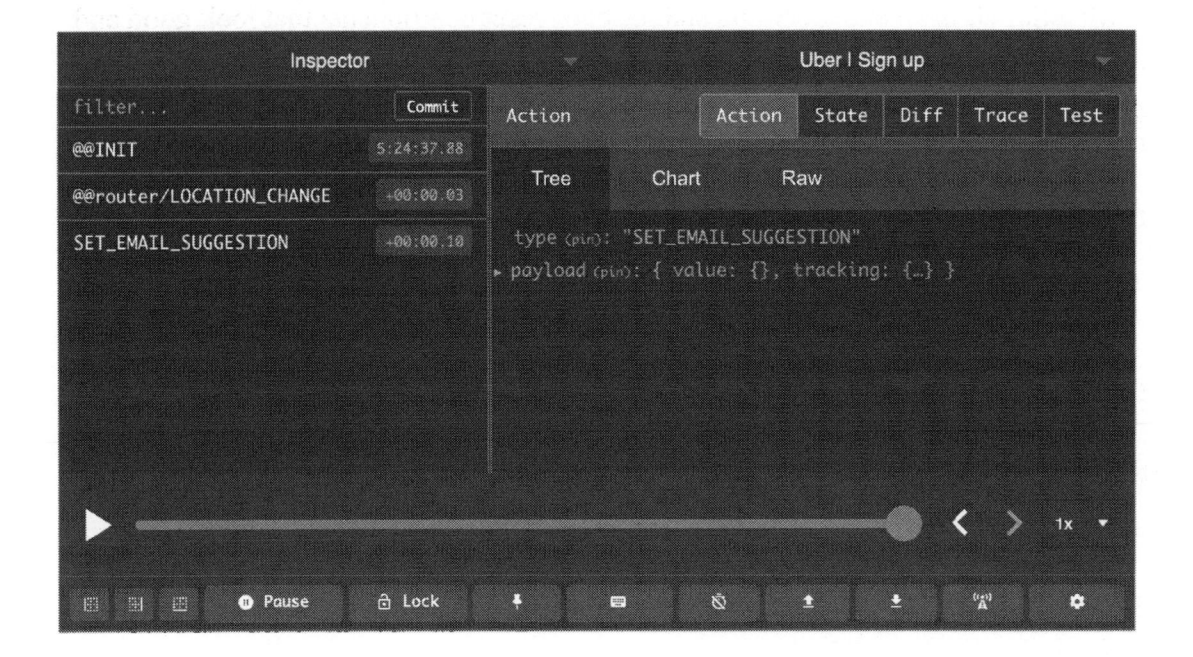

React UI Component Libraries/Frameworks

Material UI

The most popular component library for React. Material UI emulates Google's Material Design. Material UI is an excellent and stable set of react components that look good and easy to use and customize. Material UI consists of many accessible and configurable UI widgets. The components are self-supporting and only inject the styles they need to display.

https://material-ui.com/

React Bootstrap

React-Bootstrap replaces the Bootstrap for JavaScript. Each component has been built from scratch as a true React component, without dependencies like old jQuery. It simply replaces the JavaScript in the regular Bootstrap components with React code. Using React bootstrap is intuitive to use because of the number of available bootstrap themes.

https://react-bootstrap.github.io/

Ant Design

Created by Alibaba. Ant-design components provide a fully-fledged list of over 50 customizable components that you can use to create a beautifully crafted application. It is specially made for internal desktop applications and is based on several principles and unitary specifications. Ant Design has rich components that are easily customizable.

https://ant.design/

Grommet

Developed by Hewlett Packard. It is a React-based framework that provides accessibility, modularity, responsiveness, and themes in a tidy package. Grommet helps build responsive and accessible mobile-first projects for the web to use the component library. You can easily integrate it with existing projects.

https://v2.grommet.io/

Fluent UI

Developed by Microsoft. Fluent UI can help you build MS Office-like user experiences, similar behavior, and graphics. Fluent UI provides compatibility with Desktop, Android, and iOS devices. It is used by sites such as Office 365, OneNote, Azure DevOps, and others.

https://github.com/microsoft/fluentui

Shards React

A high-quality React UI kit featuring a modern design system with dozens of custom components. Shards React has one of the best options and free if you want to build a standard website.

https://designrevision.com/downloads/shards-react/

Tailwind CSS

Tailwind CSS, a utility-first CSS framework, provides pre-made class names. Unlike a component library, a utility class library comes with pre-made classes to style your elements. You can style your app by applying className to each element. You don't have to write any styles by hand any longer by using Tailwind UI, which is a collection of professionally designed, pre-built, fully responsive HTML snippets.

https://tailwindcss.com/

react-admin

Open sourced and maintained by Marmelab. A front-end framework for building admin applications running in the browser. The react admin comes with lots of useful features for B2B applications. Built on top of REST/GraphQL APIs and Material UI. React-admin uses an adapter approach with a concept called Data Providers. Existing providers can be used as a blueprint to design your API, or you can write your own Data Provider to query an existing API. Writing a custom Data Provider is very simple.

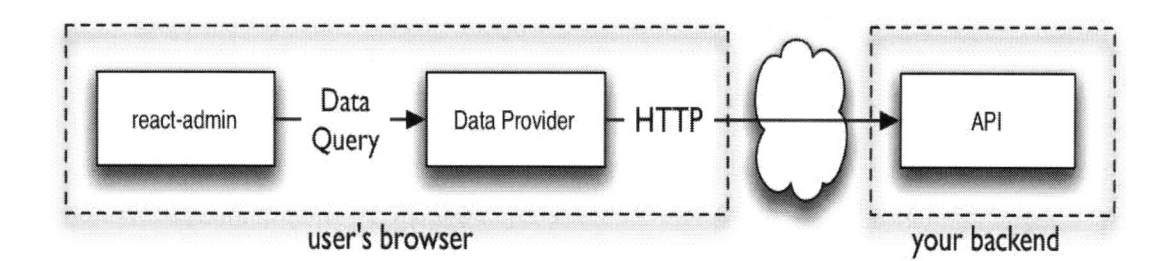

https://marmelab.com/react-admin/

SSG/SSR Frameworks

Gatsby.js

A free and open-source framework, Gatsby is a Static Site Generator (SSG) based on React and GraphQL. With Gatsby, the HTML content is statically generated using React DOM server-side. And this static HTML content can then be enhanced with client-side JavaScript via React hydration, which allows for app-like dynamic features in Gatsby sites.

Gatsby can work without any server at all. Gatsby lets you build websites powered by the JAMStack, without requiring the use of a database or server-side programming language.

Running Gatsby build starts up a Node.js server that processes your site: it creates a GraphQL schema, fetches data that your pages will pull in by extracting queries from your code and executing them, and it then renders each page's HTML.

Gatsby loads only the critical HTML, CSS, data, and JavaScript, so your site loads as fast as possible. Once loading is completed, React takes over as a single page application, and at the same time, Gatsby prefetches resources for other pages to improve speed. Gatsby uses GraphQL to manage data throughout the application. GraphQL is no longer used when building for production, but the data is persisted into JSON files instead.

Using Gatsby results in better performance and great SEO. Additionally, Gatsby comes with several plugins. Gatsby is perfect for hooking up to a CMS (such as WordPress). Furthermore, Gatsby automatically generates your site as a PWA, with a service worker that speeds up page loading and resources caching.

Gatsby.js official docs are easy to understand:
https://www.gatsbyjs.com/

The following example is hello world from the official site.
https://codesandbox.io/s/30op436nw5

Next.js

An open-source framework created by Vercel. Next.js is a flexible, full-stack, React-based framework that can help you deliver statically optimized content and fall back on serverless functions for API routes and SSR when you need to generate content dynamically. While Gatsby generates pure HTML/CSS/JS at build time, Next.js creates HTML/CSS/JS at run time. Each time a new request comes in, it dynamically creates a new HTML page from the server.

Next.js can create applications that run both on the client and the server, otherwise known as Universal JavaScript applications. Next.js framework helps you build universal apps faster by streamlining basic features like client-side routing and page layout while simplifying advanced features like server-side rendering and code splitting.

Next.js 9.3, released in 2020, comes with Static Site Generation support. These build time methods are called getStaticPaths and getStaticProps, and users can use them to build static websites, just like Gatsby.

Next.js has many other advantages, including automatic optimization of page bundles, automatic image optimization with the new Image tag, and built-in performance analytics.

If you use GitHub and Vercel, you'll also get automatically deployed on Vercel. Next.js is used in tens of thousands of production websites and web applications, including many of the world's largest brands.

Next.js official docs:
https://nextjs.org/

The following example is a hello world from the official site.
https://codesandbox.io/s/github/zeit/next.js/tree/master/examples/hello-world

About an author

Satoshi Yoshida started his professional carrier in the 1980s, developing CPU circuits, mobile phone modem LSIs and firmware. He also had management and architect experiences in various multinational companies in Japan, Canada, France, and Germany. He has 16 patents in wireless communication and has been working as a freelance consultant (wireless hardware, IoT, smart metering, UI software) since 2018.

About a co-author

Simona Yoshida has been working on web-based UI software and e-commerce platform since 2015. Sample codes in chapter 2, chapter 3, and chapter 4 were written and tested by her. In her spare time, she takes care of dogs and cats from animal shelters.

Contact us:

If you have any suggestions to improve this book, we would appreciate your feedback.

email: react3001@gmail.com

Printed in Poland
by Amazon Fulfillment
Poland Sp. z o.o., Wrocław